Savvas A. Cha
Yiannis S. Bou

Compact Composite Descriptors for Content Based Image Retrieval

Savvas A. Chatzichristofis
Yiannis S. Boutalis

Compact Composite Descriptors for Content Based Image Retrieval

Basics, Concepts, Tools

VDM Verlag Dr. Müller

Impressum/Imprint (nur für Deutschland/ only for Germany)

Bibliografische Information der Deutschen Nationalbibliothek: Die Deutsche Nationalbibliothek verzeichnet diese Publikation in der Deutschen Nationalbibliografie; detaillierte bibliografische Daten sind im Internet über http://dnb.d-nb.de abrufbar.

Alle in diesem Buch genannten Marken und Produktnamen unterliegen warenzeichen-, marken- oder patentrechtlichem Schutz bzw. sind Warenzeichen oder eingetragene Warenzeichen der jeweiligen Inhaber. Die Wiedergabe von Marken, Produktnamen, Gebrauchsnamen, Handelsnamen, Warenbezeichnungen u.s.w. in diesem Werk berechtigt auch ohne besondere Kennzeichnung nicht zu der Annahme, dass solche Namen im Sinne der Warenzeichen- und Markenschutzgesetzgebung als frei zu betrachten wären und daher von jedermann benutzt werden dürften.

Coverbild: www.ingimage.com

Verlag: VDM Verlag Dr. Müller GmbH & Co. KG
Dudweiler Landstr. 99, 66123 Saarbrücken, Deutschland
Telefon +49 681 9100-698, Telefax +49 681 9100-988
Email: info@vdm-verlag.de

Herstellung in Deutschland:
Schaltungsdienst Lange o.H.G., Berlin
Books on Demand GmbH, Norderstedt
Reha GmbH, Saarbrücken
Amazon Distribution GmbH, Leipzig
ISBN: 978-3-639-37391-2

Imprint (only for USA, GB)

Bibliographic information published by the Deutsche Nationalbibliothek: The Deutsche Nationalbibliothek lists this publication in the Deutsche Nationalbibliografie; detailed bibliographic data are available in the Internet at http://dnb.d-nb.de.

Any brand names and product names mentioned in this book are subject to trademark, brand or patent protection and are trademarks or registered trademarks of their respective holders. The use of brand names, product names, common names, trade names, product descriptions etc. even without a particular marking in this works is in no way to be construed to mean that such names may be regarded as unrestricted in respect of trademark and brand protection legislation and could thus be used by anyone.

Cover image: www.ingimage.com

Publisher: VDM Verlag Dr. Müller GmbH & Co. KG
Dudweiler Landstr. 99, 66123 Saarbrücken, Germany
Phone +49 681 9100-698, Fax +49 681 9100-988
Email: info@vdm-publishing.com

Printed in the U.S.A.
Printed in the U.K. by (see last page)
ISBN: 978-3-639-37391-2

To Andreas, Maro, Margarita and Giota
Savvas A. Chatzichristofis Xanthi,Greece - 2011

To Vaso, Argyro, Savvina and Artemi
Yiannis S. Boutalis Xanthi,Greece - 2011

i

Preface

In the past few years there has been a rapid increase in the field of multimedia data, mostly due to the evolution of information technology. One of the main components of multimedia data is its visual content, which includes digital images and video. While the issue of producing, compressing and propagating such media might have been a subject of scientific interest for a long time, in the past few years, exactly due to the increase in the range of data, a large part of the research was turned towards the management of retrieval of such material.

The first steps in automated management and retrieval of visual multi-media, can be traced back to 1992, where the term *Content Based Retrieval* was initially used. Since then, a new research field was created, which, approximately 20 years later, still remains active. And while initially this field of research seemed to be a research element classified under the general spectrum of information retrieval, as the years progressed, it managed to attract scientists from various disciplines.

Even though there is a large number of scientists working in this area, there is still lack of widely accredited solutions, keeping the field active and open to new ideas. The first Chapter of this book[1] introduces the reader in the field by giving the fundamental concepts and tools for Content-Based Image Retrieval. It includes the current standards and a brief description of existing image retrieval software solutions.

From Chapter 2 to Chapter 4, particular emphasis is given in recent computational intelligence techniques for producing compact content based descriptors comprising color, texture and spatial distribution information. They are used for fast image retrieval from large probably distributed inhomogenous databases. These descriptors can be described by the general term *Compact Composite Descriptors (CCDs)*. In contrast to MPEG-7, each type of multimedia data will be described by a specific group of descriptors.

Compact Composite Descriptors can describe the visual content of the following types of multimedia material:

---

[1]This book contains parts of a Ph.D. dissertation material presented at Xanthi, Greece, Democritus University of Thrace, Department of Electrical and Computer Engineering, 2010

1

- Images/ Video with natural content

- Images/ Video with artificially generated content

- Grayscale Images/ Images with medical content

For the description and retrieval of multimedia material with natural content, 4 descriptors were developed:

- CEDD - Color and Edge Directivity Descriptor

- C.CEDD - Compact Color and Edge Directivity Descriptor

- FCTH - Fuzzy Color and Texture Histogram

- C.FCTH - Compact Fuzzy Color and Texture Histogram

The CEDD includes texture information produced by the six-bin histogram of a fuzzy system that uses the five digital filters proposed by the MPEG-7 EHD. Additionally, for color information the CEDD uses a 24-bin color histogram produced by the 24-bin fuzzy-linking system. Overall, the final histogram has $6 \times 24 = 144$ regions.

The FCTH descriptor includes the texture information produced in the eight-bin histogram of a fuzzy system that uses the high frequency bands of the Haar wavelet transform. For color information, the descriptor uses a 24-bin color histogram produced by the 24-bin fuzzy-linking system. Overall, the final histogram includes $8 \times 24 = 192$ regions.

The method for producing the C.CEDD differs from the CEDD method only in the color unit. The C.CEDD uses a fuzzy ten-bin linking system instead of the fuzzy 24-bin linking system. Overall, the final histogram has only $6 \times 10 = 60$ regions. Compact CEDD is the smallest descriptor requiring less than 23 bytes per image.

The method for producing C.FCTH differs from the FCTH method only in the color unit. Like its C.CEDD counterpart, this descriptor uses only a fuzzy ten-bin linking system instead of the fuzzy 24-bin linking system. Overall, the final histogram includes only $8 \times 10 = 80$ regions.

To restrict the Compact Composite Descriptors' length, the normalized bin values of the descriptors are quantized for binary representation in a three bits/bin quantization.

Experiments conducted on several benchmarking image databases demonstrate the effectiveness of the CCDs in outperforming the MPEG-7 Descriptors as well as other state-of-the-art descriptors from the literature. These descriptors are described in details in Chapter 2.

Chapter 3 describes the Spatial Color Distribution Descriptor (SpCD). This descriptor combines color and spatial color distribution information. Since this descriptor capture the layout information of color features, they can be used for image retrieval by using hand-drawn sketch queries. In addition, the descriptors of this structure are considered to be suitable for colored graphics, since such images contain relatively small number of color and less texture regions than the natural color images. This descriptor uses a new fuzzy-linking system, that maps the colors of the image in a custom 8 colors palette.

The rapid advances made in the field of radiology, the increased frequency in which oncological diseases appear, as well as the demand for regular medical checks, led to the creation of a large database of radiology images in every hospital or medical center. There is now the imperative need to create an effective method for the indexing and retrieval of these images. Chapter 4 describes a new method of content based radiology medical image retrieval using the Brightness and Texture Directionality Histogram (BTDH). This descriptor uses brightness and texture characteristics as well as the spatial distribution of these characteristics in one compact 1D vector. The most important characteristic of this descriptor is that its size adapts according to the storage capabilities of the application that is using it.

The requirements of the modern retrieval systems are not limited to the achievement of good retrieval results, but extend to their ability for quick results. The majority of the Internet users would accept a reduction in the accuracy of the results in order to save time from searching. Chapter 5 describes how CCDs may be modified, in order to achieve a faster retrieval from databases. Test results indicate that the developed descriptors are in a position to execute retrieval of approximately 100,000 images per second, regardless of dimensions.

In Chapter 6 the procedure of early fusion of the two descriptors which describe visual multi-media material with natural content, is described. Given the fact that this category includes more than one descriptors, the procedure for combining these descriptors in order to further improve on the retrieval results, is analyzed.

Compact Composite Descriptors are capable of describing images with a specific content. The descriptors developed for use with images with natural content cannot be used to retrieve grayscale medical images and vice versa. Due to this, the calculation of the efficiency of each descriptor is made using image databases with homogenous content, suitable for the specific descriptor. However, the databases mostly used in the Internet are heterogeneous, and include images from every category. Chapter 7 describes how late fusion techniques can be used to combine all the CCDs, in order to achieve high retrievals scores in databases of this kind. Linear and non linear methods, which were adopted from the information retrieval field, have proven that the combination of descriptors yields very satisfactory results when used in heterogeneous data bases.

In the same Chapter, a retrieval scenario from distributed image databases is considered. In this scenario, the user executes a search in multiple databases. However, it is possible that each database uses its own descriptor(s) for the images it contains. Adopting once more methods from the information retrieval field and combining them with a method developed in this book it is possible to achieve high retrieval scores.

Chapter 8 describes a relevance feedback algorithm. The aim of this algorithm is to better readjust or even to alter the initial results of the retrieval, based on user preferences.

During this process, the user selects from the retrieved results those images which are similar to his/her expected results. Information extracted from these images is in the sequel used to alter the descriptor of the query image.

Chapter 9 describes the implementation of CCDs into free and open source software packages.

- img(Rummager)

- img(Anaktisi)

img(Rummager) was employed for the demonstration of the results of the research carried out in this book. In addition to the developed descriptors, the software implements a large number of descriptors from the literature (including the MPEG-7 descriptors), so that the application constitutes a platform for retrieving images via which the behaviour of a number of descriptors can be studied. The application can evaluate the retrieval results, both via the use of the new image retrieval evaluation method as well as via MAP and ANMRR. The application was programmed using C# and is freely available via the "Automatic Control, Systems and Robotics Laboratory" webpage, Department of Electrical and Computer Engineering, Democritus University of Thrace. The reader of this book may download the latest version of img(Rummager) application from http://www.img-rummager.com.

img(Anaktisi) was developed in collaboration with "Electrical Circuit Analysis Laboratory", Department of Electrical and Computer Engineering, Democritus University of Thrace, and is an Internet based application which possesses the capability of executing image retrieval using the presented in these book tools in a large number of images. The application is programmed in C# . and is available on-line at http://www.anaktisi.net.

Contents

Introduction to Content-Based Image Retrieval

Image retrieval in general and Content-based image retrieval (CBIR)[1] in particular are well-known fields of research in information management where a large number of techniques have been presented and investigated but still lacking of a satisfactory general solution.

In the fields of science, arts, health and even in commerce, collections of digital images are created daily, either by conversions of older documents and images into digital form, or via the use of digital mediums. Thus, the need to index or even to find an image in a collection is now of great importance. One of the basic problems which arise from creating such collections, is that often there is no available metadata on the images, either due to omission or due to the excessive time requirements such a process would require. Thus, searches in such data are undertaken via the use of content-based image retrieval methods.

Content-based image retrieval (CBIR) is defined as any technology that in principle helps to organize digital picture archives by their visual content. By this definition, anything ranging from an image similarity function to a robust image annotation engine falls under the purview of CBIR [35].

The retrieval of images based on content has peaked the interest of researches, but also of many companies. It is now used in a multitude of applications such as publications, historical and medical research, advertising, graphic arts, architectural and mechanical drawings, crime prevention, etc.

An important feature of the CBIR field is that it has managed to attract research interest of scientists from different fields, such as computer vision, machine learning, information retrieval, human-computer interaction, database systems, Web and data mining, information theory, statistics, and psychology [111].

This chapter describes the fundamentals of content-based image retrieval, several descriptors from the literature and the MPEG-7 standard.

---

[1]Recommendations for further literature on CBIR: [122][46][113]

1.1 Introduction

Content-based image retrieval extracts several features that describe the visual information of the image, mapping its content into a new space called the feature space. The feature space values for a given image are stored in a vector (*descriptor*) that can be used for retrieving similar images. The key to a successful retrieval system is to choose the right features that represent the images as accurately and uniquely as possible. The features chosen have to be discriminative and sufficient in describing the objects being present in the image.

The first steps in automated management and retrieval of visual multi-media, can be traced back to 1992, where the term *Content Based Retrieval* was initially used. Since then, a new research field was created, which, approximately 20 years later, still remains active. And while initially this field of research seemed to be a research element classified under the general spectrum of information retrieval, as the years progressed, it managed to attract scientists from various disciplines. Figure 1.1 illustrates a study of post-1995 publications in this field.

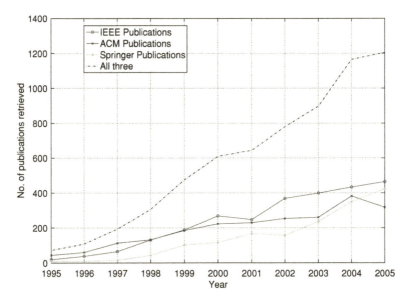

Figure 1.1: *Publisher, wise break-up of publication count on papers containing "image retrieval" [35]*

In CBIR, there are two different main approaches:

- The discrete approach

- The continuous approach

The discrete approach is directly inspired by information retrieval research (Text Retrieval). According to this approach, each image is described by a bag of features. Each image feature is treated like a word in a text document. The most popular system to follow this approach is the VIPER system developed at the University of Geneva [171].

The continuous approach is inspired by nearest neighbor classification [63]. It is actually the approach which is most frequently used in the field of image retrieval. According to this method, each image is represented by one, ore more than one feature vectors and these are compared using various similarity matching techniques. The images with lowest distances are ranked highest in the retrieval process while the images with highest distances are ranked lowest. Detailed comparison of the two approaches can be found in [38].

1.2 A Typical CBIR System

Figure 1.2 shows a block diagram of a generic CBIR system, whose main components are:

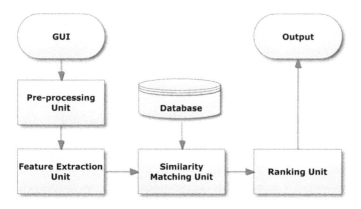

Figure 1.2: *A Typical CBIR System*

- GUI - Graphical User Interface allows the users to interactively query the database and browse the results. The user interface is a crucial component of CBIR system. According to [122], ideally, such interface should be simple, easy, friendly, functional and customizable and should provide integrated browsing, viewing, searching, and querying capabilities.

- Pre-processing Unit (Optional Unit): This unit performs several enchantment techniques to the query image in order to increase its quality.

- Feature Extraction Unit: This is the core unit of the system. Several features are extracted from the image. These features describe the image content and are to be used in the search procedure.

- Database: This is the database that includes the features extracted from the images, which are stored in the system in which the searching procedure is taking place.

- Similarity Matching Unit: This unit is used, with the assistance of a similarity matching technique, to calculate the distance between the features of a query image to the features of each image which is stored in the database.

- Ranking Unit: This unit undertakes the classification for images which are located in the database, so that they are ranked according to their similarity with the query image.

- Output: This is the unit which interacts with the GUI in order to present the results.

1.3 Features Classification and Selection

Features can be generally classified in three categories[122]:

1. Low Level Features: Visual information, such as color, texture or shape, extracted directly from the pixel values

2. Middle Level Features: Regions or blobs obtained as a result of image segmentation

3. High Level Features: Semantic information about the meaning of an image.

Low level features can be extracted by using image processing and computer vision techniques, some of which are described along this chapter. Middle level features require further processing. High level features are even harder to be automatically extract without explicit human assistance. In most of the cases, as high level features are defined the metadata that accompanying the image (EXIF information, image label, tags,etc.)

1.4 Low Level Features

In this chapter, some of the most commonly used low level features, are outlined. Low level features are used for describing the visual content of the image and that is why they must be appropriately selected on occasion. The visual content of the images is mapped into a new space named the *feature space*. The features that are chosen have to be discriminative and sufficient for the description of the objects. Basically, the key to attaining a successful retrieval system is to choose the right features that represent the images as *strong* as possible.

The features are measurable quantities or specifiers of the *YES-NO* type. Features of the second category are called binary. For example, the answer to the question whether an object has or does not have edges might be YES or NO. Non binary features are continuous or discontinuous quantities, such as for example features which are derived from moments or transformations.

Regarding their type, features can be classified to the following categories:

- Color Features

- Texture Features

- Shape Features

Some techniques adopt methods in which more than one feature types are involved. Limitations are imposed due to the requirements of each application and the type of classifier it uses.

In general, it could be said that a set of well determined features must have the following attributes:

- Discrimination. Features must be capable of separating objects from one another.

- Reliability. For similar objects there must be suitably similar values for their features.

- Low Computational Cost. Depending on the application, the computational cost must be low.

However, in addition to this, the extracted features must be independent of scale, turning and shifting, and also sould have a low sensitivity to noise.

Typically, an image can be represented by a global feature or several local features. In a small image databases, a simple sequential scan is usually employed for K nearest-neighbor (*K-NN*) search. However, if we want to exploit large-scale, say millions or billions images, efficient indexing algorithms are imperative [108].

High-dimensional indexing still remains a challenging problem in the database field. Existing methods for exact K-NN search are outperformed on average by sequential scanning if the number of dimensions increases [52], which is known as the curse of dimensionality. In many cases, the precision of search results is much more important than the recall rate when the database is large enough, e.g. millions or billions. In this case, an approximate yet efficient indexing technique can be employed [108].

In what follows, a brief description of some low level features is given. These features are selected from the literature and are widely used by many applications for image retrieval. Although it is impossible to include the entirety of all such features in a single chapter, an effort has been made to include the most widely used features. More features are described in [113].

15

1.5 Color Features

Color is a low level feature that is widely used in Content Based Image Retrieval systems. Several approaches have been used to describe the color information appearing in the images.

1.5.1 Color Histograms

Computer screens are the most classical example of the use of an RGB (Red - Green - Blue) color model. The image dimension denotes the number of image pixels, each one being expressed as a vector with three basic color components. A graphical representation of these values can be constructed in relation to the number of pixels in which they are presented. Thus, a graphical representation can be created for each one of the 3 basic colors, in which the horizontal axis will have values from 0 up to 255, which correspond to color levels, while the vertical axis will declare the number of pixels in which each color hue appears.

In order for graphical representations to constitute a feature which can be used for image comparison, the values of the pixels which correspond to the shades of the color must be normalized to 1. This can be easily achieved, if each value of the graph is divided by the number of image pixels (image dimensions).

The design process for the normalized graphs is often referred to in literature as representation of color distribution. Color histograms are among the most basic approaches and widely used in image retrieval [46].

1.5.2 Luminosity Histogram

One of the most important features, that is used in color models which are nearest to the field of human vision, is luminosity. This trait, which in the present document will retain the symbol Y, contains the huge amount of information and could by itself render very good retrieval results.

As a feature, luminosity is directly connected with color and can be derived from a transformation, different for each color space, of the pixel color. In the literature, there are various methods, for calculating luminosity. In most cases, the transformation of the YIQ color space is used:

$$\begin{bmatrix} Y \\ I \\ Q \end{bmatrix} = \begin{bmatrix} 0.299 & 0.587 & 0.114 \\ 0.596 & -0.275 & -0.321 \\ 0.212 & -0.523 & 0.311 \end{bmatrix} \begin{bmatrix} R \\ G \\ B \end{bmatrix} \qquad (1.1)$$

where $R, G, B \in [0, 255]$, $Y \in [0, 255]$

The luminosity histogram of an image (Y) is a graph with its horizontal axis depicting the luminosity levels (in the range $0, \dots, 255$), while the vertical axis counts the number of image pixels having that luminosity. In its normalized version each vertical value is divid-ed by the total number of image pixels, providing this way the frequency of appearance of each luminosity level (in the range $0, \ldots, 1$).

The shape of the histogram gives out significant information concerning the image character. Thus, a histogram with a narrow lobe denotes a low contrast image. On the other hand, a histogram with 2 clear lobes which are at a considerable distance to each other, indicates that this image consists of an object and a background having considerably different shades of grey.

It should be stressed that the importance of a histogram also lays in its relative in-variance under actions of rotation, partial shifting, changing of dimensions and reflection, imposed on the image.

1.5.3 Histogram Features (Color and Luminosity)

Each histogram can be defined by a set of elements which are derived from it.

The first element which can be directly extracted by knowing the number of pixels is the distribution probability:

$$P(b) = \frac{N(b)}{M} \tag{1.2}$$

where:

(b) is the number of pixels in the area which have a color or luminosity level equal to b,

M the total number of pixels in the area.

The distribution probability, in addition to being able to normalize graphs is also used for extracting a significant number of other useful statistical measures, used as features describing the content of the image:

Mean Value:

$$m = \sum_{0}^{255} bP(b) \tag{1.3}$$

Standard Deviation:

$$s = \left[\sum_{0}^{255} (b-m)^2 P(b) \right]^{\frac{1}{2}} \tag{1.4}$$

Variability:

$$\mu_2 = \sum_{0}^{255} (b-m)^2 P(b) \tag{1.5}$$

Skewness:

$$\mu_3 = \sum_{0}^{255} (b-m)^3 P(b) \tag{1.6}$$

Kurtosis:

$$\mu_4 - 3 = \sum_{0}^{255} (b-m)^4 P(b) \tag{1.7}$$

Energy:

$$E = \sum_{0}^{255} [bP(b)]^2 \qquad (1.8)$$

Entropy:

$$H = -\sum_{0}^{255} P(b)Log_2[P(b)] \qquad (1.9)$$

1.5.4 Color Coherence Vector

Using Color Coherence Vector (CCV) [138], each pixel is partitioned into two types, *coherent* and *incoherent*. When a pixel belongs to a uniformly-colored area then it is referred to as coherent, otherwise it is called incoherent [164]. For a given color, some of the pixels with this color will be coherent and some will be incoherent. In order to make clear the CCV production process, the following example is given.

Using a color reduction method we cluster the N colors of an image into only c color clusters, where $c << N$. To keep our example easy, we assume that $c = 4$. Suppose that the pixel values for an image after the color reduction method are as follows:

$$
\begin{array}{cccc}
1 & 1 & 3 & 2 \\
1 & 3 & 4 & 4 \\
1 & 2 & 4 & 4 \\
2 & 2 & 2 & 4 \\
\end{array}
$$

In the sequel, we extract the connected components. Individual components will be labeled with letters $(A, B, \dots)$. The resulting image is:

$$
\begin{array}{cccc}
A & A & B & E \\
A & B & C & C \\
A & D & C & C \\
D & D & D & C \\
\end{array}
$$

Then, we calculate how many pixels participate in each connected component. If the number of the pixels in a connected component is greater than a given threshold t, then the connected component is classified as coherent, otherwise as incoherent.

To our example, A consists of 4 pixels, B consists of 2 pixels, C consists of 5 pixels, D consists of 4 pixels and finally, only one pixel participates in the connected component E. If $t = 4$, the pixels in A,C and D are classified as coherent, while the pixels in B and E are classified as incoherent

Due to its additional spatial information, it has been shown that CCV provides better retrieval results than the color histogram, especially for those images which have either mostly uniform color or mostly texture regions [113].

1.5.5 Color Correlogram

Color correlogram [71] extends the Color Coherence Vector in order to characterize not only the color distribution of pixels, but also the spatial correlation between pair of colors. A color correlogram expresses how the spatial correlation of pairs of colors changes with distance.

In general, a color correlogram of an image is a table indexed by color pairs, where the k-th entry for (i, j) specifies the probability of finding a pixel of color j at a distance k from a pixel of color i in the image.

Let I be an $n \times n$ image and $I_{c(i)}$ represent the set of pixels with color $c(i)$. Then, the color correlogram for a given d is defined as:

$$\gamma_{c(i),c(j)}^{(k)}(I) = \Pr_{p_1 \in I_{c(i)}, p_2 \in I} \left[p_2 \in I_{c(j)} \, |p1 - p2| = k \right] \tag{1.10}$$

where $i, j \in 1, 2, \ldots, n$, $k \in 1, 2, \ldots, d$, and $|p_1 - p_2|$ is the distance between pixels p_1 and p_2.

Given any pixel of color $c(i)$ in an image I, $\gamma_{c(i),c(j)}^{(k)}(I)$ gives the probability that a pixel at distance k away from this pixel is of color $c(j)$.

A simplified version of color correlogrma is the color autocorrelogram. The color autocorrelogram captures only the spatial correlation between identical colors.

$$\alpha_c^{(k)}(I) = \gamma_{c,c}^{(k)}(I) \tag{1.11}$$

Compared to the color histogram and CCV, the color autocorrelogram provides better retrieval results, but is also the most computational expensive due to its high dimensionality [113].

1.5.6 Color Distribution Entropy

Rao et al. [147] introduced the annular color histograms. In this method, the centroid C_i and the radius r_i of each color are calculated.

Let A_i be the count of the pixels with the same color i. Let $C_i = (x_i, y_i)$ be the centroid of the color i. x_i and y_i defined as:

$$x_i = \frac{1}{A_i} \sum_{(x,y) \in A_i} x \tag{1.12}$$

$$y_i = \frac{1}{A_i} \sum_{(x,y) \in A_i} y \tag{1.13}$$

Let r_i be the radius of the color i which is defined as:

$$r_i = \max_{(x,y) \in A_i} \sqrt{(x - x_i)^2 + (y - y_i)^2} \tag{1.14}$$

Given a number N, draw N concentric circles centered at C_i and with $j \times \frac{r_i}{N}$, $1 \leq j \leq N$ as the radius for each circle. A_{ij} is the count of the pixels with the same color i inside circle j.

Sun et al. [177] proposed the Color Distribution Entropy (CDE) descriptor which describes the spatial information of an image and is based on the Normalized Spatial Distribution Histogram (NSDH) and the definition of entropy. This method presents low dimension indexes and is therefore very efficient in CBIR. Furthermore, the NSDH is size invariant because annular color histograms are normalized by the number of pixels of the color bins. Thus, CDE is also size invariant.

Based on the annular color histogram, the Normalized Spatial Distribution Histogram (NSDH) can be defined as:

$$P_i = (P_{i1}, P_{i2}, \dots, P_{iN}) \tag{1.15}$$

where

$$P_{ij} = |A_{ij}|/|A_i| \tag{1.16}$$

The Color Distribution Entropy (CDE) for a given color i can be defined as:

$$E_i(P_i) = -\sum_{j=1}^{N} P_{ij} \log_2(P_{ij}) \tag{1.17}$$

The CDE index for an image can be written as:

$$(A_1, E_1, A_2, E_2, \dots, A_n, E_n) \tag{1.18}$$

where A_i is the number of the the pixels with the same color i, E_i is the CDE of these pixels and n is the total number of the colors.

1.5.7 Color Moments

The basis of color moments lays in the assumption that the distribution of the color in an image can be interpreted as a probability distribution. So far, color moments have been successfully used in many retrieval systems [113].

Stricker et al.[174] proposed the first three central moments to describe the color distribution in an image. These moments are defined as:

- Mean:

$$\mu_1 = \frac{1}{N} \sum_{j=1}^{N} f_{ij} \tag{1.19}$$

- Variance:

$$\sigma_1 = \left(\frac{1}{N} \sum_{j=1}^{N} (f_{ij} - \mu_1)^2 \right)^{0.5} \tag{1.20}$$

20

- Skewness:

$$s_i = \left(\frac{1}{N} \sum_{j=1}^{N} \left(f_{ij} - \mu_i \right)^3 \right)^{0.333} \tag{1.21}$$

where f_{ij} is the value of the i-th color component of the image pixel j, and N is the number of pixels in the image.

Mean value describes the average color value in the image. The standard deviation value is the square root of the variance of the distribution and Skewness is a measure of the degree of asymmetry in the distribution.

Given that we have three moments for each one of the three color components, color moments can provide a very compact representation of the visual content of the image since, only 9 values are used to represent the color content of each image.

1.6 Texture Features

Texture representation methods can be classified into two categories:

- Structural

- Statistical

Structural texture refers to statistical distributions of image structures such as lines, edges, or bumps [49]. In other words, structural methods, describe textures by identifying structural primitives and their placement rules. They tend to be most effective when applied to textures that are very regular.

Statistical approaches compute different properties and are suitable if texture primitive sizes are comparable with the pixel sizes [172]. These include Fourier transforms, co-occurrence matrix, spatial autocorrelation, fractals, etc.

1.6.1 Tamura Texture Features

The Tamura texture includes 6 features selected by psychological experiments: *Coarseness, contrast, directionality, line likeness, regularity* and *roughness* [180]. The first three components have been used in several image retrieval systems. A detailed description of these three features is given below.

Coarseness gives information in regards to the size of the texture elements of the image. The higher the value of coarseness, the coarser the texture of the image is. The coarseness of the image is calculated as follows:

- For each point (n_0, n_1) the average value of the neighbor area is calculated. The size of the neighbor area is determined by use of powers of 2. For example: 1×1, 2×2, 4×4, ..., 32×32.

$$A_k(n_0, n_1) = \frac{1}{2^{2k}} \sum_{i=1}^{2^{2k}} \sum_{j=1}^{2^{2k}} X(n_0 - 2^{k-1} + i, n_1 - 2^{k-1} + j) \qquad (1.22)$$

where X denotes the image pixel intensity.

- For each point (n_0, n_1) the differences between non overlapping neighbor areas are calculated in the horizontal and vertical distances.

$$E_k^h(n_0, n_1) = |A_k(n_0 + 2^{k-1}, n_1) - A_k(n_0 - 2^{k-1}, n_1)| \qquad (1.23)$$

$$E_k^v(n_0, n_1) = |A_k(n_0, n_1 + 2^{k-1}) - A_k(n_0, n_1 - 2^{k-1})| \qquad (1.24)$$

- For each point (n_0, n_1) the value which leads to the maximum difference is selected.

$$S(n_0, n_1) = \arg \max_{k=1...5 \, d=h,v} E_k^d(n_0, n_1) \qquad (1.25)$$

- Finally, the average value of all 2^S terms is taken as a standard for measuring the coarseness of the image

$$F_{crs} = \frac{1}{N_0 N_1} \sum_{n_0=1}^{N_0} \sum_{n_1=1}^{N_1} 2^{S(n_0, n_1)} \qquad (1.26)$$

Contrast is derived from the following four factors:

- Dynamic range of levels of grey

- Polarization of the white-black distribution in the grey level histogram

- Edge Sharpness

- Frequency of repeated patterns

The contrast of an image can be calculated as follows:

$$F_{con} = \frac{\sigma}{\alpha_4^z} \qquad (1.27)$$

with

$$a_4 = \frac{\mu_4}{\sigma_4} \qquad (1.28)$$

where z has been experimentally found to be equal to $\frac{1}{4}$, with σ^2 being the deviation of the values of grey in the image.

$$\mu_4 = \frac{1}{N_0 N_1} \sum_{n_0=1}^{N_0} \sum_{n_1=1}^{N_1} (X(n_0,n_1) - \mu)^4 \tag{1.29}$$

Tamura *Directionality* histogram is a graph of local edge probabilities against their directional angle.

The extraction method of the traditional Tamura Directionality histogram utilizes the fact that gradient is a vector, so it has both magnitude and direction. In the discrete case, the magnitude $|\Delta G|$ and the local edge direction θ are approximated as follows:

$$|\Delta G| = \frac{|\Delta_H| + |\Delta_V|}{2} \tag{1.30}$$

$$\theta = tan^{-1}\left(\frac{\Delta_V}{\Delta_H}\right) + \frac{\pi}{2} \tag{1.31}$$

where $|\Delta_H|$ and $|\Delta_V|$ are the horizontal and vertical differences computed using approximate pixel-wise derivatives measured by the Sobel edge detector in the 3×3 moving window.

The resultant θ is a real number $(0 < \theta < \pi)$ measured counter clockwise so that the horizontal direction is zero. The desired histogram H_D can be obtained by quantizing θ in n values and counting the points with the magnitude $|\Delta G|$ over the threshold t;

$$H_D(k) = \frac{N_\theta(k)}{\sum_{i=0}^{n-1} N_\theta(i)} \quad k = 0,1,\ldots n-1 \tag{1.32}$$

where $N_\theta(k)$ is the number of points at which $|\Delta G| \geq t$.

Thresholding by t aims at preventing counting of unreliable directions which cannot be regarded as edge points. The most classic approach, uses $n = 16$ and $t = 12$. Note that the shape of each histogram is not sensitive to the value of t.

1.6.2 Co-occurrence Matrix

The co-occurrence matrix [27] of an $N \times N$-pixel image I, comprises the probabilities $p_{d,}(i,j)$ of the transitions from a grey-level i to a grey-level j in a given direction at a given intersample spacing d:

$$p_{d,\theta}(i,j) = \frac{C_{d,\theta}(i,j)}{\sum_{i=1}^{N_g} \sum_{j=1}^{N_g} C_{d,\theta}(i,j)} \tag{1.33}$$

where

$$C_{d,\theta}(i,j) = (m,n),(u,v) \in N \times N : f(m,n) = j, f(u,v) = i \tag{1.34}$$

23

$$|(m,n) - (u,v)| = d, \angle((m,n),(u,v)) = \theta \tag{1.35}$$

denotes the number of elements in the set, $f(m,n)$ and $f(u,v)$ correspond to the grey-levels of the pixel located at (m,n) and (u,v) respectively, and N_g is the total number of grey-levels in the image.

Several features can be extracted directly from the co-occurrence matrix:

Energy:
$$\sum_i \sum_j p_{\theta,d}^2(i,j) \tag{1.36}$$

Contrast:
$$\sum_i \sum_j (i-j)^2 p_{\theta,d}(i,j) \tag{1.37}$$

Homogeneity:
$$\sum_i \sum_j \frac{p_{\theta,d}(i,j)}{1+(i-j)^2} \tag{1.38}$$

Inverse Difference Moment:
$$\sum_i \sum_j \frac{p_{\theta,d}(i,j)}{|i-j|^2}, i \neq j \tag{1.39}$$

Entropy:
$$-\sum_i \sum_j p_{\theta,d}(i,j) \log p_{\theta,d}(i,j) \tag{1.40}$$

Correlation:
$$\frac{\sum_i \sum_j (i-\mu_x)(j-\mu_y) p_{\theta,d}(i,j)}{\sigma_x \sigma_y} \tag{1.41}$$

where μ_x, μ_y, σ_x and σ_y are the mean values and typical deviations given by the equations:

$$\mu_x = \sum_i i \sum_j p_{\theta,d}(i,j) \tag{1.42}$$

$$\mu_y = \sum_i j \sum_j p_{\theta,d}(i,j) \tag{1.43}$$

$$\sigma_x^2 = \sum_i (i-\mu_x)^2 \sum_j p_{\theta,d}(i,j) \tag{1.44}$$

$$\sigma_y^2 = \sum_i (i-\mu_y)^2 \sum_j p_{\theta,d}(i,j) \tag{1.45}$$

$\mu = \mu_x = \mu_y$ for symmetric matches.

It is obvious that the choice of the vector d has a direct impact on the co-occurrence matrix. Thus, the co-occurrence matrix must be calculated for various different values of d after which a selection of the prominent features must be undertaken.

1.6.3 Autocorrelation

The autocorrelation equation $p(k,l)$ for an image $N \times M$ is defined as follows:

$$p(k,l) = \frac{MN}{(N-k)(M-l)} \frac{\sum_{i=1}^{N-k}\sum_{j=1}^{M-l} f(i,j)f(i+k,j+l)}{\sum_{i=1}^{N}\sum_{j=1}^{M} f^2(i,j)} \qquad (1.46)$$

where $f(i,j)$ is the image intensity of pixel (i,j), $0 \le k \le N-1, 0 \le l \le M-1$,

For images consisting of repeating texture elements, the autocorrelation equation exhibits a standard periodicity, with a period equal to the distance between neighbor elements in the texture. If the texture is coarse, the autocorrelation equation drops slowly, as opposed to a fine texture where there is a steep drop. The equation is used as a measure of the periodicity of the texture, as well as a measure of the scale of the texture elements.

1.6.4 Law's Texture

The texture analysis technique based on the texture energy measure, developed by K. I. Laws [100], has been used for many applications of image analysis for classification and segmentation [101]. The texture energy measurements for 2D images are computed by applying three convolution filters [178]:

- L3 = (1 2 1)

- E3 = (-1 0 1)

- S3 = (-1 2 -1)

The initial letters of these filters indicate:

- (L) Local average (or Level)

- (E) Edge detection

- (S) Spot detection

The numbers followed by the initial letters indicate the length of the filters. In this case, the length of the filters is three.

The extension of the filters can be done by convolving the pairs of these filters together.

- L5 = L3 * L3 = (1,4,6,4,1)

- E5 = L3 * E3 = (-1 -2 0 2 1)

- S5 = L3 * S3 = (-1 0 2 0 -1)

- W5 = -E3 * S3 = (-1 2 0 -2 1)

25

- R5 = S3 * S3 = (1 -4 6 -4 1)

The initial letters of these filters stand for Local average (or Level), Edge, Spot, Wave, and Ripple. Please note that all filters are zero-sum filters except for the L5 filter.

From these one dimensional vectors, 25 different two dimensional filters can be produced, as follows:

$$LE = L5^T E5 = \begin{bmatrix} 1 \\ 4 \\ 6 \\ 4 \\ 1 \end{bmatrix} \begin{bmatrix} -1 & -2 & 0 & 2 & 1 \end{bmatrix} = \begin{bmatrix} -1 & -2 & 0 & 2 & 1 \\ -4 & -8 & 0 & 8 & 4 \\ -6 & -12 & 0 & 12 & 6 \\ -4 & -8 & 0 & 8 & 4 \\ -1 & -2 & 0 & 2 & 1 \end{bmatrix} \quad (1.47)$$

A list of all 25 names for the filters is given below:

LL	EL	SL	WL	RL
LE	EE	SE	WE	RE
LS	ES	SS	WS	RS
LW	EW	SW	WW	RW
LR	ER	SR	WR	RR

The sum of elements in these filters is equal to zero, except for filter LL which has the following form:

$$LL = L5^T L5 = \begin{bmatrix} 1 \\ 4 \\ 6 \\ 4 \\ 1 \end{bmatrix} \begin{bmatrix} 1 & 4 & 6 & 4 & 1 \end{bmatrix} = \begin{bmatrix} 1 & 4 & 6 & 4 & 1 \\ 4 & 16 & 24 & 16 & 4 \\ 6 & 24 & 36 & 24 & 6 \\ 4 & 16 & 24 & 16 & 4 \\ 1 & 4 & 6 & 4 & 1 \end{bmatrix} \quad (1.48)$$

the sum of its elements is 256.

Via the use of these 25 filters, 14 texture features can be extracted. These features are derived by the application of the filters on the image, and the subsequent measurement of the energy contained in the resulting images.

1.6.5 Haar Wavelet Features

To export texture information from the images, three features that represent energy in high frequency bands of wavelet transforms are used. These elements are the square roots of the second order moment of wavelet coefficients in high frequency bands [36]. To obtain these features, the Haar transform is applied to the Y (Luminosity in the YIQ color space) component of an *Image Block*. The choice of *Image Block* size depends on the image dimensions. Suppose for instance that the block size is 4×4. After a one-level wavelet transform, each block is decomposed into four frequency bands: LL: Low-Low, LH: Low-High, HL: High-Low and HH: High-High. Each band contains 2×2 coefficients. The coefficients in the HL band are $\{C_{kl}, C_{k,l+1}, C_{k+1,l}, C_{k+1,l+1}\}$. One feature is then computed as:

$$f = \left(\frac{1}{4} \sum_{i=0}^{1} \sum_{j=0}^{1} C_{k+i,l+j}^2 \right)^{\frac{1}{2}} \tag{1.49}$$

The other two features are computed similarly from the LH and HH bands. The motivation for using these features is their relation to texture properties. Moments of wavelet coefficients in various frequency bands are proven effective for discerning texture[189, 183]. For example, a large coefficient value on the HL band shows high activity in the horizontal direction. Thus, an image with vertical stripes has high energy in the HL band and low energy in the LH band. Research shows that this texture feature is a good compromise between computational complexity and effectiveness [189].

1.7 Shape Features

Shape is one of the most important low level features used in content based image retrieval. In most cases it is used in identifying objects. These can be derived directly from the geometrical form of the objects and help in depicting, recognizing and determining content. Most methods proposed in the literature are applied to the contours of the image.

In this context we consider as edge a curve, in the two sides of which there are significant differences(for example of luminosity). In most applications, but especially in issues of retrieval, edge detection is a stage which precedes any other sort of process. Edges are defined by various geometrical characteristics, such as for examples height and grade.

1.7.1 Geometric Moments

Moments can be considered as being a very useful set of object features. Their use has been proven in a multitude of shape analysis applications and especially in character recognition. The two dimensional continuous moments $p + q$ of an image $f(x,y)$ are given by the equation:

$$m_{pq} = \int\limits_{-\infty}^{\infty} \int\limits_{-\infty}^{\infty} x^p y^q f(x,y) dx dy \tag{1.50}$$

p and q have non negative number values and this creates an unlimited set of moments. The more moments there are available, the better they can describe the original image $f(x,y)$.

In other words, each image corresponds to a set of moments, and vice versa. In the case of discrete images their relation with moments can be expressed as follows:

$$m_{pq} = \sum_X \sum_Y x^p y^q f(x,y) \tag{1.51}$$

The center of weight for an object can be defined from the following equations:

$$\bar{x} = \frac{m_{10}}{m_{00}}, \bar{y} = \frac{m_{01}}{m_{00}} \tag{1.52}$$

Based on the coordinates of the center of weight, moments can be determined regardless of the position of the object. This means that in effect, moments can be determined regardless of any possible movements of the object. These moments are called central and are calculated by the equation:

$$\mu_{pq} = \sum_x \sum_y (x-\bar{x})^p (y-\bar{y})^q f(x,y) \tag{1.53}$$

It is obvious that for discrete images, the moment equations are as follows:

$$m_{pq} = \sum_x \sum_y x^p y^q \tag{1.54}$$

$$\mu_{pq} = \sum_x \sum_y (x-\bar{x})^p (y-\bar{y})^q \tag{1.55}$$

Central moments can be determined from the normal moments. For instance, 0 to 3 class central moments are given by the following equations:

$$\mu_{10} = \sum_x \sum_y (x-\bar{x})^1 (y-\bar{y})^0 f(x,y) = m_{10} - \frac{m_{10}}{m_{00}} m_{00} = 0 \tag{1.56}$$

$$\mu_{11} = \sum_x \sum_y (x-\bar{x})^1 (y-\bar{y})^1 f(x,y) = m_{11} - \frac{m_{10}m_{01}}{m_{00}} \tag{1.57}$$

$$\mu_{20} = \sum_x \sum_y (x-\bar{x})^2 (y-\bar{y})^0 f(x,y) = m_{20} - \frac{2m_{10}^2}{m_{00}} + \frac{m_{10}^2}{m_{00}} \tag{1.58}$$

$$\mu_{02} = \sum_x \sum_y (x-\bar{x})^0 (y-\bar{y})^2 f(x,y) = m_{02} - \frac{m_{01}^2}{m_{00}} \tag{1.59}$$

$$\mu_{30} = \sum_x \sum_y (x-\bar{x})^3 (y-\bar{y})^0 f(x,y) = m_{30} - 3\bar{x}m_{20} + 2\bar{x}^2 m_{10} \tag{1.60}$$

$$\mu_{12} = \sum_x \sum_y (x-\bar{x})^1 (y-\bar{y})^2 f(x,y) = m_{12} - 2\bar{y}m_{11} - \bar{x}m_{02} + 2\bar{y}^2 m_{10} \tag{1.61}$$

$$\mu_{21} = \sum_x \sum_y (x-\bar{x})^2 (y-\bar{y})^1 f(x,y) = m_{21} - 2\bar{x}m_{11} - \bar{y}m_{02} + 2\bar{x}^2 m_{10} \tag{1.62}$$

$$\mu_{03} = \sum_x \sum_y (x - \bar{x})^0 (y - \bar{y})^3 f(x,y) = m_{03} - 3\bar{y}m_{02} + 2\bar{y}^2 m_{01} \qquad (1.63)$$

Normalized central moments can be calculated as follows:

$$\eta_{pq} = \frac{\mu_{pq}}{\mu_{00}^{\gamma}}, \gamma = \frac{p+q}{2} + 1 \qquad (1.64)$$

When using moments for object recognition, it is desirable that they be immutable. Hu [70] determined that the following sum of 7 moments are invariant to scaling, rotation and skew. Moments $\varphi1$ to $\varphi6$ as well as the measure of $\varphi7$ are also invariant to reflection.

$$\varphi1 = \eta_{20} + \eta_{02} \qquad (1.65)$$

$$\varphi2 = (\eta_{20} - \eta_{02})^2 + 4\eta_{11}^2 \qquad (1.66)$$

$$\varphi3 = (\eta_{30} - 3\eta_{12})^2 + (\eta_{11} - \eta_{03})^2 \qquad (1.67)$$

$$\varphi4 = (\eta_{30} - \eta_{12})^2 + (\eta_{21} - \eta_{03})^2 \qquad (1.68)$$

$$\varphi5 = (\eta_{30} - 3\eta_{12})(\eta_{30} + \eta_{12})\left[(\eta_{30} + \eta_{12})^2 - 3(\eta_{21} + \eta_{03})^2\right]$$
$$+ (3\eta_{21} - \eta_{03})(\eta_{21} + \eta_{03})\left[3(\eta_{30} + \eta_{12})^2 - (\eta_{21} + \eta_{03})^2\right] \qquad (1.69)$$

$$\varphi6 = (\eta_{20} - \eta_{02})\left[(\eta_{30} + \eta_{12})^2 - (\eta_{21} + \eta_{03})^2\right]$$
$$+ 4\eta_{11}(\eta_{30} + \eta_{12})(\eta_{21} + \eta_{03}) \qquad (1.70)$$

$$\varphi7 = (3\eta_{21} - \eta_{03})(\eta_{30} + \eta_{12})\left[(\eta_{30} + \eta_{12})^2 - 3(\eta_{21} + \eta_{03})^2\right]$$
$$+ (3\eta_{21} - \eta_{03})(\eta_{21} + \eta_{03})\left[3(\eta_{30} + \eta_{12})^2 - (\eta_{21} + \eta_{03})^2\right] \qquad (1.71)$$

As shown, these seven moments are low level features and are calculated using second and third class moments. It is obvious that for the description or recognition of an object these seven moments are insufficient, however the advantage of their immutability render them suitable for supplementing other features.

1.7.2 Compact Shape Portrayal Descriptor

The recently proposed Compact Shape Portrayal Descriptor (CSPD) [200] is a compact (123 bits) forty-one dimensions vector MPEG-like descriptor that contains conventional contour and region shape features. It is based on three prominent features which they are effective identifying similarities between shapes and rejecting small differences due to remained noise. The three-feature set is: Width to Height Ratio, Vertical - Horizontal Projection and Top-Bottom Shape Projections. Each vector value is non-linearly quantized in three bits to reduce its storage cost and increase its retrieval efficiency. Figure 1.3

illustrates the CSPD calculation block diagram. Each feature can be computed separately and easily in parallel.

The advantage of the CSPD is the tradeoff between its very small size, its low computation cost and its retrieval effectiveness. It is appropriate for retrieval systems that want to add shape capabilities without conceding any existing storing and computational specifications.

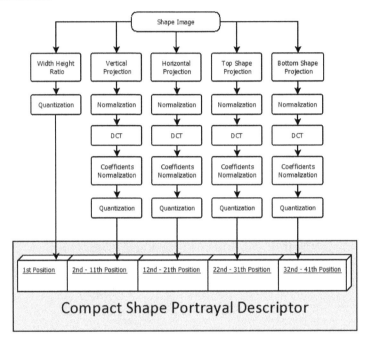

Figure 1.3: *CSDP Implementation Diagram*

1.8   Local Features

Local features provide slightly better retrieval results than global features [1]. These features represent the visual content of images using multiple **points of interest** and they are more expensive computationally due to the high dimensionality of their feature spaces[142]. Note that high-dimensional indexing and retrieval is a very challenging problem in the database field. Thus, global features are still popular in content based image retrieval systems, as they are easier to handle and still provide basic retrieval mechanisms. In any case, CBIR with either local or global features does not scale up well to large databases efficiency-wise. In a small database, a simple sequential scan may be acceptable, however, scaling up to millions images efficient indexing algorithms are imperative [109].

1.8.1 Points of Interest - Extraction and Description

As humans, when we observe a scene, we concentrate on certain points more than others. In computer vision these are called points of interest [116]. According to [191], a point of interest is a point in the image which in general can be characterized as follows:

- it has a clear and complete definition.

- it has a well-defined position in the image.

- the local image structure around the interest point is rich in terms of local information contents.

- it is stable under local and global perturbations in the image domain, including deformations as those arising from perspective transformations

- Optionally, the notion of interest point should include an attribute of scale, to make it possible to compute interest points from real-life images as well as under scale changes.

The term *interest points* goes back to the earlier notion of corner detection. Corners detection are based on the principle that if you place a small shifted patch over an area of an image, if that patch is placed on a corner then if it is moved in any direction there will be a large variation in its intensity. If the patch is over a uniform area of an image, then there will be no intensity change when the patch moves. If the patch is over an edge (Figure 1.4(a)) there will be an intensity change only if the patch moves in one direction. But, if the patch is over a corner then there will be a change in all directions, and therefore we know there must be a corner (Figure 1.4(b)).

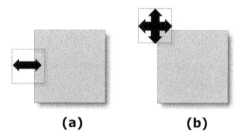

(a) **(b)**

Figure 1.4: *Corner Detection*

The term *points of interest* originally defined by Moravec[128], back in 1980. According to Moravec, interest points are points where there are large intensity variations in all directions. In 1988, Harris et al.[62] revised Moravec's corner detector by considering the differential of the corner score with respect to direction directly. The Harris corner detector computes the locally averaged moment matrix from the image gradients, and then combines the Eigenvalues of the moment matrix to compute a corner measure.

For a given shift $(\Delta x, \Delta y)$, the auto correlation function at point (x, y) in an image I is defined as:

$$c(x,y) = \sum_W [I(x_i, y_i) - I(x_i + \Delta x, y_i + \Delta y)]^2 \qquad (1.72)$$

$I(x_i + \Delta x, y_i + \Delta y)$ is approximated by a Taylor expansion:

$$I(x_i + \Delta x, y_i + \Delta y) \approx I(x_i, y_i) + \left[I_x(x_i, y_i) I_y(x_i, y_i) \begin{bmatrix} \Delta x \\ \Delta y \end{bmatrix} \right] \qquad (1.73)$$

where I_x and I_y is the partial derivatives of image I in x and y, respectively. Combining these 2 equations:

$$
\begin{aligned}
c(x,y) &= \sum_W [I(x_i, y_i) - I(x_i + \Delta x, y_i + \Delta y)]^2 &(1.74)\\
&= \sum_W \left[I(x_i, y_i) - I(x_i, y_i) - \left[I_x(x_i, y_i) I_y(x_i, y_i) \begin{bmatrix} \Delta x \\ \Delta y \end{bmatrix} \right] \right]^2 &(1.75)\\
&= \sum_W \left[-I_x(x_i, y_i) I_y(x_i, y_i) \begin{bmatrix} \Delta x \\ \Delta y \end{bmatrix} \right]^2 &(1.76)\\
&= [\Delta x, \Delta y] \begin{bmatrix} \sum_W I_x(x_i, y_i)^2 & \sum_W I_x(x_i, y_i) I_y(x_i, y_i) \\ \sum_W I_x(x_i, y_i) I_y(x_i, y_i) & \sum_W I_y(x_i, y_i)^2 \end{bmatrix} \begin{bmatrix} \Delta x \\ \Delta y \end{bmatrix} &(1.77)\\
&= [\Delta x, \Delta y] C(x,y) \begin{bmatrix} \Delta x \\ \Delta y \end{bmatrix} &(1.78)
\end{aligned}
$$

where $C(x,y)$ is the structure tensor and captures the intensity structure of the local neighborhood.

Assume that $\lambda 1$ and $\lambda 2$ are the eigenvalues of matrix $C(x,y)$.

- If both λ values are small then the windowed image region is of approximately constant intensity (no features of interest).

- If one eigenvalue approximates zero while the other eigenvalue is a large positive number, then an edge is found.

- If both eigenvalues have large positive values, then a corner is found.

Given that the computation of the eigenvalues is computationally expensive, the Harris color operator can be define by positive local extrema of the following operator:

$$M_c = \det(C(x,y)) - k \times \text{Trace}^2(C(x,y)) \qquad (1.79)$$

where k is a tunable sensitivity parameter (usually is equal to 0.04).

The evaluation of interest point extraction methods in Schmid et al. [162] demonstrate the effectiveness of the Harris detector compared to other existing approaches. However this detector is not invariant to scale changes.

The multi-scale Harris-Laplace detector is based on a second moments matrix [104], which reflects the local distribution of gradient directions in the image. This matrix must be adapted to scale changes to make it independent of the image resolution [190]. The multi-scale Harris-Laplace detector is merely suitable for grayscale images.

Given that this book mainly deals with global features, more sophisticated point of interest extraction methods are beyond our scope and are not discussed further. Nevertheless, here's a list of the state of the art methods for further research:

- Laplacian-of-Gaussian (LoG) [112].

- Difference of Gaussians (DoG) Filter [114] applied in scale space.

- Salient region detector proposed by Kadir and Brady [86].

- Hessian matrix on integral images [8].

- Salient region detector proposed by Kadir and Brady [86].

- The edge-based region detector proposed by Jurie and Schmid [85].

- The Wang and Brady corner detection algorithm [188].

- The SUSAN: Smallest Univalue Segment Assimilating Nucleus corner detector proposed in [170].

- The MSER: Maximally Stable Extremal Regions [123].

- The Kadir's detector [87].

Local descriptors are describing the content of the points of interest (or blobs) for an image. A list of the most commonly used local descriptors for further research is given below:

- SIFT: Scale-Invariant Feature Transform [114].

- SURF: Speeded Up Robust Features[8].

- GLOH: Gradient Location and Orientation Histogram [125].

- LESH: Local Energy based Shape Histogram [160].

- HOG: Histogram of oriented gradients [133].

Local features are used in the literature mainly to solve the problem of Simultaneous Localization And Mapping based on visual information (SLAM). A Comparative Evaluation of Interest Point Detectors and Local Descriptors for Visual SLAM is given in [56].

1.8.2 Bag of Visual Words

Bag-of-visual-words (BOVW) [33] approach is inspired by the bag-of-words model, a widely used method in information retrieval (text retrieval), where a document is represented by a set of distinct keywords. The same concept governs the BOVW model, in which an image is represented by a set of distinct local features, known as visual words. BOVWs are becoming a widely used representation for content-based image retrieval, for two reasons: their retrieval effectiveness on near duplicate images, and their better efficiency than local feature representations. However, experimental results show that visual words are still not as expressive as the text words [202].

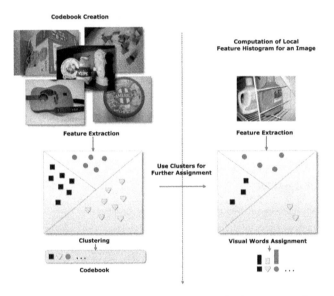

Figure 1.5: *Illustration of the process employed for codebook creation and visual words assignment.*

Using Bag-of-visual-words approach, the extracted local features (usually SURF or SIFT) are clustered (usually using K-means classifier) into a preset number of classes, and the calculated cluster centers (i.e. the mean vectors) are called visual words. The set of visual words forms a visual vocabulary also known as codebook. For every new image added in the collection, its local features must be extracted and assigned to the best fitting visual word from the existing codebook. By the end of that process a local feature histogram is composed for each image in the collection. Multiple approaches to enhance the bag of visual words approach have been proposed in literature [94][83][107][69][44].

1.9 MPEG-7

Before MPEG-7, there were no acceptable standards available for the description of the visual contents of multimedia. MPEG-7, also known as "Moving Pictures Expert Group Multimedia Content Description Interface - 7" [75][76][30] is the first attempt in this direction. MPEG-7 goal is to determine a standardized method for describing the various types of multimedia information. Its objective goal is to facilitate the fast and efficient recognition and management of the information, which exists in multimedia.

Even without MPEG-7, there are many methods for describing the visual content of an image. Many of them are employed today in various commercial and research systems used in image management. However, these systems do not allow for searching multiple information storage sites and do not facilitate exchange of content between various data bases which use different description systems. All these incompatibility issues can be solved with the creation of a standard. A standardized method for describing multimedia information allows for exchange between different systems not only of content, but also of its description. Moreover, this determines an environment, in which tools from different systems can collaborate with each other in order to create a platform for the transparent management of multi-media information. The main results of MPEG-7 is increasing intra-functionality, the prospect of achieving low cost products through the creation of a market in which services will be based on a common standard, as well as an increasing base of users which will employ this standard. This agreement (a standard is in essence and agreement) between users, has the potential for simplifying the entire process for content identification. Of course, this standard must be technologically powerful and correct, otherwise there will be various commercial standards created, which will impede intra-functionality. MPEG-7 meets these prerequisites based on current demands, in as much as it bridges what is feasible with what is useful.

1.9.1 The Basic Principles of MPEG-7

The creation of the MPEG-7 standard, caused the formation of a set of basic principles. The participating groups which contributed to the creation of MPEG-7 followed these basic principles, which are more or less high level demands and express the vision behind MPEG-7.

Some of these basic principles are:

1. Wide Range of Application. MPEG-7 must be compatible for use in all applications.

2. Content-Based. MPEG-7 allow the creation of various descriptors so that they can be used:

    - Individually, for example for the summary of an image content.

35

- In conjunction with the content, for example for transmission along with the content.

- Attached more than once with the content, for example in an Internet based medium.

3. Wide range of data formats. MPEG-7 must support a wide range of data formats, such as sounds, speech, images, graphics, 3D models, synthesized sound, video etc.

4. Independent of medium. MPEG-7 must be independent of medium, through which the content is distributed. This medium may be paper, film, cassette, CD, hard drive, digital recording, the Internet, etc

5. Object-oriented. MPEG-7 must allow object-oriented description of the image content. Thus, the content must be described as a composition of multi-media objects. Moreover, there must exist the capability of independent access to the description data of the specific objects.

6. Expansive. MPEG-7 must allow the expansion of the entire range of basic tools for content description, in a specific manner.

A standard such as MPEG-7, cannot incorporate all the structures which might be required from an application. Thus, it must allow and describe the expansion of the standard, so that it is to the greater extent possible, and if feasible, intra-functional.

These basic principles, don't just describe the vision of MPEG-7 but also highlight its differences in regards to other standards.

1.9.2   MPEG-7 Descriptors

More than a hundred descriptors have been developed. The relations between these descriptors in MPEG-7 are outlined in Figure 1.6.

The basic components found in low level deal with the basic data forms, the mathematic structures, the schema tools, the link and media localization tools, as well as the basic description schemes, which are the elementary components of more complex description schemes. The section of the schematic mapping tools is defined by the components for the creation of valid MPEG-7 schema instance documents and sections of the descriptions.

Moreover, in this level, the tools for the management and organization of the elements and types of structures of the schema are defined. Based on the low level, the content descriptors and management components are defined. These elements describe the content from different visual angles. At present there are five visual angles defined: creation and production, treatment, structural dimension and conceptual dimension. The first three manage information related to content management, while the last two mainly deal with the content description of the received information.

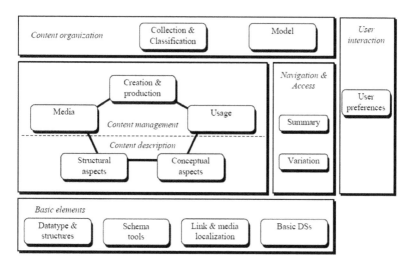

Figure 1.6: *Multimedia Description Scheme[84]*

An overview of the Visual Description Tools, proposed by MPEG-7, is illustrated in Figure 1.7.

Dominant Color Descriptor (DCD)

DCD is a compact color descriptor which is formed by a small number of representative colors that are obtained by using clustering and color quantization. This descriptor consists of these representative colors, their percentages in a region, spatial coherency of the color, and color variance. Its benefits are small storage requirements and high speed retrieval.

The traditional color histogram contains some high-dimensional indexing problems. In contrast, the representative colors can be indexed in the 3-D color space, bypassing those problems. For similarity retrieval and in order to find regions containing a representative color, each one of these colors are used independently in the query image or region.

The descriptor is computed making use of the following steps. First, the colors present in a given image or region are first clustered having a result of a small number of colors. The dominant color extraction method is based the generalized Lloyd algorithm[75] for color clustering. After that, the percentages of these colors are calculated. These percentage values are quantized to 5 bits each. The color quantization depends on the color space specifications defined for the entire database.

Furthermore, the spatial coherency value is computed. This value differentiates between large color blobs versus colors that are spread all over the image. Mainly it is a single number that represents the overall spatial homogeneity of the dominant colors in

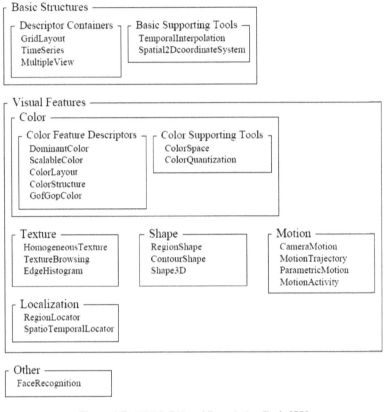

Figure 1.7: *MPEG-7 Visual Description Tools [75]*

the image. The number of dominant colors can vary from image to image and a maximum
of eight dominant colors can be used to represent the region. The definition of the above
is presented with the following equation:

$$F = \{(c_i, p_i, v_i), s\}, (i = 1, 2, \ldots, N) \tag{1.80}$$

where

- N the total number of the dominant colors;

- c_i is the ith dominant color;

- p_i its percentage value;

- v_i its color variance. (optional field)

The dissimilarity between two DCDs can be computed as:

Figure 1.8: *Dominant Color Descriptor: The Representative Colors of an Image*

$$D^2(F_1, F_2) = \sum_{i=1}^{N1} p_{1i}^2 + \sum_{j=1}^{N2} p_{2j}^2 - \sum_{i=1}^{N1}\sum_{j=1}^{N2} 2a_{1i,2j} p_{1i} p_{2j} \tag{1.81}$$

where:

$F_1 = \{\{c_{1,i}, p_{1,i}, v_{1,i}\}, s_1\}$, the DCD of the first image, $F_2 = \{\{c_{2,i}, p_{2,i}, v_{2,i}\}, s_2\}$ the DCD for the second image, and $a_{k,l}$ is the similarity coefficient between two colors c_k and c_l:

$$a_{k,l} = \begin{cases} 1 - d_{k,l}/d_{\max}, & d_{k,l} \leq T_d \\ 0, & d_{k,l} > T_d \end{cases} \tag{1.82}$$

where:

- $d_{k,l}$ is the Euclidean distance between two colors c_k and c_l

- T_d is maximum distance for two colors to be considered similar

- $d_{\max} = aT_d$

In particular, this means that any two dominant colors from one single description are at least T_d distance apart [120].

Scalable Color Descriptor (SCD)

In the SCD implementation, the HSV color space has been employed.

$$H_1 = \cos^{-1}\left(\frac{\frac{1}{2}[(R-G)+(R-B)]}{\sqrt{(R-G)^2 + (R-B)(G-R)}} \right) \tag{1.83}$$

$$H = \begin{cases} H_1, & B \leq G \\ 360 - H_1, & B > G \end{cases} \tag{1.84}$$

$$S = \frac{\max(R,G,B) - \min(R,G,B)}{\max(R,G,B)} \tag{1.85}$$

$$V = \frac{\max(R,G,B)}{255} \tag{1.86}$$

where $R,G,B \in [0,255]$, $H \in [0,360]$ and $S,V \in [0,1]$.

HSV space is uniformly quantized into a total of 256 bins defined by sixteen levels in H (Hue), four levels in S (Saturation) and four levels in V (Value). The values of H, S and V are calculated for every pixel and are then linearly quantized in the ranges [0 , 15], [0 , 3] and [0 , 3] respectively. Afterwards, the modified histogram is formed using the function:

$$H_{Quantized} + 16 \times S_{Quantized} + 64 \times V_{Quantized} \qquad (1.87)$$

Each bin value is non uniformly quantized to a 11-bit value. To achieve a more efficient encoding, the 11-bit integer values are first mapped into a nonlinear 4-bit representation.

This has the result of higher significance to the small values with higher probability. The problem faced is that this 4-bit representation of the 256-bin HSV histogram would require 1024 bits/histogram, which is too large a number in the context of many MPEG-7 applications. The idea is to lower this number make application scalable. So, the histograms are encoded using a Haar tranform.

This 4-bit representation of the 256-bin HSV histogram would require 1024 bits/histogram, which is too large a number in the context of many MPEG-7 applications. To lower this number and make the application scalable, the histograms are encoded using a Haar transform. More specific, by matching the coefficients and by using the size conversion of Haar transform, a simple histogram intersection for similarity measure and a comparison among different sized histograms can be achieved respectively.

SCD binary representation is scalable in terms of bin numbers and bit representation accuracy over a broad range of data rates.

Color Structure Descriptor (CSD)

The main purpose of the CSD is to express the local color features in images and it is mostly used for still image retrieval. More specific, an 8×8 sized structuring block scans the image in a sliding window approach. With each shift of the structuring element, CSD counts the number of times a particular color is contained within the structuring element.

Suppose that $c_0,c_1,c_2,\ldots,c_{M-1}$ denote the M quantized colors. A color structure histogram can then be denoted by:

$$CSD = \bar{h}_s(m), m \in \{1,\ldots M\} \qquad (1.88)$$

where the value in each bin represents the number of structuring elements in the image containing one or more pixels with color c_m. The HMMD color space, which is supported in MPEG-7 is used in this descriptor. In the MPEG-7 core experiments for image retrieval, the HMMD color space appeared to be very effective and compared favorably with the

HSV color space. Note that it is a slight twist on the HSI color space, where the diff component is scaled by the intensity value.

For further deepening, the hue has the same meaning as in the HSV space, and max and min are the maximum and minimum among the R, G, and B values, respectively. The diff component is defined as the difference between max and min. Only three of the four components are sufficient to describe the HMMD space. This color space can be depicted using the double cone structure.

$$Max = max(R,G,B)$$
$$Min = min(R,G,B) \qquad (1.89)$$
$$Diff = Max - Min$$

The CSD is defined using four color space quantization operating points: 184, 120, 64, and 32 bins. The bin values of the CSD are normalized by the number of locations of the structuring element and lie in the range $[0.0, 1.0]$. The bin values are then nonlinearly quantized to 8 bits/bin.

If there is need of similarity measure, a simple histogram intersection can be used.

Color Layout Descriptor (CLD)

The CLD is designed to describe the spatial distribution of color in an image in a very compact form. The spatial distribution of color recommends an effective descriptor for sketch based image retrieval, content filtering using image indexing, and visualization. In addition the most of this descriptor can be achieved by using a combination of grid structure descriptor and grid-wise dominant colors. However, such a combination would require a relatively large number of bits, and matching will be more complex and expensive. For several applications, a compact yet effective descriptor is needed, and the CLD satisfies these needs.

Figure 1.9: *Color Layout Descriptor: The Representative Color of Each Tile.*

CLD is formed by dividing the image into an 8×8 grid, and then the representative color of each tile is obtained, using th YCbCr color space.

41

$$\begin{bmatrix} Y \\ Cb \\ Cr \end{bmatrix} = \begin{bmatrix} 16 \\ 128 \\ 128 \end{bmatrix} + \begin{bmatrix} 65.481 & 128.553 & 24.966 \\ -37.797 & -74.203 & 112 \\ 112 & -93.768 & -18.214 \end{bmatrix} \begin{bmatrix} R \\ G \\ B \end{bmatrix} \quad (1.90)$$

where $R, G, B \in [0, 1]$, $Y \in [16, 235]$ and $Cb, Cr \in [16, 240]$.

A Discrete Cosine Transform (DCT) is performed on the 8×8 block and the DCT coefficients are used as the descriptor.

According to the DCT, N real numbers $x_0, x_1, \ldots, x_{N-1}$ are transformed into N real numbers $y_1, y_2, \ldots, y_{N-1}$ according to the following formula:

$$y(k) = a(k) \sum_{x=0}^{N-1} x(n) \cos \left[\frac{(2n+1)k\pi}{2N} \right] \quad (1.91)$$

where $k = 0, 1, \ldots, N-1$.

$$a(k) = \begin{cases} \sqrt{1/N}, & k = 0 \\ \sqrt{2/N}, & k > 0 \end{cases} \quad (1.92)$$

The default number of bits for CLD is 63. This includes six coefficients for the Y channel, and three coefficients for each one of Cr and Cb channel. The DC (first coefficient of the DCT transform) values are quantized to 6 bits and the remaining to 5 bits each.

Similarity between CLDs can be measured by the root of squared differences of each matched coefficients.

In details, for matching two CLDs, (DY, DCb, DCr) and (DY', DCb', DCr') the following distance measure is used:

$$D = \sqrt{\sum_i w_{yi}(DY_i - DY_i')^2} + \sqrt{\sum_i w_{bi}(DCb_i - DCb_i')^2} + \sqrt{\sum_i w_{ri}(DCr_i - DCr_i')^2} \quad (1.93)$$

where (DY, DCb, DCr) represent the DCT coefficients of the respective color components. The distances are weighted appropriately, with larger weights given to the lower frequency components.

It should be noted that representation of CLD is in frequency domain, the coefficient represents the visual pattern in three separated channels of YCbCr, information of particular colors cannot be directly accessed.

Inverse DCT is needed for accessing spectral information. Inverse DCT is calculated as follows:

$$x(n) = \sum_{k=0}^{N-1} a(k) y(k) \cos \left[\frac{(2n+1)k\pi}{2N} \right] \quad (1.94)$$

where $n = 0, 1, \ldots, N-1$

The detail of colors is not as accurate as other color descriptors.

Group-of-Pictures (GoP) Color Descriptor

By aggregating SCD descriptor and using the same similarity measure as SCD, another descriptor was proposed for joint representation of color feature for multiple images, such as frames in video sequences. This is GoP descriptor and it consists of average, median, and intersection histograms of groups of frames calculated based on the individual frame histograms.

Region-Based Shape Descriptor (RBSD)

The MPEG-7 Region-Based Descriptor is based on Angular Radial Transformation (ART)[92]. The ART coefficients are used to describe the visual pattern in a circular region. An important characteristic, is that this descriptor is suitable for shapes that can be best described by shape regions rather than contours. The benefits of using it, is that it is invariant to transformations and it can represent complex objects as well as simple objects.

Contour-Based Shape Descriptor (CBSD)

MPEG-7 Contour Shape Descriptor uses Contour Shape Space (CSS) [12] to represent shapes using curves, in a vector valued functions. The descriptor also includes eccentricity and circularity values of the original and filtered contours. All these make a size of 122 bits/contour in average for the descriptor. Finally to changes of object shape in videos such as non-rigid motion, partial occlusion or perspective distortion the behavior of CBSD is robust.

Edge Histogram Descriptor (EHD)

The edge histogram descriptor captures the spatial distribution of edges which is a good texture signature that is useful for image to image matching even when the underlying texture is not homogeneous.

Edge Histogram Descriptor is computed using the follow method. A given image is first sub-divided into sub-images. Then, local edge histograms for each of these sub-images is computed. Edges are broadly grouped into five categories: vertical, horizontal, 45 diagonal, 135 diagonal, and isotropic (non-directional edge). Thus, each local histogram has five bins corresponding to the above five categories.

Since there are 16 sub-images in the image, a total of $5 \times 16 = 80$ histogram bins is required. These bins are non uniformly quantized using 3 bits/bin, resulting in a descriptor of size 240 bits.

A fuzzy version of the five digital filters presented by the MPEG-7 EHD as well as more details about the descriptor are presented in Section 2.2.2.

Homogeneous Texture Descriptor (HTD)

The HTD provides a quantitative characterization of texture for similarity-based image-to-image matching. This descriptor is computed by first filtering the image with a bank of orientation and scale sensitive filters, and computing the mean and standard deviation of the filtered outputs in the frequency domain. That happens because during the MPEG-7 Core Experiments,it was realized that the computational complexity of this descriptor can be reduced significantly using frequency domain and an efficient implementation using Radon transform is described in [150].

Texture Browsing Descriptor (TBD)

Texture Browsing Descriptor is a compact descriptor that requires only 12 bits (maximum) to characterize a texture's regularity (2 bits), directionality bits , and coarseness bits. Because a texture may have more than one dominant direction and associated scale the specification allows a maximum of two different directions and coarseness values.

The regularity of a texture is graded on a scale of 0 to 3, with 0 indicating an irregular or random texture and 3 indicating a periodic pattern with well-defined directionality and coarseness values. Between values 1 and 2 there is some or implied ambiguity. Additionally, the directionality of a texture is quantized to six values, ranging from 0 degrees to 150 degrees in steps of 30 degrees.

1.10 Similarity Matching Techniques

A similarity matching unit can perform with the assistance of a similarity matching technique, to calculate the distance between the features of a query image to the features of each image which is stored in the database. The choice of the appropriate similarity matching method is directly related to the type of data which will be used. Therefore, during system design, the selection of features and the similarity matching method must be simultaneous. In this section, some of the most usual methods for measuring similarity are outlined.

The first and most basic classification which can be applied to the similarity matching methods is their classification as similarity and dissimilarity metrics. Normalized forms of the similarity matching methods have values in the range of $[0,1]$. Deviation from this range depends on the method. Dissimilarity metrics converge towards 0 while on the other hand similarity metrics converge towards 1.

These two types of classifiers are linked to each other and the conversion between them is very easy. If the dissimilarity of two vectors is taken to be D, then their similarity S is equal to $S = 1 - D$.

1.10.1 Dissimilarity Metrics

The similarity matching methods in this category are more commonly known as *Distance Measures*, since their function is to present the distance between two given vectors.

Minkowski Metric

This is the most widely used method for determining distance between feature vectors and is defined as follows:

$$d_p(i,j) = \left(\sum_{k=1}^{m} |x_{ik} - x_{jk}|^p \right)^{\frac{1}{p}} \tag{1.95}$$

x_i and x_j are descriptors which describe images i and j. x_{ik} and x_{jk} are the K-th element for x_i and x_j, while m is the number of the elements. Higher values of p give weight to larger values of absolute distance (more emphasis is given in more inhomogeneous pairs). Three special cases of the Minkowski Metric which are of special interest are the following:

- **City Block or Manhattan Distance** In this case the distance between 2 $m - D$ vectors is taken to be the sum of absolute distance between the elements.

$$d_p(i,j) = \left(\sum_{k=1}^{m} |x_{ik} - x_{jk}| \right) \tag{1.96}$$

- **Euclidean Distance** In this case the distance is taken to be the square root of the sum of differences of elements squared.

$$d_p(i,j) = \left(\sum_{k=1}^{m} |x_{ik} - x_{jk}|^2 \right)^{\frac{1}{2}} \tag{1.97}$$

- **Chess Distance** In this case the distance between vectors is equal to the highest value of the absolute differences of the elements.

$$d_p(i,j) = \max \left\{ |x_{i1} - x_{j1}|, |x_{i2} - x_{j2}|, \dots |x_{im} - x_{jm}| \right\} \tag{1.98}$$

Canberra Metric

Canberra Metric[11] is defined as:

$$d_p(i,j) = \sum_{k=1}^{m} \frac{|x_{ik} - x_{jk}|}{(x_{ik} + x_{jk})} \tag{1.99}$$

x_{ik} and x_{jk} is the K-*th* element of x_i and x_j, while m is the number of the elements. The sum in the equation is set to zero only if x_{ij} and x_{jk} are equal. This type of measurement is applied to groups of vectors which cannot be set to negative values, such as color.

1.10.2   Similarity Metrics

The problem of determining the similarity distance between 2 multi- dimensional points can also be solved via the use of a symmetric equation which has a value of one when the 2 given vectors are identical. Any non-parametric equation $S(x_i, x_j)$ can be used for the comparison of 2 multidimensional points x_i and x_j. Examples of similarity equations are:

Mahalanobis Distance

The Mahalonobis distance [37] is given by the following formula:

$$M_{ij} = r^2(x_i, x_j) = (x_i - x_j)^T C^{-1}(x_i - x_j) \qquad (1.100)$$

where $r(\vec{x}_i, \vec{x}_j)$ the Mahalanobis distance between two vectors $\vec{x}_i$ and $\vec{x}_j$ and C^{-1} the inverse of the scatter matrix for the two vectors.

Tanimoto Coefficient

The Tanimoto coefficient for two vectors $\vec{x}_i$ and $\vec{x}_j$ is given by the following formula [181]:

$$T_{ij} = t(x_i, x_j) = \frac{x_i^T x_j}{x_i^T x_i + x_j^T x_j - x_i^T x_j} \qquad (1.101)$$

where x^T is the transpose vector of the descriptor x.

In the absolute congruence of the vectors, the Tanimoto coefficient takes the value 1, while in the maximum deviation the coefficient tends to zero.

1.10.3   Special Classes of Classifiers

Histogram Intersection

Histogram Intersection is defined as:

$$H(H_q, H_c) = \frac{\sum\limits_{i=1}^{N} \min(H_q(i), H_c(i))}{\min(\sum\limits_{i=1}^{i=N} H_q(i), \sum\limits_{i=1}^{i=N} H_c(i))} \qquad (1.102)$$

where H_q and H_c are the query and challenging vectors respectively and N is the number of bins. Histogram Intersection remains one of the best methods for comparing histograms in image retrieval applications. The similarity ratio belongs to the interval [0, 1].

Simple Match

Let us assume that there is a need for comparison of two images based on their histograms. The two histograms have elements. The intersection of the histogram of the one image $h(i)$, with the histogram of the sample $M, h(m)$, is defined as the sum of lowest values of the k relevant elements, as shown in the following equation [165].

$$T((h(i), h(m)) = \sum_{j-1}^{k} \min\{h(i)[j], h(m)[j]\} \tag{1.103}$$

The value of T is normalized with the sum of the pixels of the image-sample (m) and a match value is given.

$$B.O.(h(i), h(m)) = \frac{\sum\limits_{j-1}^{k} \min\{h(i)[j], h(m)[j]\}}{\sum\limits_{j-1}^{k} h(m)[j]} \tag{1.104}$$

he metric $B.O.(h(i), h(m))$ approaches the value 1 when the two images are similar in regards to their color content, while for completely different images it approaches zero.

QBIC Distance

The QBIC distance is one more metric which is used in histogram comparison. Its name originates in the QBIC system which is a standard IBM application, which is used in image retrieval. The user inputs an image-sample and the system, via the use of appropriate algorithms returns with images from the database using only the color distance of these images. The QBIC system determine histogram distance as follows [77]:

$$d(I, Q) = [(h(I) - h(Q)]^T x A x [(h(I) - h(Q)] \tag{1.105}$$

where $h(I)$ and $h(Q)$ are the histograms for K-positions of images I and Q respectively, while A is a $K \times K$ similarity matrix. In this matrix, very similar colors will have similarity values approaching one (1), while colors which are very different must have similarity values approaching zero (0). The similarity matrix will have the following form:

$$A = \begin{bmatrix} 1 & 0.99 & 0.98 & 0.96 & \cdots & 0 \\ 0.99 & 1 & 0.99 & 0.98 & \cdots & 0.01 \\ \vdots & \vdots & \vdots & \vdots & \vdots & \vdots \\ 0.01 & 0.02 & \cdots & 0.99 & 1 & 0.99 \\ 0 & 0.01 & \cdots & 0.98 & 0.99 & 1 \end{bmatrix} \tag{1.106}$$

Two chromatically similar images, have $d(I, Q)$ near zero, while on the other hand, images with chromatic deviation have a $d(I, Q)$ near one.

Earth Movers Distance

The earth movers distance (EMD) [153] is describing the minimal cost that must be paid to transform one distribution into the other. The EMD is based on a solution to the *transportation problem* from linear optimization.

The transportation problem is a special linear programming problem to distribute any commodity from any group of supply centers, called sources, to any group of receiving centers, called destinations, in such a way as to minimize the total distribution cost [66].

Computing the EMD requires a transportation problem to be solved. The EMD $d_{EMD}(H, H')$ between the histograms H and H' is calculated as:

$$d_{EMD}(H, H') = \frac{\sum_{i,j} d_{i,j} g_{i,j}}{\sum_{i,j} g_{i,j}} \tag{1.107}$$

Here d_{ij} denotes the dissimilarity between bin i and bin j and $g_{i,j} \geq 0$ is the optimal flow between the two distributions such that the total cost $\sum_{i,j} d_{i,j} g_{i,j}$ is minimized. The following constraints have to be taken into account for all i, j:

$$\sum_i g_{i,j} \leq H'_j \tag{1.108}$$

$$\sum_j g_{i,j} \leq H_i \tag{1.109}$$

$$\sum_{i,j} g_{i,j} = \min(H_i, H'_j) \tag{1.110}$$

The earth movers distance is more robust than histogram matching techniques.

1.11 Evaluating an Image Retrieval System

The objective of an image retrieval system is to retrieve images in rank order, where the rank is determined from the relevance to the query at hand [167].

The performance of a content based image retrieval system is measured using the following procedure. A certain benchmark image database is initially used. Classical examples of such databases are the Wang [189] database, the UCID database [161] and the Nister database [136]. Each database is comprised of a number of N images, Q of them been designated as queries. Queries are images used as input to the retrieval system in order to evaluate its performance. For each query there is a given total number of images with visual similarity which are considered as the ground truth. The system's performance is calculated using a technique to evaluate the order in which the images which form the ground truths for all the queries appear. Many of the methods that are used in the field of information retrieval have been adopted in order to evaluate the image retrieval results.

48

1.11.1 Retrieval Evaluation Methods

The overall retrieval effectiveness can be calculated only if the actual relevancies' (ground truth) are known [167]. Let the database $\{x_1, x_2, \cdots, x_i, \cdots, x_N\}$ be a set of images represented by low level features. To retrieve images similar to a query q, each database image x_i is compared with the query image using an appropriate distance function $d(q, x_i)$. The database images are then sorted according to the distance such that $d(q, x_i) \leq d(q, x_{i+1})$ holds for each pair of images x_i and x_{i+1} in the sequence $(x_1, x_2, \cdots, x_N)$ [41].

A very important parameter that contributes to the evaluation of a retrieval system is the $Rank(k)$ index. This index describes the retrieval rank of the kth ground truth image. Consider a query q and assume that the kth ground truth image is found to be the Rth position of the retrieval rank. Then $Rank(k) = R$. $NG(q)$ describes the total number of relevant images for the query q.

In [131], the most important image retrieval evaluation methods are described. The most commonly used indices which contribute to the formation of performance measures for information retrieval systems are as follows [167][131]:

Detections - True Positives: $A_k = \sum\limits_{n=1}^{k} V_n$, where $V_n \in \{0, 1\}$ describes the relevance of the image that appears at position n. If the image belongs to the ground truth of the query then $V_n = 1$, otherwise $V_n = 0$. If k corresponds to the final image of the ground truth, then A_k indicates the number of relevant images retrieved in the first k results.

False Alarms - False Positives: $B_k = \sum\limits_{n=1}^{k} (1 - V_n) = k - A_k$. This indicator essentially counts the incorrect results that appear in the first k retrieved images.

Misses: $C_k = \sum\limits_{n=1}^{N} V_n - A_k = NG(q) - A_k$, where N is the total number of images in the database.

Correct Dismissals: $D_k = \sum\limits_{n=1}^{N} (1 - V_n) - B_k$.

By using these indices the following standard information retrieval measures are implemented.

Recall: $R_k = \frac{A_k}{A_k + C_k} = \frac{A_k}{NG(q)} = \frac{|\text{retrieved} \cap \text{relevant}|}{|\text{relevant}|}$. Recall essentially describes the ratio of the number of the relevant images within the first k results, to the number of the total relevant images.

Precision: $P_k = \frac{A_k}{A_k + B_k} = \frac{A_k}{k} = \frac{|\text{retrieved} \cap \text{relevant}|}{|\text{retrieved}|}$. Precision essentially describes the ratio of the number of the relevant images within the first k results, to the number of the retrieved images.

Using the standard information retrieval measures, the following evaluation methods are shaped [167]:

- Retrieval effectiveness: P_k vs R_k.

- Receiver operating characteristic: A_k vs V_k.

- Relative operating characteristic: A_k vs F_k.

- 3-point average: average P_k at $R_k = 0.2, 0.5, 0.8$.

- 11-point average: average P_k at 11 recall points

- AVRR: average relevant rank in top $k, (\frac{1}{k}A_k)$.

- MT: relevant and missing in top $k, (C_k)$.

- First page score: R-Value at $k = 20, (P_{20})$.

- Visual inspection of top $k, (P_k)$ and

- Response ratio: $\frac{A_k}{B_k}$ vs A_k.

A very popular evaluation method is the retrieval rate (RR):

$$RR(q) = \frac{NF(\alpha, q)}{NG(q)} \qquad (1.111)$$

$NF(\alpha, q)$ is the number of ground truth images found within the $\alpha \times NG(q)$ first retrievals.

At [74] the error rate which was first used to evaluate the results of object and face recognition was given.

$$\text{Error Rate} = \frac{\text{Number of NON Relevant Images Retrieved}}{\text{Number of Images Retrieved}} = \frac{B_k}{k} \qquad (1.112)$$

Muller and Rigoll present in [121] the retrieval efficiency. If the number of images retrieved is lower than the number or relevant images, retrieval efficiency is the precision, otherwise it is the recall of a query. This definition can be misleading since it mixes two standard measures [131].

A commonly used image retrieval evaluation method is retrieval effectiveness: P_k vs R_k. Precision and recall values are usually presented in a precision-recall graph $(R, P(R))$.

The average precision AP for a single query q is the mean over the precision scores after each relevant retrieved image:

$$AP(q) = \frac{1}{NG(q)} \sum_{k=1}^{NG(q)} P_q(R_k) \qquad (1.113)$$

where R_k is the recall after the kth relevant image. Mean Average Precision (MAP) is the mean of the average precision scores over all queries and is equal to:

$$MAP = \frac{1}{|Q|} \sum_{q \in Q} AP(q) \tag{1.114}$$

where Q is the set of queries q.

An advantage of the MAP is that it contains both precision and recall oriented aspects and is sensitive to the entire ranking.

MPEG-7, presented a new evaluation method, the Averaged Normalized Modified Retrieval Rank (ANMRR) [129].

ANMRR is always in a range of 0 to 1, and the smaller the value of this measure the better the matching quality of the query is. ANMRR is the evaluation criterion used in all of the MPEG-7 color core experiments. Evidence has shown that the ANMRR measure coincides approximately linearly with the results of the subjective evaluation of the retrieval accuracy of search engines [105].

The average rank $AVR(q)$ for a given query q is:

$$AVR(q) = \sum_{k=1}^{NG(q)} \frac{Rank(k)}{NG(q)} \tag{1.115}$$

where

- $NG(q)$ is the number of ground truth images for the query q

- $Rank(k)$ is the retrieval rank of the ground truth image.
  If this image is in the first K retrievals then $Rank(k) = R$ else $Rank(k) = 1.25 \times K$

  - K is the top ranked retrievals examined where:
    $K = min(X \times NG(q), 2 \times GMT)$
  - If $NG(q) > 50$ then $X = 2$ else $X = 4$
  - $GMT = max\{NG(q)\}$ for all q's of a data set

The modified retrieval rank is:

$$MRR(q) = AVR(q) - 0.5 \times [1 + NG(q)] \tag{1.116}$$

The normalized modified retrieval rank is computed as follows:

$$NMRR(q) = \frac{MRR(q)}{1.25 \times K - 0.5 \times [1 + NG(q)]} \tag{1.117}$$

Finally, the average NMRR over all queries is defined as:

$$ANMRR = \frac{1}{Q} \sum_{q=1}^{Q} NMRR(q) \tag{1.118}$$

One of the most significant advantages of ANMRR is that, similar to MAP, each system is evaluated on the basis of one value only, thus making it easier to compare the performance of different systems. ANMRR has already been used by several retrieval systems [199] [195].

1.12 Image Retrieval Systems

In this section some of the content based retrieval systems are presented. Their presentation is undertaken in order to highlight the research dynamic in this sector as well as the diversity of systems which exist, using different approaches for image retrieval.

1.12.1 LIRe

LIRe [117] is an open source Java library which is intended for developers and researchers, who want to integrate content based image retrieval features in their applications. More specific, LIRe extracts several image low level features from raster images and stores them in a Lucene index for later retrieval while the same time provides means for searching the index. Because of the simplicity of the approach it is an easy way to test the capabilities of classical CBIR approaches for single application domains.

Currently the following image features are included in LIRe:

1. Color histograms in RGB and HSV color space.

2. MPEG-7 descriptors scalable color, color layout and edge histogram.

3. The Tamura texture features coarseness, contrast and directionality.

4. Color and edge directivity descriptor, CEDD.

5. Fuzzy color and texture histogram, FCTH.

6. Auto color correlation feature.

7. Scale-invariant feature transform (SIFT).

8. SIFT based visual words.

In addition to LIRe, there is also a demo package called LIRe Demo. This package allows to test selected CBIR features of LIRe with a graphical user interface. Speed and simplicity are achieved by making indexing in parallel using multiple threads and photos from Flickr can be indexed instead of specifying a local image collection for testing purposes, respectively.

Both, LIRe and LIRe Demo, are available licensed under GPL online[2]. LIRe is hosted as sub project within the project 'Caliph and Emir', which provides Java based tools MPEG-7 image annotation and retrieval.

---

[2]http://semanticmetadata.net/LIRe

1.12.2 LISA

The ALISA (Adaptive Learning Image and Signal Analysis) was developed by ALIAS Corporation in collaboration with George Washington University and the Research Institute for Applied Knowledge Processing in Germany. The system employs an algorithm called Collective Learning for the statistical reproduction of an image.

LISA has the capability to extract features for the whole image or for segments of it. The algorithm can be taught to identify a new structure or shape, with only a few images. It extracts characteristic data for color, texture and image shape.

Successful applications of the system include the detection of intruders in a contained environment, vehicle detection in a desert environment, detecting aneurisms in the heart, classification of batteries per brand, coins, fruits, stamps etc. It has seen use for years now in industrial applications [130].

1.12.3 Blobworld

Blobworld was developed by the University of California, Berkeley. It extracts features by calculating the color and texture, the position and shapes of blobs of the images. The user first selects a category which defines the search parameters of the system. Then the user selects an area in an initial picture and denotes importance of color, texture, position and shape [16].

1.12.4 Behold

Behold implements two content-based image indexing techniques, automated image annotation and image similarity network construction. These techniques are complementary to extracting image metadata. The first one generates probabilities of keywords from a finite vocabulary for every image and allows the user to specify desired image content using keywords in addition to, or instead of, regular metadata search. The second one links visually similar images together allowing one to explore the indexed images freely based on their visual similarity. A typical search will start with a text query, and can be followed up by browsing the image network starting from an image in the search results that is visually close to the user's target.

Amazon Elastic Compute Cloud (EC2) provides computational power to Behold so it can handle large volumes of images [196].

1.12.5 QBIC

QBIC (Query By Image Content) [77] was the first commercial CBIR system. It was developed by IBM in the first half of the 90s. It consists of a search engine that sorts through database images according to colors, textures, shapes, sizes, and their positions. Its structure and techniques used have made a great effect on most of the later image retrieval systems. QBIC supports queries based on example images, user-constructed sketches and drawings, selected color and texture patterns, camera and object motion, and other graphical information. Any resulting image can be used as a new query in order to improve the search. Moreover, text-based keyword search can be combined with content-based similarity search. QBIC also takes into account the high dimensional feature indexing. The main aim of IBM was to design a good search engine to the detriment of designing a more attractive web-like interface.

As an extension of QBIC, IBM proposed the IMARS [132] system. IBM Multimedia Analysis and Retrieval System (IMARS) is a powerful system that can be used to automatically index, classify, and search large collections of digital images and videos. IMARS works by applying computer-based algorithms that analyze visual features of the images and videos, and subsequently allows them to be automatically organized and searched based on their visual content[151].

1.12.6   VisualSEEk

VisualSEEk [169] is a content-based search engine developed at Columbia University which was the first search engine which allowed users to flexibly query for images by specifying both visual features and spatial properties of the desired images. VisualSEEk supports queries based on spatial properties, such as size, location and relationships to other regions. This happens because this system uses visual features such as color set and wavelet transform-based texture feature and the same time it extended local queries at the region level. The user interface let the formulation of queries under the form of sketches by using a graphical editor.

VisualSEEk was developed following a server-client architecture on the Internet, where the client was a Java application and the server contained a test-bed of 12,000 images. The server side of the system was extended to the WebSEEk [168], which is a web-oriented search engine[151].

1.12.7   FIRE

The FIRE (Flexible Image Retrieval Engine) system was created in Aachen University in Germany. It extracts features regarding color, shape and structure of images. The user initiates the search by selecting an image from a series of images and has the capability of refreshing the relevance of his query by denoting under each image whether it is relevant, irrelevant or neutral to his query.

The specific system is probably the largest open source library for image retrieval. The main aim of FIRE is to investigate different image descriptors and evaluate their performance. FIRE was developed in C++ and Python and is meant to be easily extensible [134] [40].

1.12.8 Photobook

Photobook[139] is a computer system that allows the user to browse large image databases quickly and efficiently. To achieve that Photobook uses two techniques. First it uses text annotation information which is stored in an AI database and second it makes the computer search the images directly based on their content.

The most common use of Photobook is the following. Users use to select one (or several) of the currently-displayed images. Then they want Photobook to sort the entire set of images in terms of their similarity to the selected image (or set of images). Thus, Photobook re-presents the images to the user, now sorted by similarity to the selected images.

There are three well known different types of image descriptions which are available in Photobook and can be made rotation and scale invariant. Fot the beginning, there is the 'Appearance Photobook', which is applied to face and keyframe databases. There are also texture descriptions ('Texture Photobook') applied to texture-swatch and keyframe databases. Finally there are shape descriptions ('Shape Photobook') applied to hand-tool and fish databases.

Photobook was implemented by the Vision and Modeling Group, Media Laboratory at Massachussets Institute of Technology (MIT).

1.12.9 ALIPR

ALIPR (Automatic Linguistic Indexing of Pictures), processes an image and assigns it a batch of a preset number of words, arranged in order of perceived relevance. To achieve that it uses a combination of statistical techniques.

ALIPR has the advantage to combine a new annotation method that achieves real-time operation and better optimization properties while preserving the architectural advantages of the generative modeling approach. Models are established for a large collection of semantic concepts. This approach has the benefit that the computer only needs to learn from the new images as it has stored all the previous information in the form of profiling models that it obtained until that time. With fewer words it needs no retraining.

The revolution in computational efficiency results from a fundamental change in the modeling approach. In ALIP [105], every image is described by a set of feature vectors residing on grids at several resolutions. The profiling model of each concept is the probability law governing the generation of feature vectors on 2-D grids. Under the new approach, every image is characterized by a statistical distribution. The profiling model specifies a probability law for distributions directly [106].

1.12.10 MiPai

MiPai is an image search system that provides visual similarity search and text-based search functionalities on the CoPhIR collection [13] consisting of 106 million images crawled from the Flickr photo sharing website.

The similarity search functionality is implemented by means of the Permutation Prefix Index (PP-Index), which is a novel and approximate similarity search data structure that belongs to the family of the permutation-based indexes (PBI), independently introduced by Amato and Savino [3], and Chavez et Al. [26]. The text-based search functionality is based on a traditional inverted list index data structure.

More detailed, each image is represented by five MPEG-7 visual descriptors, used to perform visual the similarity search, and it has structured textual content associated (e.g., title, description, tags, comments), used by the text search component[51].

1.12.11   MUFIN

MUFIN (Multi-Feature Indexing Network)[7] indexing and searching mechanisms are based on the concept of structured Peer-to-Peer (P2P) networks.

The MUFIN system is based on a four-tier architecture. In first tier the executive core of the system is composed by several independent P2P overlays Each one of them maintains only the data of a specific feature, e.g. shape descriptors of images, color histograms, or protein spectra vectors. While operating, overlay's peers exchange messages. It must be mentioned that they are completely independent of the specific hardware infrastructure.

In the second tier, the independent overlays are linked together into a single virtual multi-overlay system where any peer from any overlay can access all the other overlays. For instance, a peer maintaining shapes of images can ask for similar color histograms or similar protein spectra vectors. In the third tier we find interfaces for maintaining data and posing queries. In particular, MUFIN offers a native API, a web service interface and a plug-in interface for linking with external indexes. Finally, the fourth level comprises of a variety of user interfaces.

1.12.12   Real-World Image Retrieval Systems

Not many image retrieval systems are deployed for public usage, save for Google Image Search, Bing Image Search, ASK Images Search and Yahoo! Images [35]. These web image search works as other textual search engines. The meta data of the image is indexed and stored in a large scale database and when a search query is performed the image search engine looks up the index, and queries are matched with the stored information. The results are presented in order of relevancy. The usefulness of an image search engine depends on the relevance of the results it returns, and the ranking algorithms are one of the keys to becoming a big player. Recently, Google announced a new image search user interface. Users can upload images and search for similar images over the Internet based on visual information.

For web-based retrieval systems, the user is concerned with the validity of the first results, without requiring the system to retrieve the entire ground truth for a query. For example, in Google images, the user is concerned for the proper presentation of the relevant results in the first pages. Even if a relevant result is retrieved in further pages, it is quite possible that it will not be detected by the users. There are cases in which the retrieval of the entire ground truth is required.

2

Describing Natural Color Images

The family of compact composite descriptors includes descriptors for 3 types of images. A group of 2 descriptors combines color and texture information in order to describe natural color images. One descriptor combines brightness and texture characteristics in order to describe grayscale images (primarily radiology medical images), and the other combines color and spatial distribution characteristics in order to describe artificially generated images (computer graphics, color sketches etc.).

This chapter [1] describes the Compact Composite Descriptors for Natural Color Images: the Color and Edge Directivity Descriptor (CEDD) and the Fuzzy Color and Texture Histogram (FCTH). The structure of these descriptors consists of n texture areas. In particular, each texture area is separated into 24 sub-regions, with each sub-region describing a color.

CEDD and FCTH use the same color information, as it results from 2 fuzzy systems that map the colors of the image in a 24-color custom palette. To extract texture information, CEDD uses a fuzzy version of the five digital filters presented by the MPEG-7 EHD, forming 6 texture areas. In contrast, FCTH uses the high frequency bands of the Haar Wavelet Transform in a fuzzy system to form 8 texture areas. An important characteristic of these 2 descriptors is the small size needed for indexing images. The CEDD length is 54 bytes per image while FCTH length is 72 bytes per image.

2.1 Color Information Extraction

Color is a low level feature that is widely used in Content Based Image Retrieval systems. Several approaches have been used to describe the color information that appears in the images. In most cases, color histograms are used, which on the one hand are easily ex-

[1]This Chapter is Based on: "ACCURATE IMAGE RETRIEVAL BASED ON COMPACT COMPOSITE DESCRIPTORS AND RELEVANCE FEEDBACK INFORMATION", S. A. Chatzichristofis, K. Zagoris, Y. S. Boutalis and N. Papamarkos, International Journal of Pattern Recognition and Artificial Intelligence (IJPRAI), Volume 24, Number 2 / February, 2010, pp. 207-244, Copyright @ 2010 World Scientific.

tracted from the images and, on the other hand, present independence on some distortions such as rotation and scaling. [135]

An easy way to extract color features from an image is by linking the color space channels. Linking is defined as the combination of more than one histogram to a single one. One example is the Scalable Color Descriptor (SCD) [121] demonstrated in MPEG-7 [120]. In the SCD implementation, the HSV color space is uniformly quantized into a total of 256 bins defined by sixteen levels in H (Hue), four levels in S (Saturation) and four levels in V (Value). The values of H, S and V are calculated for every pixel and are then linearly quantized in the ranges [0 , 15], [0 , 3] and [0 , 3] respectively. Afterwards, the modified histogram is formed using the function:

$$H_{Quantized} + 16 \times S_{Quantized} + 64 \times V_{Quantized} \tag{2.1}$$

Konstantinidis et Al. [97] propose the extraction of a fuzzy-linking histogram based on the color space CIE-L*a*b*. Their 3-input fuzzy system uses the L*, a* and b* values from each pixel in an image to classify that pixel into one of 10 preset colors, transforming the image into a palette of the 10 preset colors.

In this method, the defuzzyfication algorithm classifies the input pixel into one and only one output bin (color) of the system (crisp classification). Additionally, the required conversion of an image from the RGB color space to CIEXYZ and finally to CIE-L*a*b* color space makes the method noticeably time-consuming.

This chapter presents a new two-stage fuzzy-linking system using the HSV color space, which demands smaller computational power than CIELAB because HSV converts directly from the RGB color space. The first stage of the presented fuzzy system produces a fuzzy-linking histogram that uses the three HSV channels as inputs and forms a 10-bin histogram as output. Each bin represents a preset color: (0) White, (1) Gray, (2) Black, (3) Red, (4) Orange, (5) Yellow, (6) Green, (7) Cyan, (8) Blue and (9) Magenta.

The shaping of the input membership value limits is based on the position of the vertical edges of specially constructed artificial images representing channels H (Hue), S (Saturation) and V (Value). Figure 2.1(a.iii) illustrates the vertical edges of the image that represents the channel H, which were used for determining the position of membership values of Figure 2.2(a). The selected hue regions are stressed by dotted lines in Figure 2.1(a.iv). The membership value limits of S and V are identified with the same process.

Coordinate logic filters (CLF) [126](Chapter 11) [182] [124] are found to be the most appropriate among edge detection techniques for determining the fine differences and extracting these vertical edges in the specially constructed artificial images representing channels H, S, and V. In our procedure, every pixel of the images that represent the channels H, S and V is replaced by the result of the coordinate logic filter "AND" operation on its 3×3 neighborhood. The values of Red, Green and Blue of the nine pixels of every neighborhood are expressed in binary form. The nine binary values of every channel from R, G and B are combined with the use of the logical operator 'AND'. The result is a

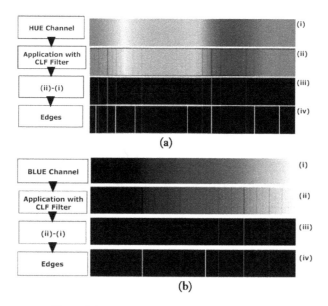

Figure 2.1: *Edges Extraction with CLF-AND Filter.*

binary number for each of the 3 channels R, G and B. Converting these numbers to byte form produces the value that the neighborhood's central pixel will have. This process is repeated for all the pixels and in the 3 specially constructed artificial images. The result of this action stresses the edges of the image (Figure 2.1(a.ii)). The difference between the initial and the filtered image indicates the total edges. The position of these edges is the boundaries (Limits) of the system's Membership values.

Based on these edges, the inputs of the system are analyzed as follows: Channel H is divided into eight fuzzy areas. Their borders are shown in Figure 2.2(a) and are defined as: (0) Red to Orange, (1) Orange, (2) Yellow, (3) Green, (4) Cyan, (5) Blue, (6) Magenta and (7) Magenta to Red.

Channel S is divided into two fuzzy areas. The first area, in combination with the fuzzy area activated in channel V, determines whether the input color is clear enough to be ranked in one of the H histogram colors, or if it is simply a shade of white or gray.

The third input, channel V, is divided into three areas. The first area defines whether the input will be black, independently from the other input values. The second fuzzy area combined with the value of channel S defines gray.

A set of 20 TSK-like rules [204] with fuzzy antecedents and crisp consequents is used. These rules are given in Appendix B. The consequent section contains variables that count the number of original pixels mapped to each specific bin of the 10-bin histogram. Four of the rules depend on two only inputs (S and V) and are decided independently of the H value.

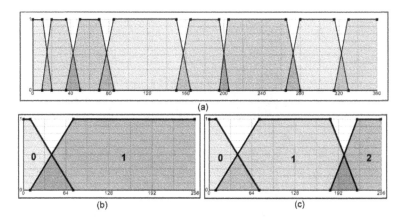

Figure 2.2: *Membership Functions of (a) Hue, (b) Saturation and (c) Value.*

For evaluating the consequent variables, two algorithms were compared. First, an LOM (Largest of Maximum) algorithm was used. This method assigns the input to the output bin of the rule with the greatest activation value. Second, a Multi-Participant algorithm was used. This method assigns the input to the output bins which are defined by all the rules that are being activated with a participation rate to each bin proportional to the activation rate of the rule that is activated. Experimental results reveal that the second algorithm performs better [189, 19, 17].

In the second stage of the fuzzy-linking system, a fuzzy system categorizes each color into one of three hues, producing a 24-bin histogram as output. Each bin represents a preset color as follows: (0) White, (1) Grey, (2) Black, (3) Light Red, (4) Red, (5) Dark Red, (6) Light Orange, (7) Orange, (8) Dark Orange, (9) Light Yellow, (10) Yellow, (11) Dark Yellow, (12) Light Green, (13) Green, (14) Dark Green, (15) Light Cyan, (16) Cyan, (17) Dark Cyan, (18) Light Blue, (19) Blue, (20) Dark Blue, (21) Light Magenta, (22) Magenta, (23) Dark Magenta.

The system developed to assign these shades is based on the determinations of the subtle vertical edges appearing in images with smooth single-color transition from absolute white to absolute black. The use of a coordinate logic filter (CLF) "AND" is also found to be appropriate for determining these vertical edges (Figure 2.1(a.iv)) [126](Chapter 11) [182] [124].

The values of S and V from each pixel as well as the position number of the bin (or bins) resulting from the previous fuzzy 10-bin stage are the inputs to this 24-bin Fuzzy Linking system. If the previous fuzzy 10-bin stage outputs bin position number three or lower, which defines that pixel as grayscale, the fuzzy system classifies the pixel directly into the corresponding output bin without using the fuzzy rules.

If the position number of the bin from the previous fuzzy 10-bin stage is greater than three, the system classifies the input pixel as belonging to one or more of the three hue areas produced by the vertical edge extraction procedure described above. These hues are labeled as follows: Light Color, Color and Dark Color (where Color is the color attribute produced by the first 10-bin stage).

The fuzzy 24-bin linking system inputs are analyzed by dividing channels S and V into 2 fuzzy regions as depicted in Figure 2.3(a) and Figure 2.3(b) respectively.

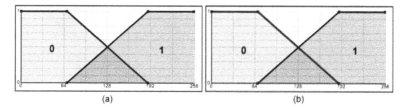

(a)   (b)

Figure 2.3: *Membership Functions for (a) Saturation and (b) Value for the expansion at 24-bin.*

A set of four TSK-like rules [204] with fuzzy antecedents and crisp consequents are used. These rules are defined in Appendix C. For the evaluation of the consequent variables, the Multi-Participant method is also employed.

2.2 Texture Information Extraction

Texture is one of the most important attributes used in image analysis and pattern recognition. It provides surface characteristics for the analysis of many types of images including natural scenes, remotely sensed data and biomedical modalities [72]. The present chapter focuses on two new methods of texture information extraction based on fuzzy techniques. The first method creates an 8-bin histogram using the high-frequency bands produced by the Haar Wavelet transform. The second method creates a 6-bin histogram using the five digital filters that were presented in the MPEG-7 Edge Histogram Descriptor. In both methods each bin corresponds to a texture form.

2.2.1 Extraction of Texture Information Using High Frequency Bands of Wavelet Transforms

To export texture information from the images, three features that represent energy in high frequency band of wavelet transforms are used. These elements are the square root of the second order moment of wavelet coefficients in high frequency bands [36]. To obtain these features, the Haar transform is applied to the Y (Luminosity in the YIQ color space) component of an *Image Block*. The choice of *Image Block* size depends on the image dimensions and is discussed in Section 2.4. Suppose for instance that the block size is 4×4. After a one-level wavelet transform, each block is decomposed into four frequency bands. Each band contains 2×2 coefficients. The coefficients in the HL band are $\{C_{kl}, C_{k,l+1}, C_{k+1,l}, C_{k+1,l+1}\}$. One feature is then computed as:

$$f = \left(\frac{1}{4} \sum_{i=0}^{1} \sum_{j=0}^{1} C_{k+i,l+j}^2 \right)^{\frac{1}{2}} \tag{2.2}$$

The other two features are computed similarly from the LH and HH bands. The motivation for using these features is their relation to texture properties. Moments of wavelet coefficients in various frequency bands are proven effective for discerning texture [189, 183]. For example, a large coefficient value on the HL band shows high activity in the horizontal direction. Thus, an image with vertical stripes has high energy in the HL band and low energy in the LH band. Research shows that this texture feature is a good compromise between computational complexity and effectiveness [189].

Elements f_{LH}, f_{HL} and f_{HH} from each image block are normalized and applied as inputs to a three-input fuzzy system that creates an 8-bin (areas) histogram as output. This method classifies the input image block into one or more output bins with the following preset texture form labels: TextuHisto(0) Low Energy Linear area, TextuHisto(1) Low Energy Horizontal activation, TextuHisto(2) Low Energy Vertical activation, TextuHisto(3) Low Energy Horizontal and Vertical activation, TextuHisto(4) High Energy Linear area, TextuHisto(5) High Energy Horizontal activation, TextuHisto(6) High Energy Vertical activation, TextuHisto(7) High Energy Horizontal and Vertical activation.

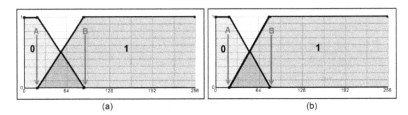

Figure 2.4: *Membership Functions for (a) f_{LH} and f_{HL}, (b) f_{HH}.*

To shape the domain limits of membership values of the three fuzzy-system inputs over eight texture areas, a simple genetic algorithm is used.

A database of 100 images cropped from a set of 80 texture types selected from the Brodatz Album [14] is used. For these images the corresponding ideal texture histograms were manually formed. The simple genetic algorithm then determines off-line the limits of membership values with an AFT (Auto Fuzzy Tuning) method.

Every fuzzy input is separated into two parts with trapezoidal membership functions, as illustrated in Figure 2.4. Also, it is assumed that, due to the structure of the information carried by the inputs f_{HL} and f_{LH}, these two can share the same membership value limits. This assumption facilitates the algorithm's implementation. The chromosomes used by the genetic algorithm include four values, allocated in two pairs. The first pair includes the zero points (points A,B of Fig.2.4(a)) of the two membership values f_{HL} and f_{LH} while the second pair contains the two zero points (points A,B of Fig. 2.4(b)) of f_{HH}.

The algorithm begins with a sample of 50 chromosomes. The chromosomes are in an integer and non-binary form. An additional control parameter assures that the second number of each pair is always greater than the first and that the number values can not exceed the limit of their range. The zero point values from all the chromosomes are used by the fuzzy system to determine the texture type for each of the 100 images from the database.

For each image the texture histogram produced by the fuzzy system is compared with the corresponding ideal texture histogram using the Euclidean distance. The fitness function is chosen to be the sum of these Euclidean distances. The chromosomes are then sorted and the best 10 are kept for the formation of the next generation. A crossover procedure is applied to the next 10 best chromosomes with the algorithm using the point that separates the two pairs as the crossover point. The next best five chromosomes are mutated by increasing or decreasing only one contributor value of the chromosome. Finally, 25 additional chromosomes are randomly inserted. In all cases the new chromosomes are not allowed to violate the control parameter restrictions. The procedure is repeated until the fitness function is minimized and there is no further improvement.

Figure 2.4(a) shows the f_{HL} and f_{LH} inputs while the f_{HH} input is shown in Figure 2.4(b). A set of eight TSK-like rules [204] with fuzzy antecedents and crisp consequents are used. These rules are defined in Appendix C. For the evaluation of the consequent variables, the Multi-Participant method is also employed.

2.2.2 Extraction of Texture Information Using the Five Digital Filters Proposed by the MPEG-7 EHD

The five digital filters presented by the MPEG-7 Edge Histogram Descriptor (EHD), are shown in Figure 2.5(a) [194]. These filters are used for the extraction of texture information. They are able to characterize the edges being present in the applied region as one of the following texture types: vertical, horizontal, 45-degree diagonal, 135-degree diagonal and non-directional edges. In this section a novel approach is presented that uses these filters and permits the applied region to participate in more than one texture type.

The presented texture feature extraction begins by dividing the image into a specified number of *Image Blocks*. Each *Image Block* contains four *Sub Blocks*. The average gray level of each *Sub-Block* at (i,j)th *Image Block* is defined as $a_0(i,j)$, $a_1(i,j)$, $a_2(i,j)$, and $a_3(i,j)$. The filter coefficients for vertical, horizontal, 45-degree diagonal, 135-degree diagonal, and non-directional edges are labeled as $f_v(k)$, $f_h(k)$, $f_{d-45}(k)$, $f_{d-135}(k)$, and $f_{nd}(k)$, respectively, where $k = 0,\ldots,3$ represents the location of the Sub Block. The respective edge magnitudes $m_v(i,j)$, $m_h(i,j)$, $m_d-45(i,j)$, $m_{d-135}(i,j)$, and $m_{nd}(i,j)$ for

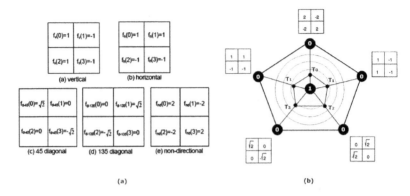

Figure 2.5: *(a) Filter coefficients for edge detection, (b) Edge Type Diagram.*

the (i, j)th *Image Block* can be obtained as follows:

$$m_v(i,j) = \left| \sum_{k=0}^{3} a_k(i,j) \times f_v(k) \right| \tag{2.3}$$

$$m_h(i,j) = \left| \sum_{k=0}^{3} a_k(i,j) \times f_h(k) \right| \tag{2.4}$$

$$m_{nd}(i,j) = \left| \sum_{k=0}^{3} a_k(i,j) \times f_{nd}(k) \right| \tag{2.5}$$

$$m_{d-45}(i,j) = \left| \sum_{k=0}^{3} a_k(i,j) \times f_{d-45}(k) \right| \tag{2.6}$$

$$m_{d-135}(i,j) = \left| \sum_{k=0}^{3} a_k(i,j) \times f_{d-135}(k) \right| \tag{2.7}$$

then the *max* is calculated:

$$max = MAX(m_v, m_h, m_{nd}, m_{d-45}, m_{d-135}) \tag{2.8}$$

and all *m*s normalized

$$m'_v = \frac{m_v}{max}, m'_d = \frac{m_d}{max}, m'_{nd} = \frac{m_{nd}}{max}, m'_{d-45} = \frac{m_{d-45}}{max}, m'_{d-135} = \frac{m_{d-135}}{max} \tag{2.9}$$

The output of the unit that extracts texture information from each *Image Block* is a 6-bin (area) histogram. Each bin corresponds to a preset region as follows: EdgeHisto(0) Non Edge, EdgeHisto(1) Non Directional Edge, EdgeHisto(2) Horizontal Edge, Edge-Histo(3) Vertical Edge, EdgeHisto(4) 45-Degree Diagonal and EdgeHisto(5) 135-Degree Diagonal. The system classifies each *Image Block* in a two step process: First, the system calculates the *max* value. The *max* value must be greater than the defined threshold for the the *Image Block* to be classified as a *Texture Block*, otherwise it is classified as a Non Texture Block (Linear). Then, if the *Image Block* is classified as a *Texture Block*, each m value is placed on the pentagonal diagram of Figure 2.5(b) along the line corresponding to the digital filter from which it was calculated. The diagram's center corresponds to the value 1 and the outer edge corresponds to value 0. If any m value is greater than the threshold on the line where it participates, the *Image Block* is classified in the particular type of edge. Thus an *Image Block* can participate in more than one edge type. The following source code describes the process:

```
program SetEdgeType(max, m#nd, m#h, m#v, m#d#45, m#d#135)

  if (max LT TEdge) then EdgeHisto(0)++
  else
     (
     if (m#nd GT T0)      then EdgeHisto(1)++
     if (m#h GT T1)        then EdgeHisto(2)++
     if (m#v GT T1)        then EdgeHisto(3)++
     if (m#d#45 GT T2)  then EdgeHisto(4)++
     if (m#d#135 GT T2) then EdgeHisto(5)++
     )
  endif
return(EdgeHisto)
```

where **LT** means *Less Than* and **GT** means *Greater Than*.

For the calculation of the thresholds, the genetic algorithm described in the previous section is used again. In this case, the chromosome length is only three values that correspond to T_{edge}, T_0 and T_1. For convenience, the implementation assumes that $T_1 = T_2$. To avoid decimal numbers, the values of T_0 and T_1 are transformed into space [0 , 100], thereby avoiding modifications to the mutation method. The extra control parameter used by the fuzzy system in the previous section is replaced by a new parameter that limits the threshold values to their allowable boundaries. Furthermore, the crossover point is determined to allow a crossover procedure between T_0 and T_1.

The threshold values are set as: $T_{Edge} = 14$, $T_0 = 0.68$, $T_1 = T_2 = 0.98$.

2.3 Descriptor Implementation

The color and texture features described in the previous sections are combined to produce four descriptors. In order to form the presented descriptors, the image is initially separated into 1600 *Image Blocks*. This number is chosen as a compromise between the image detail and the computational demand. Considering that the minimum size of each *Image Block* must be 2×2 pixels (a restriction that comes from the Texture units), the presented descriptors are used for images larger than 80×80 pixels.

The presented descriptors are constructed as follows: The unit associated with color information extraction in every descriptor is called the *Color Unit*. Similarly, the *Texture Unit* is the unit associated with texture information extraction. The descriptors' structure has n regions determined by the *Texture Unit*. Each *Texture Unit* region contains m individual regions defined by the *Color Unit*. Overall, each presented descriptor contains $m \times n$ bins. On the completion of the process, each descriptor's histogram is normalized within the interval $[0, 1]$ and then quantized into three bits/bin. The quantization process and the quantization tables are described in Section 2.5.

2.3.1 CEDD - Color and Edge Directivity Descriptor

The CEDD includes texture information produced by the 6-bin histogram of the fuzzy system that uses the five digital filters presented by the MPEG-7 EHD. Additionally, for color information the CEDD uses the 24-bin color histogram produced by the 24-bin fuzzy-linking system. Overall, the final histogram has $6 \times 24 = 144$ regions.

Each *Image Block* interacts successively with all the fuzzy systems. Defining the bin produced by the texture information fuzzy system as n and the bin produced by the 24-bin fuzzy-linking system as m, then each *Image Block* is placed in the bin position: $n \times 24 + m$. The process of generating the descriptor is described in the flowchart Figure 2.6(a).

In the *Texture Unit*, the *Image Block* is separated into four regions called *Sub Blocks*. The value of each *Sub Block* is the mean value of the luminosity of the pixels it contains. The luminosity values are derived from a YIQ color space transformation. Each *Image Block* interacts with the five digital filters presented by MPEG-7 EHD, and with the use of the pentagonal (Fig.2.5(b)) diagram it is classified in one or more texture categories. For illustration purposes let us assume that the *Texture Unit* classifies a given *Image Block* into the second bin which is defined as NDE (Non Directional Edge). Then, in the *Color*

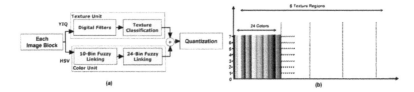

Figure 2.6: *CEDD (a) Implementation Flowchart, (b) Structure.*

Unit, every *Image Block* is converted to the HSV color space. The mean values of H, S and V are calculated and become inputs to the fuzzy system that produces the fuzzy 10-bin histogram. Let us again assume that the classification resulted in the fourth bin which indicates that the color is red. Then, the second fuzzy system (24-bin Fuzzy Linking System), using the mean values of S and V as well as the position number of the bin (or bins) resulting from the previous fuzzy 10-bin unit, calculates the hue of the color and produces the fuzzy 24-bin histogram. And let us assume that the *Color Unit* system classifies this block in the fourth bin which indicates the color as (3) Light Red. The combination of the three fuzzy systems finally will classify the *Image Block* in the 27th bin ($1 \times 24 + 3$). The process is repeated for all the image blocks. On the completion of the process, the histogram is normalized within the interval $[0, 1]$ and quantized according to the process described in Section 2.5. Figure 2.6(b) illustrates the CEDD structure.

2.3.2 C.CEDD - Compact Color and Edge Directivity Descriptor

The method for producing the C.CEDD differs from the CEDD method only in the color unit. The C.CEDD uses the fuzzy 10-bin linking system instead of the fuzzy 24-bin linking system. Overall, the final histogram has only $6 \times 10 = 60$ regions. It is the smallest descriptor of the presented set. The flowchart in Figure 2.7(a) describes the generation of the C.CEDD while Figure 2.7(b) shows its structure.

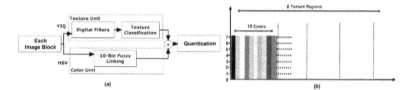

Figure 2.7: *C.CEDD (a) Implementation Flowchart, (b) Structure.*

2.3.3 FCTH - Fuzzy Color and Texture Histogram

The FCTH descriptor includes the texture information produced in the 8-bin histogram of the fuzzy system that uses the high frequency bands of the Haar wavelet transform. For color information, the descriptor uses the 24-bin color histogram produced by the 24-bin fuzzy-linking system. Overall, the final histogram includes $8 \times 24 = 192$ regions.

Each *Image Block* interacts successively with all the fuzzy systems in the exact manner demonstrated in CEDD production. The FCTH descriptor generation is described in the Figure 2.8(a) flowchart.

Each *Image Block* is transformed into the YIQ color space and transformed with the Haar Wavelet transform. The f_{LH}, f_{HL} and f_{HH} values are calculated and with the use of the fuzzy system that classifies the f coefficients, this *Image Block* is classified in one of the eight output bins. Suppose, for example, that the classification assigns this block to the second bin defined as Low Energy Horizontal activation. Next, the same *Image Block* is transformed into the HSV color space and the mean H, S and V block values are calculated. These values become inputs to the fuzzy system that forms the 10-bin fuzzy color histogram. Let us assume that this system classifies a given block into the fourth bin defined as the color (3) Red. Then, the next fuzzy system uses the mean values of S and

69

V as well as the position number of the bin (or bins) resulting from the previous fuzzy 10-bin unit, to calculate the hue of the color and create the fuzzy 24-bin histogram. Let us assume that the system classifies this *Image Block* in the fourth bin which defines that color as (3) Light Red. The combined three fuzzy systems therefore classify the *Image Block* into the 27th bin $(1 \times 24 + 3)$. The process is repeated for all the blocks of the image. At the completion of the process, the histogram is normalized within the interval $[0, 1]$ and quantized according to the procedures described in Section 2.5. Figure 2.8(b) illustrates the FCTH descriptor structure.

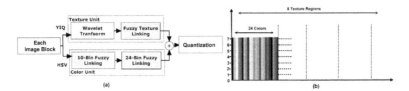

Figure 2.8: *FCTH (a) Implementation Flowchart, (b) Structure.*

2.3.4 C.FCTH - Compact Fuzzy Color and Texture Histogram

The method for producing C.FCTH differs from the FCTH method only in the color unit. Like its C.CEDD counterpart, this descriptor uses only the fuzzy 10-bin linking system instead of the fuzzy 24-bin linking system. Overall, the final histogram includes only $8 \times 10 = 80$ regions. The flowchart in Figure 2.9(a) describes the procedure for generating the C.FCTH descriptor while Figure 2.9(b) shows the C.FCTH structure.

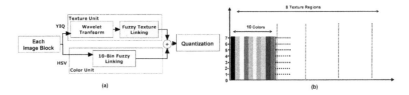

Figure 2.9: *C.FCTH (a) Implementation Flowchart, (b) Structure.*

2.4 Descriptor Quantization

To restrict the presented descriptors' length, the normalized bin values of the descriptors are quantized for binary representation in a three bits/bin quantization. For example, the 144-bin CEDD is limited to $144 \times 3 = 432$ bits. Because most of the values are concentrated within a small range (from 0 to 0.25), they are nonlinearly quantized. Also, the descriptor bins are divided into separate quantization groups with differing quantization values.

In order to calculate the CEDD quantization table, a sample of 10,000 images is used. First, CEDD vectors are calculated for all images. The combined 10000×144 elements constitute inputs into the fuzzy Gustafson Kessel classifier, [61] which separates the volume of the samples into eight regions, mapping the bin values from the decimal area [0 , 1] into the integer area [0 , 7]. The Gustafson Kessel parameters are selected as: clusters=8, repetitions=2000, $e = 0.002$, and $m = 2$. The resulting quantization is given in Table 2.1. The values of the histogram appearing in bins 0 - 23 are assigned to one of the values [0 , 7] according to the minimum distance of each bin value from one of the eight entries in the first row of the table. The same procedure is followed for the entries in bins 24 - 47, 48 - 95 and 96 - 143 using the quantization values shown in each of their corresponding rows in the table.

CEDD Bin: 0 - 23 / C.CEDD Bin: 0 - 9							
000	001	010	011	100	101	110	111
0.00018	0.0237	0.0614	0.1139	0.1791	0.2609	0.3417	0.5547
CEDD Bin: 24 - 47 / C.CEDD Bin: 10 - 19							
000	001	010	011	100	101	110	111
0.00020	0.0224	0.0602	0.1207	0.1811	0.2341	0.3256	0.5207
CEDD Bin: 48 - 95 / C.CEDD Bin: 20 - 39							
000	001	010	011	100	101	110	111
0.00040	0.0048	0.0108	0.0181	0.0270	0.0381	0.0526	0.0795
CEDD Bin: 96 - 143 / C.CEDD Bin: 40 - 59							
000	001	010	011	100	101	110	111
0.00096	0.0107	0.0241	0.0415	0.0628	0.0930	0.1369	0.2628

Table 2.1: *CEDD Quantization Table.*

The quantization table for FCTH descriptor is calculated in a similar manner, limiting its total length to $192 \times 3 = 576$ bits. The resulting quantization is presented in Table 2.2. The values of the histogram appearing in bins 0 - 47 are assigned to one of the values [0 , 7] according to the minimum distance of each bin value from one of the eight entries in the first row of the table. The same procedure is followed for the entries in bins 48 - 143 and 144 - 191 using the quantization values shown in each of their corresponding rows.

For convenience in the implementation of systems that use the presented descriptors, the quantization tables of the compact versions of the descriptors are the same as the quantization tables of the non-compact versions. The C.CEDD quantization table is the same as the CEDD quantization table. Likewise, the C.FCTH quantization table is the same as the FCTH quantization table. The CEDD length is 54 bytes per image, FCTH length is 72 bytes per image, C.CEDD requires less than 23 bytes per image and C.FCTH uses 30 bytes per image.

Figure 2.10: *Query examples in the (a) WANG's database, (b) MPEG-7 CCD database, (c) UCID database and, (d) img(Rummager) database and (e) Nister database. The first image on the top left of each group is also the query image.*

FCTH Bin: 0 - 47 / C.FCTH Bin: 0 - 19

000	001	010	011	100	101	110	111
0.00013	0.0093	0.0224	0.0431	0.0831	0.1014	0.1748	0.224

FCTH Bin: 48 - 143 / C.FCTH Bin: 20 - 59

000	001	010	011	100	101	110	111
0.00023	0.0173	0.0391	0.0693	0.0791	0.0910	0.1618	0.185

FCTH Bin: 144 - 191 / C.FCTH Bin: 60 - 79

000	001	010	011	100	101	110	111
0.00018	0.0273	0.0414	0.0539	0.0691	0.0820	0.0918	0.128

Table 2.2: *FCTH Quantization Table.*

2.5 Experiments

Recently, standard benchmark databases and evaluation campaigns have been created allowing a quantitative comparison of CBIR systems. These benchmarks allow the comparison of image retrieval systems under different aspects: usability and user interfaces, combination with text retrieval, or overall performance of a system [42]. The presented descriptors are integrated into the retrieval software system img(Rummager) [20] and the on-line application img(Anaktisi) [199] where they can be quantitatively evaluated.

To evaluate the performance of the descriptors, experiments are performed on five image databases: WANG's database, [189] MPEG-7 CCD database, UCID [161] database, img(Rummager) database and Nister database [136]. All the results are available on-line.[2] Figure 2.11 illustrates the ANMRR values for the five benchmarking image databases.

2.5.1 Similarity Measure

For similarity matching, the distance $D(i, j)$ of two image descriptors x_i and x_j is calculated using the non-binary Tanimoto coefficient. The Tanimoto Coefficient was found to be preferable than the similarity L1, L2 (Euclidean Distance), Jensen-Shannon [152] and Bhattacharyya because it presented better results.

2.5.2 Experiments on the WANG database

The WANG database [189] is a subset of 1000 manually-selected images from the Corel stock photo database and forms 10 classes of 100 images each. This image database is available on-line.[3] In particular, queries and ground truths presented by the MIRROR [195] image retrieval system are used. MIRROR separates the WANG database into 20 queries. A sample query is illustrated in Figure 2.10(a).

---

[2]http://orpheus.ee.duth.gr/anaktisi/results
[3]http://wang.ist.psu.edu/docs/home.shtml

The presented descriptors are used in the retrieval procedure and the results are compared
with the corresponding results of the following MPEG-7 [120, 75, 76] descriptors:
Color Descriptors: Dominant Color Descriptor (DCD 8 colors), Scalable Color De-
scriptor (SCD-32 colors), Color Layout Descriptor (CLD), Color Structure Descriptor
(CSD-32 colors).
Texture Descriptors: Edge Histogram Descriptor (EHD), Homogeneous Texture Descriptor (HTD).
The NMRR values for the MPEG-7 descriptors in WANG's database are available in
[195]. Table 2.3 shows indicative examples of query results and the ANMRR scores for
all 20 queries.
The results of the presented descriptors are also compared with the results of the RGB
Color Histogram, Tamura Directionality Histogram [180] and Auto Color Correlograms
[71].

Descriptor	Query					ANMRR
	204	327	522	600	703	
MPEG-7 Descriptors						
DCD MPHSM-8 Colors	0.543	0.407	0.556	0.215	0.306	0.39460
DCD QHDM-8 Colors	0.420	0.469	0.537	0.610	0.781	0.54680
SCD-32 Colors	0.442	0.406	0.508	0.083	0.211	0.35520
CLD	0.616	0.542	0.454	0.454	0.252	0.40000
CSD-32 Colors	0.323	0.348	0.526	0.066	0.146	0.32460
EHD	0.782	0.317	0.690	0.277	0.307	0.50890
HTD	0.887	0.594	0.734	0.445	0.615	0.70540
Other Descriptors						
RGB Color Histogram	0.618	0.899	0.715	0.569	0.820	0.59134
Tamura Directionality	0.889	0.682	0.806	0.690	0.574	0.63622
Correlograms	0.493	0.458	0.674	0.334	0.664	0.50107
CCDs						
CEDD	0.314	0.127	0.347	0.059	0.115	**0.25283**
FCTH	**0.235**	**0.114**	**0.323**	0.026	0.092	0.27369
C.CEDD	0.316	0.140	0.452	0.069	**0.088**	0.30637
C.FCTH	0.320	0.224	0.493	**0.013**	0.116	0.31537

Table 2.3: *ANMRR Results on the WANG Image Database.*

As the results in Table 2.3 show, on the WANG database the presented descriptors achieve
better retrieval scores than the other descriptors.
In order to be able to compare the results of the presented descriptors with even more
descriptors in the bibliography, the following experiment was carried out. For each image
in the Wand database, a search was carried out over the total of 1000 and the AP (Average

74

Precision) was calculated, assuming the Ground Truth to be the remaining 99 images belonging to the same group as the query image. Then the mean of all these average precisions (MAP) was taken. The results are presented in Table 2.4. The values of the remaining descriptors are taken from [42]. The bigger the MAP, the better the descriptor is. As the results show, the CEDD presents the best results out of all the descriptors.

Descriptor	MAP	Descriptor	MAP
CEDD	**50.6**	32x32 image	37.6
FCTH	50.1	MPEG7: color layout	41.8
C.CEDD	49.3	Xx32 image	24.3
C.FCTH	47.6	Tamura texture histogram	38.2
color histogram	50.5	LF SIFT signature	36.7
LF SIFT global search	38.3	gray value histogram	31.7
LF patches histogram	48.3	LF patches global	30.5
LF SIFT histogram	48.2	MPEG7: edge histogram	40.8
inv. feature histo. (mon.)	47.6	inv. feature histo. (rel.)	34.9
MPEG7: scalable color	46.7	Gabor vector	23.7
LF patches signature	40.4	global texture feature	26.3
Gabor histogram	41.3		

Table 2.4: *Mean average precision [%] for each of the features for the WANG Image Database.*

The deviation that appears between the MAP and the ANMRR is due to the difference between experiments. In the first experiment, only 20 queries were used, with an average ground truth of about 30 images, whereas in the second, 1000 queries (all the images) were used, with 99 images for each ground truth.

2.5.3 Experiments on the MPEG-7 CCD database

The Common Color Dataset (MPEG-7 CCD) contains approximately 5000 images and a set of 50 common color queries (CCQ). Each query is specified with a set of ground truth images. This is the image database where the MPEG-7 descriptors have been tested. CCD contains images that originated from consecutive frames of television shows, newscasts and sport shows. It also includes a large number of photomaps. MPEG-7 CCD is a database that is clearly designed to be tested with color descriptors, frequently causing texture descriptors to present very low retrieval scores. A query sample is illustrated in Figure 2.10(b). The NMRR values for the MPEG-7 descriptors in MPEG-7 CCD database are also available in [195]. Table 2.5 shows certain indicative query results and the ANMRR values for all 50 queries.

On the MPEG-7 CCD database, the presented descriptors appear to present the second best scores. The Color Structure Descriptor achieved the best score. The reason that C-

Descriptor		Query		ANMRR
	i0121_add5	img00133_add3	img00438_s3	
MPEG-7 Descriptors				
DCD MPHSM-8 colors	**0**	0.484	0.008	0.2604
DCD QHDM-8 colors	0.057	0.438	0.400	0.2834
SCD-32 Colors	**0**	0.152	**0**	0.1645
CLD	**0**	0.401	0.308	0.2252
CSD-32 Colors	**0**	**0**	**0**	**0.0399**
EHD	**0**	0.406	0.381	0.3217
HTD	0.229	0.401	0.486	0.42498
Other Descriptors				
RGB Color Histogram	0.229	0.401	0.161	0.42729
Tamura Directionality	0.314	0.770	0.714	0.65913
Correlograms	0.000	0.290	0.294	0.28749
CCDs				
CEDD	**0**	**0**	0.033	0.08511
FCTH	**0**	0.037	0.003	0.10343
C.CEDD	**0**	0.014	0.167	0.12655
C.FCTH	**0**	0.065	**0**	0.15977

Table 2.5: *ANMRR Results on MPEG-7 CCD Image Database.*

CDs failed to satisfactorily retrieve entire ground truths for some queries is due to the fact that the MPEG-7 CCD ground truths include images that are directed toward descriptors that mostly control color similarity. The very low scores presented by the MPEG-7 texture descriptors and the Tamura Directionality descriptor confirm this assertion. Another reason for less than perfect recall is the fact that many queries include rotated images in their ground truth. Due to their texture attribute, CCDs are not suitable for retrieving these images.

2.5.4 Experiments on the UCID database

The UCID database was created as a benchmark database for CBIR and image compression applications [161]. This database currently consists of 1338 uncompressed TIFF images on a variety of topics including natural scenes and man-made objects, both indoors and outdoors. The UCID database is available to fellow researchers.[4]

All the UCID images were subjected to manual relevance assessments against 262 selected images, creating 262 ground truth image sets for performance evaluation.

In the assessment, only very clearly relevant images are considered to be relevant. This relevance assumption makes the retrieval task easy because the ground truth images are

---

[4]http://vision.cs.aston.ac.uk/datasets/UCID/ucid.html

quite similar. On the other hand, it makes the task difficult, because there are images in the database with high visual similarity that are not considered relevant. Hence, it can be difficult to have highly precise results with the given relevance assessment, but because only few images are considered relevant, high recall values might be easy to obtain [137]. A query sample is presented in Figure 2.10(c). In Table 2.6, certain indicative results and ANMRR values for all of the 262 queries are demonstrated.

Because the MPEG-7 descriptor results are not available for this database, an implementation of CLD, SCD and EHD in img (Rummager)[5] application is used. The source code is a modification of the implementation that can be found in the LIRe (Lucene Image REtrieval) [117] retrieval system. The original version of the descriptors' implementation is written in Java and is available online as open source[6] under the General Public License (GPL). The img(Rummager) application results match the LIRe results. More details about img(Rummager) can be found on Chapter 9.

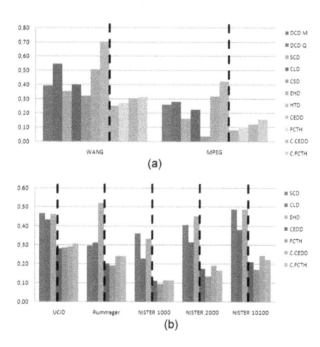

Figure 2.11: *ANMRR results for (a) Wang and MPEG-7 database and (b) UCID, img (Rummager) and Nister database.*

As shown in Table 2.6 , on the UCID database the presented descriptors achieve the best

---

[5]The prototype is available along with documentation and screenshots at http://www.img-rummager.com

[6]http://sourceforge.net/project/downloading.php?groupname=caliph-emir&filename=Lire-0.5.4.zip&use_mirror=switch

Descriptor		Query			ANMRR
	00095	00172	00297	00583	
MPEG-7 Descriptors					
SCD-32 Colors	0.471	0.058	0.471	0.384	0.46665
CLD	0.471	0.471	0.471	0.299	0.43216
EHD	0.471	0.471	**0**	0.477	0.43314
Other Descriptors					
RGB Color Hist. 0.471	0.471	0.176	0.553	0.52315	
Tamura Direct.	0.471	0.471	0.471	0.536	0.55682
Correlograms	0.059	0.471	0.294	0.360	0.41386
CCDs					
CEDD	**0**	0.471	**0**	**0.147**	**0.28234**
FCTH	0.059	**0**	**0**	0.191	0.28737
C.CEDD	**0**	0.059	**0**	0.241	0.29331
C.FCTH	0.059	**0**	0.059	0.236	0.30871

Table 2.6: *ANMRR Results on UCID Image Database.*

retrieval results.

The experiments were also repeated in this database to calculate the MAP. In this case, the ground truth used for every query image was the one suggested by the database, but without including the query image. The results are presented in Table 2.7. The values of the remaining descriptors are taken from the Ref. [42].

As can be seen from the results in Table 2.7, the CEDD presents the second best result, with the best descriptor being the LF SIFT Global Search [115], which could be expected, because database consists of very close matches that are suitable for SIFT features.

The LF SIFT Global Search descriptor is non-compact and is extracted from the Harris interest points [48] (Local). When comparing the results of the presented descriptors with the results of the corresponding global compact descriptors, it can be observed that the presented descriptors have the better MAP.

In the USID case, the deviation appearing between the ANMRR and the MAP is due to the fact that, in the latter case (experiments for MAP measurement), the ground truths did not contain the query image. Given that many ground truths contain only 2-3 images, the unsuccessful retrieval of any of these would greatly influence the results.

2.5.5 Experiments on the img (Rummager) database

The img (Rummager) database is integrated in the retrieval software system img (Rummager) and includes 22,000 images. The first 4343 images come from the Microsoft Re-

Descriptor	MAP	Descriptor	MAP
CEDD	45	32x32 image	22.3
FCTH	44.7	MPEG7: color layout	14
C.CEDD	42.1	Xx32 image	21.7
C.FCTH	40.4	Tamura texture histogram	13.9
color histogram	43.3	LF SIFT signature	33.2
LF SIFT global search	**62.5**	gray value histogram	34.1
LF patches histogram	37.5	LF patches global	11.8
LF SIFT histogram	44.7	MPEG7: edge histogram	30.3
inv. feature histo. (mon.)	41.6	inv. feature histo. (rela.)	25.2
MPEG7: scalable color	37.9	Gabor vector	14.4
LF patches signature	27.6	global texture feature	4.7
Gabor histogram	6.7		

Table 2.7: *Mean average precision [%] for each of the features for the UCID Image Database.*

search Cambridge image database,[7] and are used mostly for object detection [166, 193]. This database also includes 1000 images from the LabelME image database, [154] 2333 images from the Zubud[8] image database, 1000 Chinese art images, 1000 images of famous paintings, 3000 images from television frames, 224 images from the ICPR 2004 image set, 500 images from the VASC[9] image database and finally a set of images from personal collections. All the images are high quality, multi-object, color photographs that have been chosen according to strict image selection rules [58]. The database includes 100 queries, with an average ground truth size of approximately 15 images. A sample query is illustrated in Figure 2.10(d).

In this database, the implementation of CLD, SCD and EHD in img (Rummager) application is also used. As shown in Table 2.8, on the img (Rummager) database the presented descriptors achieve the best retrieval results.

img(Rummager) is the database that was used as the core of the experiments for the shaping of the CCDs. Table 2.9 shows the ANMRR results for the CEDD and FCTH descriptors using several similarity metric techniques. As the results show, Tanimoto Coefficient presented the best results.

2.5.6 Experiments on the Nister image database

The Nister image database consists of N groups of four images each [136]. All the images are 640x480. Each group includes images of a single object. The pictures are taken from

---

[7]http://research.microsoft.com/vision/cambridge/recognition/default.htm
[8]http://www.vision.ee.ethz.ch/datasets/index.en.html
[9]http://www.ius.cs.cmu.edu/idb/

Descriptor	Query						ANMRR
	286	133	327	400	967	703	
MPEG-7 Descriptors							
SCD-32 Colors	0.012	**0**	0.239	0.256	**0**	0.112	0.29755
CLD	0.124	0.011	0.368	0.256	**0**	**0**	0.31325
EHD	0.786	0.211	0.876	0.498	0.1225	0.2214	0.51214
Other Descriptors							
RGB Color Histo.	0.224	0.211	0.239	0.256	0.112	0.000	0.30156
Tamura Direct.	0.786	0.321	0.239	0.487	0.112	0.275	0.54211
Correlograms	0.000	0.078	0.352	0.256	0.000	0.012	0.25412
CCDs							
CEDD	**0**	**0**	**0**	0.110	**0**	**0**	0.20443
FCTH	**0**	0.078	**0**	**0**	**0**	**0**	**0.19239**
C.CEDD	0.010	**0**	0.043	**0**	**0**	0.112	0.24332
C.FCTH	**0**	0.078	**0**	0.144	**0**	0.112	0.24356

Table 2.8: *ANMRR Results on img (Rummager) Image Database.*

Descriptor	Tanimoto	L1	L2	J&S	Bhattacharyya
CEDD	0.20443	0.23554	0.20558	0.26554	0.24224
CEDD un-quantized	0.23665	0.25554	0.24013	0.26558	0.23112
FCTH	0.19239	0.21214	0.01125	0.20221	0.21112
FCTH un-quantized	0.18669	0.23325	0.23855	0.23745	0.21556

Table 2.9: *ANMRR Results on img (Rummager) Database Using Several Similarity Matching Techniques.*

different viewpoints and occasionally under different lighting conditions. The first image of every object is used as a query image. Given a query image, only images from the same group are considered relevant.

For the purpose of calculating the efficiency of the presented descriptors, the database is divided into three subsets. The first subset includes the first 1000 images of the database with 250 queries. The second subset consists of the first 2000 images with 500 queries where half (250 queries) are from the first subset. The third subset includes the entire dataset of 10200 images with the same 500 queries used in the second subset. A sample query is illustrated in Figure 2.10(e).

The Nister database retrieval difficulty is dependent on the chosen subset. Important factors are:

1. Difficulty of the objects themselves. CD-covers are much easier than flowers.

2. Sharpness of the images. Many of the indoor images are somewhat blurry and this

can affect some algorithms.

3. Similar or identical objects in different groups.

The subsets and the queries are from various difficulty levels. The images used in every subset as well as the complete results are available on-line.[10]
As shown in Table 2.10, CCDs yield better results on the Nister database as well. In fact, the FCTH descriptor approaches perfect recall (ANMRR = 0.09463) on the first subset.

As the number of the images involved in the search procedure increases, the MPEG-7 descriptor's ANMRR value also increases but the presented descriptor's ANMRR is almost stable.

2.6 Conclusions

In this chapter, four descriptors that can be used in indexing and retrieval systems are presented. The presented descriptors are compact, varying in size from 23 to 74 bytes per image. The descriptors' structure includes color and texture information. The experimental results show that the performance of the presented descriptors is better than the performance of the similarly-sized MPEG-7 descriptors.
We presented two set of descriptors which leads to similar results. However, the FCTH descriptor and its related C.FCTH descriptor produce more robust results when retrieving images with many texture areas, however, they demand higher computational power and storage space than the CEDD and C.CEDD. On the other hand, the CEDD and its companion C.CEDD satisfactorily retrieve images with a small number of texture areas and their required computational power and storage space is noticeably lower. Therefore, the choice of descriptor depends on the type of images in the search procedure and on the computational requirements of the search.

---

[10]http://orpheus.ee.duth.gr/anaktisi/results

Descriptor	Query			ANMRR
	00052	00352	00900	
1000 Images				
MPEG-7 Descriptors				
SCD-32 Colors	0.157	0.129	0.729	0.36365
CLD	0.471	0.486	0.129	0.22920
EHD	0.229	0.143	0.371	0.30060
CCDs				
CEDD	**0**	**0**	**0**	0.11297
FCTH	**0**	**0**	**0**	**0.09463**
C.CEDD	**0**	**0**	**0**	0.11537
C.FCTH	**0**	0.071	**0**	0.1152
2000 Images				
MPEG-7 Descriptors				
SCD-32 Colors	0.171	0.157	0.729	0.40589
CLD	0.471	0.571	0.386	0.3156
EHD	0.243	0.229	0.386	0.4238
CCDs				
CEDD	**0**	**0**	**0**	0.17766
FCTH	**0**	**0**	**0**	**0.13494**
C.CEDD	**0**	**0**	**0**	0.19363
C.FCTH	**0**	0.071	**0**	0.16677
10200 Images				
MPEG-7 Descriptors				
SCD-32 Colors	0.271	0.643	0.729	0.48871
CLD	0.471	0.586	0.471	0.37966
EHD	0.243	0.257	0.471	0.49863
Other Descriptors				
RGB Color Histogram	0.229	0.500	0.729	0.54437
Tamura Directionality	0.729	0.729	0.729	0.70434
Correlograms	**0**	0.471	**0**	0.35711
CCDs				
CEDD	**0**	**0**	**0**	0.21220
FCTH	**0**	**0**	**0**	**0.17111**
C.CEDD	**0**	**0**	**0**	0.24509
C.FCTH	**0**	0.271	**0**	0.22403

Table 2.10: *Results on Nister Image Database.*

3

Describing Artificially Generated Images

In this chapter [1] [2], a low level feature for content based image retrieval is presented. This feature structure combines color and spatial color distribution information and is called "Spatial Color Distribution Descriptor (SpCD)". The combination of these two features in one vector classifies the presented descriptor to the family of Composite Descriptors. In order to extract the color information, a fuzzy system is being used, which is mapping the number of colors that are included in the image into a custom palette of 8 colors. The way by which the vector of the presented descriptor is being formed, describes the color spatial information contained in images. To be applicable in the design of large image databases, the presented descriptor is compact, requiring only 48 bytes per image. Experiments presented in this chapter demonstrate the effectiveness of the presented technique especially for Hand-Drawn Sketches.

Regarding CBIR schemes which rely on single features like color and/or color spatial information several schemes have been presented. The algorithm presented in [78] makes use of multi resolution wavelet decompositions of the images. In [138], each pixel as coherent or non coherent based on whether the pixel and its neighbors have similar color. In [146] [31] [110] the Spatial Color Histograms are presented in which, in addition to the statistics in the dimensions of a color space, the distribution state of each single color in the spatial dimension is also taken into account. In [176] a color distribution entropy (CDE) method is presented, which takes account of the correlation of the color spatial distribution in an image. In [71] a color correlograms method is presented, which collects statistics of the co-occurrence of two colors. A simplification of this feature is the autocorrelogram, which only captures the spatial correlation between identical colors. The

---

[1]Part of the material presented in this chapter has been awarded with the" **Best Paper Award on Artificial Intelligence**" at the "2rd International Conference on Agents and Artificial Intelligence (ICAART) 2010"

[2]This Chapter is Based on: "COMBINING COLOR AND SPATIAL COLOR DISTRIBUTION INFORMATION IN A FUZZY RULE BASED COMPACT COMPOSITE DESCRIPTOR", S. A. Chatzichristofis, Y. S. Boutalis and M. Lux, Editors J. Filipe, A. Fred, and B. Sharp, Communications in Computer and Information Science (CCIS), Volume 129, pp. 49-60, Copyright @ 2011 Springer Verlag.

MPEG-7 standard [120] includes the Color Layout Descriptor [90], which represents the spatial distribution of color of visual signals in a very compact form.

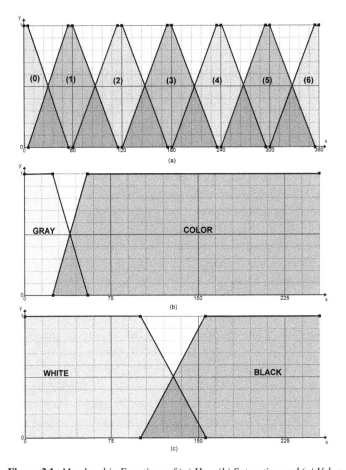

Figure 3.1: *Membership Functions of (a) Hue, (b) Saturation and (c) Value.*

In this chapter a new CCD is presented, which combines color and spatial color distribution information. The descriptors of this type can be used for image retrieval by using hand-drawn sketch queries, since this descriptor captures the layout information of color feature. In addition, this descriptor is considered to be suitable for colored graphics, since such images contain relatively small number of color and less texture regions than the natural color images.

84

3.1 Color Information

In this chapter a new fuzzy linking system is presented, that maps the colors of the image in a custom 8 colors palette. The system uses the three channels of HSV as inputs, and forms an 8-bin histogram as output. Each bin represents a present color as follows: (0) Black, (1) Red, (2) Orange/Yellow, (3) Green, (4) Cyan, (5) Blue, (6) Magenta and (7) White.

The system's operating principle is described as follows: Each pixel of the image is transformed to the HSV color space. The H, S and V values interacts with the fuzzy system as illustrated in Figure 3.1. Depending on the activation value of the membership functions of the 3 system inputs, the pixel is classified by a participation value in one or more of the preset colors, that the system uses.

For the defuzzification process, a set of 28 TSK-like [204] rules is used (See Appendix C), with fuzzy antecedents and crisp consequents.

The Membership Value Limits and the Fuzzy Rules are given in the Appendix D.

3.2 Descriptor Formation

In order to incorporate the spatial distribution information of the color to the presented descriptor, from each image, 8 Tiles with size of 4x4 pixels are created. Each Tile corresponds to one of the 8 preset colors described in Section 3.1. The Tiles are described as $T(c), c \in [0,7]$, while the Tiles' pixel values are described as $T(c)_{M,N}$, $M,N \in [0,3]$. The Tiles' creation process is described as follows: A given image J is first sub-divided into 16 sub-images according to Figure 3.2(a). Each sub image is denoted as $\acute{J}_{M,N}$. Each pixel that belongs to $\acute{J}_{M,N}$ is denoted as $P(i)_{\acute{J}_{M,N}}$, $i \in [0,I]$, I Number of pixels in $\acute{J}_{M,N}$. Each $\acute{J}_{M,N}$ contributes to the formation of the $T(c)_{M,N}$ for each c. Each $P(i)_{\acute{J}_{M,N}}$ is transformed to the HSV color space and the values of H, S and V constitute inputs to the Fuzzy-Linking system, which gives a participation value in space $[0,1]$ for each one of the 8 preset colors. The participation value of each color is defined as $MF(c)$, $c \in [0,7]$.

$$\sum_{c=0}^{7} MF(c) = 1 \qquad (3.1)$$

Each $T(c)_{M,N}$ increases by $MF(c)$. The process is repeated for all $P(i)_{\acute{J}_{M,N}}$ until $i = I$. Subsequently, the value of each $T(c)_{M,N}$ for each c is replaced according to the following formula:

$$T(c)_{M,N} = \frac{T(c)_{M,N}}{I} \qquad (3.2)$$

In this way, a normalization on the number I of the pixels, that participate in any $\acute{J}_{M,N}$ is achieved. On the completion of the process, the value of each $T(c)_{M,N}$ is quantized using a linear quantization table to an integer value within the interval $[0,7]$.

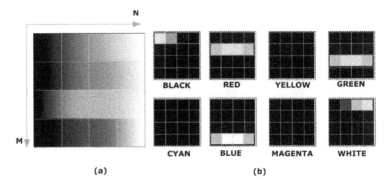

Figure 3.2: *(a) The image is divided into* 16 *sub images, (b) Result of the 8 Tiles production from the image (a).*

The described process is repeated for each (M, N). On completion of the process 8 images of 3 bits are produced, where each one of them describes the distribution (quantitative and spatial) of each color. Figure 3.2(b) shows the resulting Tiles of Figure 3.2(a).

Scanning row-by-row each tile $T(c)$, a 16-dimensional vector can be formed, with each vector element requiring 3-bits for its representation. In this vector the element's index determines position (M, N) in the tile $T(c)_{M,N}$. The element's value determines the color quantity at the position (M, N) quantized in space $[0, 7]$. By repeating the process for all the Tiles, 8 such vectors can be produced, which if combined, by placing them successively, a 48 bytes descriptor is formed.

$$16(Elements) \times 8(Tiles) \times \frac{3}{8}(bytes) = 48 bytes$$

This size compared with the size of other compact composite descriptors is considered satisfactory. The problem occurs in the length of the final vector which is set in 128 elements. During data retrieval from databases, the length of the retrieved information is of great significance. In order to compress the length of the presented descriptor the following information lossless procedure is applied. The 8 Tiles of 3 bits are combined in order to form a new 24-bit Tile ("color" Tile) of the same size. This Tile is defined as ϕ, while the values of the pixels are described as $\phi_{M,N}$, $M, N \in [0, 3]$. In order to define each $\phi_{M,N}$, 3 values are needed. $R(\phi_{M,N})$ describes the amount of red, $G(\phi_{M,N})$ describes the amount of green and $B(\phi_{M,N})$ describes the amount of blue.

The value of each $T(c)_{M,N}$ is expressed in binary form. Given that the value of each $T(c)_{M,N}$ is described by 3 bits, 3 binary digits are needed for its description.

The binary form of $T(c)_{M,N}$ value is defined as a 3 places matrix, $T(c)_{M,N}[B]$, $B \in [0, 2]$. $\phi_{M,N}$ pixel is shaped using the following rules:

$$R(\phi_{M,N}) = \sum_{c=0}^{7} 2^c \times T(c)_{M,N}[0] \qquad (3.3)$$

$$G(\phi_{M,N}) = \sum_{c=0}^{7} 2^c \times T(c)_{M,N}[1] \qquad (3.4)$$

$$B(\phi_{M,N}) = \sum_{c=0}^{7} 2^c \times T(c)_{M,N}[2] \qquad (3.5)$$

The process is repeated for each (M,N).

In order to make clear the production process of ϕ, the following example is given. The $T(c)_{M,N}$ values of the 8 Tiles for a given image J are presented in Table 3.1. Next to the 3-bit representation of each value, the binary form of the value appears. The first bit represents $T(c)_{M,N}[0]$, the second one represents $T(c)_{M,N}[1]$ and the third bit represents $T(c)_{M,N}[2]$. The value of each $\phi_{M,N}$ channel depends on the combination, using Eq. 3.3, Eq. 3.4 or Eq. 3.5, of all the $T(c)_{M,N}[B]$, $c \in [0,7]$. For example, The Blue channel of $\phi_{M,N}$ depends on the combination of all the $T(c)_{M,N}[2]$ (last column of the table). At the given example, the $B(\phi_{M,N})$ value is equal to $0 \times 2^1 + 1 \times 2^1 + 0 \times 2^2 + 1 \times 2^3 + 1 \times 2^4 + 0 \times 2^5 + 0 \times 2^6 + 1 \times 2^7 = 153$.

c	3-Bit Value	$T(c)_{M,N}[0]$	$T(c)_{M,N}[1]$	$T(c)_{M,N}[2]$
0	1	0	0	1
1	0	0	0	0
2	0	0	0	0
3	3	0	1	1
4	1	0	0	1
5	0	0	0	0
6	0	0	0	0
7	1	0	0	1
		$R(\phi_{M,N})$	$G(\phi_{M,N})$	$B(\phi_{M,N})$
		0	8	153

Table 3.1: *Combining the 8 $T(c)_{M,N}$ values to create the $\phi_{M,N}$ value.*

After applying the procedure to each (M,N) the ϕ combined "color" tile is formed. Scanning row-by-row the ϕ, a 48-dimensional vector is formed.

$$16(Elements) \times 3(Channels) = 48Elements$$

where the values of each element are quantized in the interval $[0,255]$ requiring 1 byte each. Therefore, the storage requirements of the descriptor remained the same (48 bytes), but its length in terms of number of elements was **losslessly** compressed by 62.5%. This obviously reduces the management overhead for implementation and allows for faster retrieval from the databases, in which it is stored.

3.3 Experimental Results

During the retrieval process, the user enters a query image in the form of Hand Drawn Color Sketch. From this image the 8 Tiles are exported and the 128-dimensional vector is formed. Next, each descriptor from the XML file is transformed from the 48-dimensional vector to the corresponding 128-dimensional vector, following the exact opposite procedure to that described in Section 3.2.

For the similarity matching we use, in accordance to the other Compact Composite Descriptors, the Tanimoto coefficient.

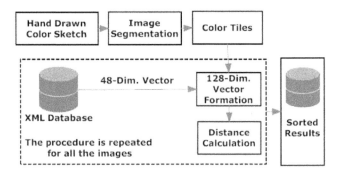

Figure 3.3: *Image Retrieval Procedure.*

After iteratively applying the process to all image descriptors contained in the XML file, the result list of best matching images is presented, ranked by distance to the query image. The process is described in Figure 3.3.

In order to evaluate the performance of the presented descriptor, experiments were carried out on 2 benchmarking image databases. The first database contains 1030 images, which they depict flags from around the world. The database consists of state flags, flags of unrecognized states, flags of formerly independent states, municipality flags, dependent territory flags and flags of first-level country subdivisions. All the images are taken from Wikipedia. We used 20 Hand Drawn Color Sketches as query images and as ground truth (list of similar images of each query) we considered only the flag that was attempted to be drawn with the Hand Drawn Color Sketch.

The "Paintings" database was also used. This database is incorporated in [199] and includes 1771 images of paintings by internationally well known artists. Also in this case, as query images were used 20 Hand Drawn Color Sketches and as ground truth was considered only the painting, which was attempted to be drawn with the Hand Drawn Color Sketch. Figure 3.4 shows a query sample from each database as well as the retrieval results.

Table 3.2 illustrates the ANMRR results in both databases. The results are compared with the corresponding results of the Color Layout Descriptor (CLD). The implementation of

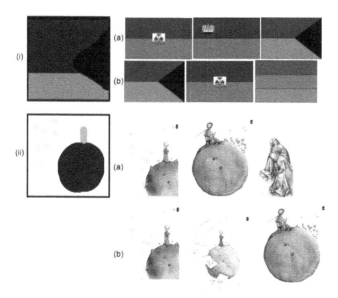

Figure 3.4: *Hand Drawn Color Sketch queries (i) for the Flags database and (ii) for the Paintings database. In each one of the queries (a) shows the first 3 results of the CLD, while (b) shows the first 3 results of the presented descriptor.*

the CLD matches the implementation in [117]. The reason for this comparison is that only the CLD, from the descriptors that were referred in the introduction, is compact.

Database	SpCD ANMRR	CLD ANMRR
Flags	0.225	0.425
Paintings	0.275	0.45

Table 3.2: *ANMRR results.*

Considering the results, it is evident that the presented descriptor is able to achieve satisfactory retrieval results by using Hand Drawn Color Sketches as queries.

3.4 Conclusions

In this chapter, a compact composite descriptor appropriate for artificially generated images has been presented. This descriptor combines color and spatial color distribution information. Characteristics of the presented descriptor are its small storage requirements (48 bytes/ per image) and its small length (48 elements). Experiments were performed at 2 databases with artificial generated images. The presented descriptor achieved very good results and outperformed the MPEG-7 CLD in both experiments.

Describing Medical Radiology Images

The last decades have witnessed significant advances in medical imaging and computerized medical image processing. The commonly used medical imaging modalities for radiological applications are: X-ray Computed Tomography (X-ray CT), Magnetic Resonance Imaging (MRI), Single Photon Emission Computed Tomography (SPECT), Positron Emission Tomography (PET) and Ultrasound [47].

Nowadays, digitized medical images are becoming more frequently used. This leads to the creation of large image databases, requiring efficient methods for indexing and retrieval of their content.

The process of automatic indexing and retrieval of medical images based on their content is known by the term Content-based medical image retrieval (CBMIR) [192]. CBMIR is quite different from CBIR as the retrieval similarity must consider the medical context (such as the subtle pathological changes) as well as the user individualized subjectivity [82]. Medical images are multimodal, heterogeneous and higher dimensional with temporal properties, which distinguish them from images in other domains [179]. In the CBMIR the basic objective is to provide diagnostic support to the physicians or radiologists by displaying relevant past cases, along with proven pathologies as ground truth [141].

Several medical image indexing and retrieval techniques have been presented in the literature. Chu et al presented an image retrieval system dedicated to brain MRI which indexes images mainly on the shape of the ventricular region [28]. Korn et al presented a system for the fast and effective retrieval of tumor shapes in mammogram X-rays [98]. Comaniciu et al described a system that aims to help physicians in the diagnosis of lymphoproliferative disorders of blood [32]. Glatard et al introduced a Texture Based Medical Image Indexing and Retrieval for Cardiac Images [57].

Most of the CBMIRs are based on visual example. The doctor/specialist uses a radiology image as input (query image), and, based on certain global or local feature vectors (FV), the system brings up similar images. This sort of feature vectors are used to describe the content of the image and that is why they must be appropriately selected on occasion. The visual content of the images is mapped in to a new space called the feature space. The feature vectors (descriptors) that are chosen have to be discriminative and sufficient for the description of the objects [17].

This chapter [1] presents a new descriptor that can be used for the indexing and retrieval of radiology medical images: the "Brightness and Texture Directionality Histogram (BTD-H)". This descriptor uses brightness and texture characteristics as well as the spatial distribution of these characteristics in one compact 1D vector. The most important characteristic of the presented descriptor is that its size adapts according to the storage capabilities of the application that is using it. This characteristic renders the descriptor appropriate for use in large medical (or gray scale) image databases.

4.1 Brightness Information

The image-acquisition system usually converts a biomedical signal or radiation carrying the information of interest to a digital image [47]. In most cases, these images are 8 bit greyscale images. The first unit of the presented system undertakes to fuzzy classify the brightness of the image pixels into L_{Bright} preset clusters. Experiments, which are described in Section 4.5, were carried out for $L_{Bright} = 8$ and $L_{Bright} = 16$. The number of clusters comes as a compromise between the low storage requirements of the application using the presented descriptor, and the need for more efficient retrieval accuracy. The center of these clusters was calculated using the following method: A sample of 3000 (8 bit grayscale) radiology medical images was used. These images included 1000 X-ray images, 1000 MRI images and 1000 Ultrasound images. All the images were resized to 128×128 pixels, ignoring the initial aspect ratio. The bicubic method was used to resize the images [91].

The aim was to classify the values of pixel brightness of all the images by using the Fuzzy Classifier Gustafson-Kessel in L_{Bright} clusters. The particularly large resulting figure of samples $3000 \times 128 \times 128 \cong 10^6$, however, would lead to out of memory problems. The Gustafson-Kessel algorithm was therefore used in each image individually, classifying the pixel brightness into 20 clusters. The Gustafson Kessel parameters are selected as: Clusters $L = 20$, Repetitions=3000, $e = 0.001$ and $m = 2$. Next, the group of 3000×20 cluster values were classified into L_{Bright} clusters using a second Gustafson-Kessel classifier. In this case, the Gustafson Kessel parameters are selected as: Clusters $L = 8, 16$, Repetitions= 2000, $e = 0.001$ and $m = 2$. The centers of the resulting clusters for $L = 8$ and $L = 16$ are shown in Table 4.1.

The resulting cluster centers $v(i), i \in [0, L-1]$ are used to form a fuzzy system. This system will classify the pixel brightness of any image, interacted with the system into L_{Bright} classes. The fuzzy system with $L_{Bright} = 8$ is illustrated in Figure 4.1.

---

[1]This Chapter is Based on: "CONTENT BASED RADIOLOGY IMAGE RETRIEVAL USING A FUZZY RULE BASED SCALABLE COMPOSITE DESCRIPTOR", S. A. Chatzichristofis and Y. S. Boutalis, Multimedia Tools and Applications, Volume 46, Numbers

	v(0)	v(1)	v(2)	v(3)	v(4)	v(5)	v(6)	v(7)
L=16	1.71	12.25	22.53	35.38	50.38	65.60	82.41	99.99
L=8	3.18	22.68	54.00	90.13	125.80	162.57	202.25	243.64
	v(8)	v(9)	v(10)	v(11)	v(12)	v(13)	v(14)	v(15)
L=16	116.92	134.31	153.65	173.36	193.70	214.88	234.91	251.23

Table 4.1: *Brightness Cluster Centers.*

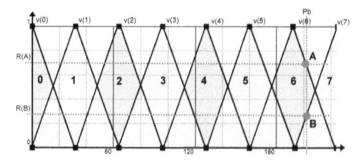

Figure 4.1: *Brightness Classification System.*

The fuzzy system output is an L_{Bright}-bin histogram. The way this system operates is described as follows: Let the image j. Every pixel of the image interacts with the system. Suppose that the brightness value of the pixel $P(x,y)$ is P_b, where P_b:

$$v(k) \le P_b \le v(k+1) \quad k \in [0, L_{Bright} - 2] \tag{4.1}$$

This value activates the membership function k by $R(A)$ and membership function $k+1$ by $R(B)$, as illustrated in Figure 4.1. Where A and B are the incision points of P_b with the membership function k and $k+1$ respectively. The fuzzy system output histogram changes as follows:

$$BrightnessHisto(k) = BrightnessHisto(k) + R(A)$$

$$BrightnessHisto(k+1) = BrightnessHisto(k+1) + R(B)$$

$$R(A) + R(B) = 1$$

Where *BrightnessHisto* is the fuzzy system output histogram.

For the example of Figure 4.1: $k = 6, R(A) = 0.7$ and $R(B) = 0.3$. The procedure is repeated for all the pixels.

2-3, pp. 493-519, Copyright @ 2010 Springer Verlag.

93

4.2 Texture Information

Most CBIMR systems use texture features. Due to the structure of medical images, texture is a very strong feature which includes huge amounts of information. A commonly used texture feature is the Tamura Texture feature [43] [59] [60]. According to [59], which compares low-level features for the automatic categorization of medical images, the histograms based on Tamura's texture features yielded the best results among the features presented for general-purpose image retrieval. The Tamura texture includes 6 features selected by psychological experiments: *Coarseness, contrast, directionality, line likeness, regularity* and *roughness* [180].

Tamura Directionality histogram is a graph of local edge probabilities against their directional angle.

In this chapter, a novel fuzzy approach of the directionality histogram is presented and used to describe the texture information to the presented descriptor.

The extraction method of the traditional Tamura Directionality histogram utilizes the fact that gradient is a vector, so it has both magnitude and direction. In the discrete case, the magnitude $|\Delta G|$ and the local edge direction θ are approximated as follows:

$$|\Delta G| = \frac{|\Delta_H| + |\Delta_V|}{2} \tag{4.2}$$

$$\theta = tan^{-1}\left(\frac{\Delta_V}{\Delta_H}\right) + \frac{\pi}{2} \tag{4.3}$$

Where $|\Delta_H|$ and $|\Delta_V|$ are the horizontal and vertical differences computed using approximate pixel-wise derivatives measured by the Sobel edge detector in the 3×3 moving window.

The resultant θ is a real number $(0 < \theta < \pi)$ measured counter clockwise so that the horizontal direction is zero. The desired histogram H_D can be obtained by quantizing θ in n values and counting the points with the magnitude $|\Delta G|$ over the threshold t;

$$H_D(k) = \frac{N_\theta(k)}{\sum\limits_{i=0}^{n-1} N_\theta(i)} \quad k = 0, 1, \dots n-1 \tag{4.4}$$

Where $N_\theta(k)$ is the number of points at which $|\Delta G| \geq t$.

Thresholding by t prevents the counting of unreliable directions which cannot be regarded as edge points. The most classic approach, uses $n = 16$ and $t = 12$. Note that the shape of each histogram was not sensitive to the value of t.

The texture information extraction unit of the system that is used for the extraction of the presented descriptor uses a fuzzy approach to extract the directionality histogram.

In our approach we used $n = L_{Textures}$ quantized values of θ. The number of $L_{Texture}$ depends as much on the storage capabilities of the application using the presented descriptor as it does on the need for more efficient retrieval accuracy. As the number of direction-ality areas increases, so does the calculating cost of extracting the presented descriptor. Experiments were carried out for $L_{Texture} = 4$ and $L_{Texture} = 16$ are described in Section 4.5.

The $L_{Texture}$ quantized values of θ are used to form a fuzzy system, similar to the system that was described in Section 4.1. The fuzzy system with $L_{Texture} = 16$ is illustrated in Figure 4.2.

For every image entered into the texture information extractor unit, an $L_{Texture}$-bin his-togram that describes the directionality of the image is extracted.

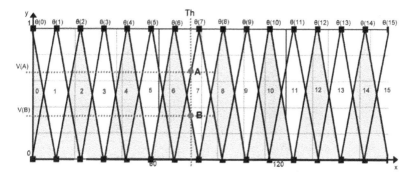

Figure 4.2: *Directionality Classification System.*

The way this system operates is described as follows: Suppose that the θ value of a moving window (3×3 pixels) is Th, where Th :

$$\theta(k-1) \leq Th \leq \theta(k) \qquad (4.5)$$

This value activates membership function k by $V(A)$ and the membership function $k+1$ by $V(B)$, as illustrated in Figure 4.2. The fuzzy system output histogram changes as follows:

$$DirectionHisto(k) = DirectionHisto(k) + V(A)$$

$$DirectionHisto(k+1) = DirectionHisto(k+1) + V(B)$$

$$V(A) + V(B) = 1$$

Where $DirectionHisto$ is the fuzzy system output histogram.

For the example of Figure 4.2: $k = 7$, $V(A) = 0.7$ and $V(B) = 0.3$. The procedure is repeated for all moving windows (Entire image).

4.3 Fractal scanning

Fractal scanning is the term given to the image scanning technique based on a predetermined fractal curve. This technique is much more efficient for capturing spatial features in digital images than other commonly used techniques such as horizontal, vertical or diagonal pixels scan [197] [135]. Such techniques do not maintain the adjacency of the features inside the image since their scanning direction is usually not identified with the one that features specify. Feature extraction is more substantial when we succeed to retain the neighborhood relationship among the pixels.

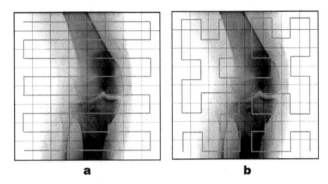

Figure 4.3: *Comparison between horizontal and fractal scanning.(a) Horizontal scanning, (b) Fractal Scanning*

A comparison between the fractal scanning technique and the linear horizontal scanning is shown in Fig. 4.3. It is obvious that horizontal scanning loses the adjacency in the vertical direction and this will be also reflected on the constructed signature.

4.3.1 Hilbert Curve Fractal scanning

To apply fractal scanning to an image, space filling curves [158] are used. The Hilbert curve which is used in this chapter is essentially a fractal that, in its two-dimensional form, can be analyzed as an L-System (Lindenmayer system) [144]. Using these systems, repetitive drawing methods that use the turtle analogy rule can be described. They are created started from one axiom, such as for example a rectilinear section and one or more drawing rules. When these rules are repeated several times the result is usually a complex fractal curve. We make this clear with the following example:

Consider the symbol "F" and the rule "replace symbol F with the string F+F-F+F". By repeating this procedure we get:

```
F
F+F-F+F
```

```
(F+F-F+F)  +  (  F+F-F+F)  -  (F+F-F+F)  +  (F+F-F+F)
. . .
```

After this, we proceed with the drawing part. This is the stage where the turtle analogy comes in. We assume that "F" says, "draw a line" (move forward), "+" says "turn left" and "-" says "turn right". Implementing the whole process by using x iterations of the rule, line length y and 60 degrees angle we get the well-known Koch curve. We characterize the curve with the factors x and y which reflects the order and the movement step, respectively. The Hilbert space-filling curve, which we use for fractal scanning, is constructed in the same way but using different rules and symbols:

```
Symbols : ''L'', ''R''
Rules : ''L->+RF-LFL-FR+'',''R->-LF+RFR+FL- ''
Angle : 90 degrees
```

The letters "L" and "R" are used to create the series of symbols, the final shape of which will relate to the levels of repetition chosen. The drawing will take place taking into consideration only the letters "F" (drawing the line), "+" (clockwise rotation) and "-" (anti-clockwise rotation). Figure 4.4 shows the first three levels of repetition of the drawing rule. A first-order Hilbert curve is a square with one open side (which is the basic element) that defines its direction. The second-order Hilbert curve replaces every square by four other in a way that depends on the direction of the first-order square [135]. The reasons we adopt the Hilbert curve are its ability to capture in its path the adjacent information of the image objects, its property to cover squared regions and that it has been successfully used in the scanning process in other image-processing applications.

4.3.2 Z-Grid Based scanning

Replacing the Hilbert Curve with the Z-Space Filling Curve, the Z-Grid fractal scanning [143] method results. The extraction method can be modeled as follows:

Consider a grid G of dimensions $W \times Q$, where $W \in \{0, w-1\}$ and $Q \in \{0, q-1\}$. Two marker labels are placed to the top and to the left of the grid, to be used for mapping the grid cells. The symbols L_W and L_Q are used as label descriptors. The marker labels are separated into W and Q positions respectively. Each position corresponds to a cell. Odd position values for each marker label are equal to 1, while even position values are equal to 0. The cell $G(w,q)$ of Grid G is described using a combination of the $L_Q(q)$ and $L_W(w)$. In the simplest case, where the grid size is equal to 2×2, $G(0,0)$ as shown in the Fig. 4.4 (ii)(a) is marked as $L_Q(0)L_W(0) = 00$, $G(0,1)$ is marked as $L_Q(1)L_W(0) = 10$, $G(1,0)$ is marked as $L_Q(0)L_W(1) = 01$ and $G(1,1)$ is marked as $L_Q(1)L_W(1) = 11$. To draw the Z-Grid fractal curve, starting from the upper left corner of the Grid $G(0,0)$ move to the next cell, according to the order in which the cells were marked.

In higher dimensions, the original Grid is separated into a new Grid G'. G' is surrounding

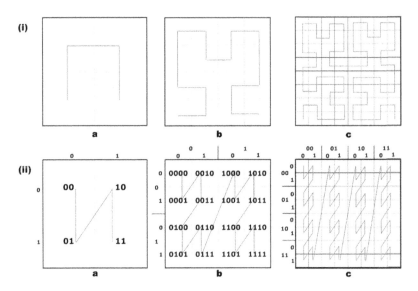

Figure 4.4: *Method of creating the (i) Hilbert and the (ii) Z-Grid based curve. (i)(a) First repetition of the drawing rule, (i)(b) Second repetition of the drawing rule and (i)(c) Third repetition of the drawing rule. (ii)(a) Designing of the Z-Grid Curve on a 2×2 grid, (ii)(b) Designing of the Z-Grid Curve on a 4×4 grid and (ii)(c) Designing of the Z-Grid Curve on a 8×8 grid*

G. The dimensions of G' are $W' \in \{0, \frac{w-1}{2}\}$ and $Q' \in \{0, \frac{q-1}{2}\}$. Given that G' has half the cells of G, each cell in G' could be considered to comprise one 2×2 Sub Grid. Two new marker labels are used to describe the cells in Grid G'. The symbols L'_Q and L'_W are used to describe the labels. Marker labels are respectively separated into $Q/2$ and $W/2$ positions. The procedure for label calibration is as follows: Starting from the top left corner of the Grid, $G(0,0)$, each cell is described by the binary number of the sequence in which it appears. As many bits as necessary are used to describe the binary number which describes the total number of cells resulting in each dimension. Cell $G(w',q')$ on Grid G' is described using the $L'_Q(q')$ and $L'_W(q')$. Finally, each cell $G(w,q)$ on Grid G is described by the combination: $L'_Q(q')L'_W(w')L_Q(q)L_W(w)$. This combination configures a binary number which specifies the order in which Z-Grid fractal scanning is configured. For example, $G(0,0)$ in the Fig. 4.4 (ii)(b) is marked as $L'_Q(0)L'_W(0)L_Q(0)L_W(0) = 0000$ while $G(1,1)$ is marked as $L'_Q(0)L'_W(0)L_Q(1)L_W(1) = 0011$. To draw the Z-Grid fractal curve in higher dimensions, starting from the upper left corner of the Grid $G(0,0)$ move to the next cell, according to the order in which the cells were marked.

For grid sized 2×2, 4×4 and 8×8, the procedure is described in Fig. 4.5 (ii).

The way in which Hilbert curve and the Z-Grid fractal scanning are used in the presented descriptor is described in Section 4.5.

4.4 Descriptor Implementation

The brightness and texture features described in the previous sections are combined to produce the presented descriptor. The production process is illustrated in Figure 4.5. Using the bicubic method, the image entered into the system is resized to the dimensions of 240×240 pixels, ignoring the initial aspect ratio. Our approach starts by performing brightness and edge enhancement in the *Pre-Filtering* unit. First, the auto brightness correction method presented in [187] is applied to the image. This method is partially inspired by the HVS (Human Vision System). It particularly adopts some of the shunting characteristics of the on-center off-surround networks, in order to define the response function for a new artificial center-surround network. This network compares every pixel to its local average and assigns a new value in order to light the dark image regions, while minimally affecting the light ones. The aim of using this filter is to cover alterations in the brightness that might result from the settings of the system used to record/capture the medical image.

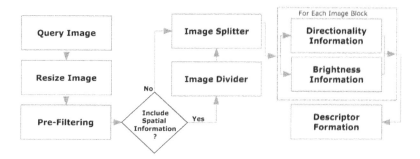

Figure 4.5: *Descriptor Implementation.*

Next, a coordinate logic filter (CLF) **-OR-** [126] [182] [124] is applied to the image. This filter enhances the edges of the image and aims to help the texture information extraction unit to reach weaker texture alternations. The result of the image enhancement is illustrated in Figure 4.6.

In the following unit, system checks whether the user chose to integrate spatial information into the descriptor.

4.4.1 Descriptor Implementation without Spatial Information

The improved image from the pre-filtering unit is transferred to the *Image Splitter* unit. In this unit, the image is divided into 3×3 pixels image blocks. Each image block is entered into the brightness information extractor unit (*Brightness Unit*) and the directionality information extractor unit (*Directionality Unit*). The combination of these two units forms

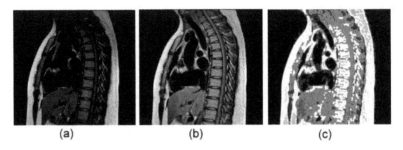

(a)   (b)   (c)

Figure 4.6: *(a) Original Image, (b) Auto Brightness Correction and (c) Application with CLF -OR- Filter. Image is taken from Auckland MRI Research Group.*

the presented descriptor which is constructed as follows: The descriptor's structure has $L_{Texture}$ regions determined by the Directionality Unit. Each Directionality Unit region contains L_{Bright} individual regions defined by the Brightness Unit. Overall, the presented descriptor histogram contains $L_{Texture} \times L_{Bright}$ bins.

Each Image Block interacts successively with the two units. Firstly, the *Directionality Unit* defines the texture type that is presented in the image block and classifies it in one or more regions $n \in [0, L_{Texture} - 1]$ with participant rate $P(n)$, for each n that participates.

$$\sum P(n) = 1$$

Meanwhile, every pixel of the image block interacts with the brightness classification unit and is classified in one or more of the $m \in [0, L_{Bright} - 1]$ preset brightness classes with participation rate $R(m)$, for each m that participates.

$$\sum R(m) = 1$$

Finally the output bin $(L_{Bright} \times n + m)$ of the presented descriptor increases by $P(n) \times R(m)$ for each n and m. The procedure is repeated in the Brightness Unit for all the pixels. On the completion of the process, the descriptor's histogram bin values are normalized within the interval $[0, 1]$.

$$bin(i)' = \frac{bin(i)}{\sum_{j=0}^{L_{Texture} \times L_{Bright}} bin(j)} \qquad i \in [0, L_{Texture} \times L_{Bright}] \qquad (4.6)$$

The structure of the presented descriptor is illustrated in Figure 4.7.

In order to reduce the storage needs of the presented descriptor, its bin values are quantized for binary representation using a three bits/bin quantization. Given that the $L_{Bright} \times L_{Texture}$ Directionality/ Brightness bin values are concentrated within a small range (from 0 to 0.053), linear quantization cannot be applied. The descriptor's histogram bins are separated into $L_{Texture}$ quantization groups (one group for each texture type). Each group is quantized with different quantization table.

Figure 4.7: *BTDH Descriptor Structure.*

In order to calculate the quantization table of each group, the same set of images described in Section 4.2 was used. First, the descriptor of all the images was calculated.

Let X_j be the presented descriptor of the image j. X_j is separated into the $L_{Texture}$ regions according to the quantization groups. Let $\left[X_j^i\right]$ the set of bin values in the group $i \in [0, L_{Texture} - 1]$ of the image j. For each i (group), the set of bin values $\left[X_j^i\right]$ of all the j (images), constitute inputs into the fuzzy Gustafson Kessel classifier, which separates the bin values into eight regions. This technique maps the bin values into the integer area $[0, 7]$. The procedure is repeated for all the $L_{Texture}$ groups. The Gustafson Kessel parameters are selected as: Clusters $L = 8$, repetitions=2000, $e = 0.002$, and $m = 2$. This quantization method was also used in [18] and [19]. The resulting quantization tables for $(L_{Texture} = 8, L_{Bright} = 8)$, $(L_{Texture} = 8, L_{Bright} = 16)$ and $(L_{Texture} = 16, L_{Bright} = 8)$ are given in Table 4.2, Table 4.3 and Table 4.4 respectively. Each row represents a quantization group. The final size of the presented descriptor is:

$$\left((L_{Texture} \times L_{Bright}) \times \frac{3}{8}\right) bytes \qquad (4.7)$$

For each image entered into the system, the presented descriptor is extracted. This descriptor is separated into $L_{Texture}$ regions according to the quantization groups. The value of each bin of the descriptor is assigned to one of the values $[0, 7]$ according to the minimum distance of the value from one of the eight entries in the corresponding row of the proper quantization table. For example, let the presented descriptor histogram $bin(4) = 0.006$ for $L_{Texture} = 16$ and $L_{Bright} = 8$. This particular bin belongs to group 1 (the first Directionality/ Brightness group), the quantization table of which is shown in the first row of Table 4.4. The minimum distance is the one with value $7.2E - 03$. Therefore the presented descriptor histogram quantized value of $bin(4) = 011 = \mathbf{3}$.

000	001	010	011	100	101	110	111
2.3E-04	1.8E-03	4.0E-03	6.8E-03	1.1E-02	1.7E-02	4.0E-02	5.7E-01
2.7E-04	1.9E-03	4.0E-03	6.5E-03	9.8E-03	1.5E-02	2.7E-02	8.3E-02
2.1E-04	1.4E-03	3.1E-03	5.1E-03	7.6E-03	1.1E-02	1.8E-02	4.5E-02
2.4E-04	1.6E-03	3.5E-03	5.7E-03	8.6E-03	1.3E-02	2.1E-02	6.2E-02
2.4E-04	1.7E-03	3.9E-03	6.7E-03	1.0E-02	1.7E-02	3.9E-02	3.6E-01
2.4E-04	1.7E-03	3.9E-03	6.7E-03	1.0E-02	1.7E-02	3.9E-02	4.6E-01
2.4E-04	1.8E-03	4.0E-03	6.9E-03	1.1E-02	1.8E-02	4.0E-02	3.9E-01
2.2E-04	1.7E-03	3.8E-03	6.5E-03	1.0E-02	1.7E-02	3.6E-02	4.0E-01

Table 4.2: *Quantization Table for $L_{Texture} = L_{Bright} = 8$.*

000	001	010	011	100	101	110	111
8.0E-04	4.6E-03	8.8E-03	1.4E-02	2.0E-02	3.0E-02	5.5E-02	4.0E-01
8.4E-04	5.1E-03	9.9E-03	1.5E-02	2.2E-02	3.3E-02	6.5E-02	5.9E-01
7.8E-04	4.5E-03	8.5E-03	1.4E-02	2.0E-02	2.8E-02	5.5E-02	5.6E-01
8.3E-04	5.0E-03	9.5E-03	1.4E-02	2.0E-02	3.0E-02	5.4E-02	2.9E-01
7.2E-04	4.1E-03	7.8E-03	1.2E-02	1.8E-02	2.7E-02	5.1E-02	3.6E-01
6.8E-04	3.9E-03	7.7E-03	1.2E-02	1.8E-02	2.6E-02	4.8E-02	3.1E-01
6.9E-04	4.2E-03	7.8E-03	1.3E-02	1.9E-02	2.8E-02	5.0E-02	3.1E-01
8.9E-04	5.2E-03	1.0E-02	1.6E-02	2.3E-02	3.3E-02	6.2E-02	3.4E-01

Table 4.3: *Quantization Table for $L_{Texture} = 8$ and $L_{Bright} = 16$.*

000	001	010	011	100	101	110	111
3.6E-04	2.3E-03	4.5E-03	7.2E-03	1.1E-02	1.6E-02	3.1E-02	5.7E-01
3.2E-04	1.9E-03	3.7E-03	5.7E-03	8.4E-03	1.3E-02	2.4E-02	5.3E-01
3.3E-04	1.9E-03	3.5E-03	5.3E-03	7.6E-03	1.1E-02	1.6E-02	4.0E-02
3.7E-04	2.1E-03	4.1E-03	6.3E-03	8.8E-03	1.2E-02	2.0E-02	6.9E-02
3.2E-04	1.8E-03	3.4E-03	5.4E-03	7.9E-03	1.1E-02	1.7E-02	3.9E-02
3.1E-04	1.7E-03	3.3E-03	5.3E-03	7.8E-03	1.1E-02	1.8E-02	5.6E-02
3.6E-04	2.0E-03	3.9E-03	6.1E-03	8.6E-03	1.3E-02	2.1E-02	7.8E-02
3.6E-04	2.1E-03	4.0E-03	6.2E-03	9.0E-03	1.3E-02	2.4E-02	1.9E-01
3.7E-04	2.3E-03	4.4E-03	7.0E-03	1.0E-02	1.6E-02	2.9E-02	2.4E-01
4.2E-04	2.5E-03	4.9E-03	7.6E-03	1.1E-02	1.9E-02	5.3E-02	6.8E-01
3.6E-04	2.1E-03	3.9E-03	6.3E-03	9.3E-03	1.4E-02	2.7E-02	4.4E-01
3.7E-04	2.2E-03	4.3E-03	6.9E-03	1.1E-02	1.6E-02	3.5E-02	3.8E-01
3.3E-04	2.0E-03	3.8E-03	6.2E-03	9.4E-03	1.4E-02	2.8E-02	3.7E-01
2.7E-04	1.8E-03	3.6E-03	5.7E-03	8.9E-03	1.3E-02	2.6E-02	3.6E-01
3.0E-04	2.0E-03	3.9E-03	6.1E-03	8.8E-03	1.3E-02	2.6E-02	3.7E-01
3.2E-04	2.1E-03	4.2E-03	6.8E-03	1.0E-02	1.5E-02	3.1E-02	4.3E-01

Table 4.4: *Quantization Table for $L_{Texture} = 16$ and $L_{Bright} = 8$.*

4.4.2 Descriptor Implementation with Spatial Information

To integrate the spatial information in relation to the distribution of Brightness and Texture, the improved image from the pre-filtering unit interacts with the *Image Divider* unit. In this unit, the image is divided into $L_{Blocks} \times L_{Blocks}$ squared sections. These sections are called *Sub Images*. Experiments were carried out for $L_{Blocks} = 4$ and $L_{Blocks} = 8$. These are described in Section 4.5.

Each *Sub Image* is transferred to the image splitter unit. The sequence in which the Sub Images are entered into the next unit relates to the fractal scanning method, as Figure 4.8 illustrates.

Fig. 4.8(b) is a schematic illustration of how the Hilbert curve is applied for the fractal scanning of Sub Images while Fig. 4.8(c) is a schematic illustration of how the Z-Grid is applied for the fractal scanning of Sub Images. Fig. 4.8(e) numerically illustrates the order in which the Sub Images are entered into the *image splitter* in case of Hilbert fractal scanning and Fig. 4.8(f) numerically illustrates the order in which the Sub Images are entered into the *image splitter* in case of Z-Grid scanning. The fractal scanning of the image plays a fundamental part in the formation of the descriptor's final shape.

In the image splitter unit, every Sub-Image is treated as an independent image and the presented descriptor is extracted using the process described. The completion of the process results in $L_{Blocks} \times L_{Blocks}$ Sub-Image descriptors.

The resulting $L_{Blocks} \times L_{Blocks}$ vectors are combined for the formation of the final descriptor shape. The Sub-Images descriptors are placed in succession, one next to the other according to the order determined by the fractal scanning method. The final length of the descriptor is:

$$L_{Blocks}^2 \times (L_{Bright} \times L_{Texture}) \tag{4.8}$$

If spatial distribution with $L_{Blocks} = 8$ is integrated in the presented descriptor, the quantization tables are given in Table 4.6 and Table 4.7. If the $L_{Blocks} = 4$, the quantization tables is given in Table 4.5.

Each Sub-Image descriptor is quantized using a different set of quantization values. The same quantization table is used for both the Hilbert fractal and the Z-Grid. The first column in the tables corresponds to the Sub-Image resulting from Linear Scanning (Fig. 4.8(d)). Depending on the method of fractal scanning implemented, the position of a given Sub-Image is defined in relation to the position of the Sub-Image in the case of Linear Scanning, and the corresponding row in the table is selected. For example: if the Hilbert fractal scanning method with $L_{Blocks} = 8$ is applied to the image, the quantization of the histogram produced by the 22nd Sub-Image is achieved using the 1st line on Table 4.6. If the Z-Grid is used, the quantization of the histogram of the 22nd Sub-Image would be achieved with the 27th row of Table 4.6. The same quantization process is followed when using $L_{Blocks} = 4$. In this case, Table 4.5 is used.

The final size of the descriptor is:

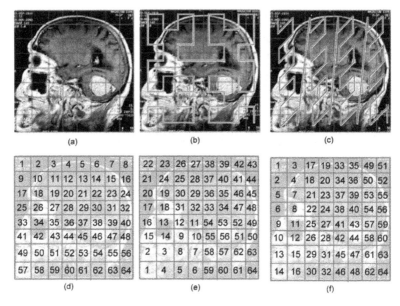

Figure 4.8: *Linear and Fractal Scanning. (a) Original image. (b) The image is divided into 64 ($L_{Blocks} = 8$) Sub Images using Hilbert Fractal. For $L_{Blocks} = 8$ the third repetition of the drawing rule is used. (c) The image is divided into 64 ($L_{Blocks} = 8$) Sub Images using Z-Grid. (d) Order Number of the Sub Images Using Linear Scanning.(e) Order Number of the Sub Images using Hilbert Fractal and (f) Order Number of the Sub Images using Z-Grid.*

$$\left(L_{Blocks}^2 \times (L_{Bright} \times L_{Texture}) \times \frac{3}{8} \right) bytes \qquad (4.9)$$

Having described the extraction method of the presented descriptor, it is now possible to justify the reason for resizing each image to the dimensions of 240×240 ignoring the initial aspect ratio. To begin with, the resizing procedure is imperative for the acceleration of the descriptor extraction process. The reason for selecting these dimensions is the following:

By applying spatial information to the descriptor, the image is divided into 8×8 or 4×4 Sub-Images. Therefore, the objective is that each side of the image is to be divisible by the L_{Blocks} without leaving a remainder. The size of each Sub-Image produced must be a multiple of 3 so that during the extraction of the non-overlapped image blocks (whose dimensions are 3×3) all pixels in the block can be included. An extension of this is also the reason why it was decided to ignore the initial aspect ratio. In many images used in the experiments described in Section 4.5, one dimension is exceedingly small compared to the other (e.g. 512×91). If resizing is attempted while maintaining the initial aspect

L	000	001	010	011	100	101	110	111
1	5.4E-06	1.2E-03	4.5E-03	9.4E-03	1.7E-02	2.7E-02	5.2E-02	4.1E-01
2	3.4E-06	9.1E-04	3.4E-03	7.2E-03	1.2E-02	2.2E-02	3.1E-02	6.8E-02
3	3.8E-06	8.6E-04	3.2E-03	6.8E-03	1.2E-02	1.9E-02	2.9E-02	6.0E-02
4	4.7E-06	1.5E-03	4.7E-03	9.8E-03	1.7E-02	2.8E-02	5.0E-02	1.3E-01
5	1.5E-06	8.2E-04	3.5E-03	7.4E-03	1.3E-02	2.1E-02	3.3E-02	7.5E-02
6	5.0E-07	1.2E-03	4.6E-03	9.8E-03	1.7E-02	2.9E-02	5.1E-02	1.3E-01
7	4.6E-06	1.2E-03	4.5E-03	9.7E-03	1.7E-02	2.2E-02	5.2E-02	4.4E-01
8	5.7E-06	1.5E-03	4.2E-03	9.0E-03	1.6E-02	2.8E-02	5.2E-02	4.9E-01
9	4.8E-06	1.2E-03	4.5E-03	9.6E-03	2.2E-02	2.8E-02	5.3E-02	3.2E-01
10	5.3E-06	1.2E-03	4.3E-03	9.6E-03	1.9E-02	3.3E-02	5.3E-02	1.9E-01
11	3.0E-06	1.1E-03	4.3E-03	9.1E-03	1.6E-02	2.5E-02	4.1E-02	1.1E-01
12	2.7E-06	1.2E-03	4.7E-03	8.0E-03	1.8E-02	3.0E-02	5.4E-02	3.3E-01
13	3.4E-06	1.7E-03	4.2E-03	9.0E-03	1.6E-02	2.8E-02	5.5E-02	1.8E-01
14	2.9E-06	8.3E-04	3.5E-03	7.5E-03	1.3E-02	2.1E-02	3.3E-02	7.4E-02
15	1.8E-06	9.6E-04	3.8E-03	6.1E-03	1.4E-02	2.2E-02	3.5E-02	8.6E-02
16	2.8E-06	1.1E-03	4.4E-03	9.5E-03	1.7E-02	3.0E-02	5.7E-02	4.1E-01

Table 4.5: *Quantization Table for* $L_{Block} = 4, L_{Texture} = 16$ *and* $L_{Bright} = 8$.

ratio, then it is very likely that Sub-Images with dimensions that are not multiples of 3 would emerge, and many pixels, and therefore useful information from the image, would be lost.

4.5 Experiments

To evaluate the performance of the presented descriptor experiments are performed on two medical image databases: The IRMA 2007 database and the IRMA 2005[2] database.

In our experiments, the Mean Average Precision is employed to evaluate the performance of the presented descriptor. The MAP was selected to compare the presented descriptor retrieval results to the results presented by other low level descriptors in the IRMA 2005 database, which are available in the bibliography.

The searching procedure is described as follows: For all benchmarking database images used in performance measurement experiments, the presented descriptor is extracted and saved in an **XML** file. For each query image there is a given ground truth. The ground truth is defined by an image set from the database exhibiting visual similarity with the query image. The descriptor is extracted from the query image and its distance from the descriptor of each image included in the XML file is measured, based on a selected measurement. The $P_Q(R_n)$ is calculated for each nth image included in the ground truth. Each resulting P_Q is a function of the total number of images retrieved in order to retrieve

---

[2]IRMA is courtesy of **TM Deserno**, Dept. of Medical Informatics, RWTH Aachen

L	000	001	010	011	100	101	110	111
1	5.5E-06	1.2E-03	4.5E-03	9.6E-03	1.7E-02	2.8E-02	5.1E-02	4.2E-01
2	3.6E-06	8.8E-04	3.4E-03	7.1E-03	1.2E-02	2.0E-02	3.2E-02	7.6E-02
3	3.6E-06	8.3E-04	3.2E-03	6.8E-03	1.2E-02	1.9E-02	2.9E-02	5.5E-02
4	3.6E-06	8.2E-04	3.1E-03	6.6E-03	1.1E-02	1.8E-02	2.8E-02	5.2E-02
5	5.4E-06	1.1E-03	4.4E-03	9.5E-03	1.7E-02	2.9E-02	5.4E-02	4.3E-01
6	5.0E-06	1.1E-03	4.4E-03	9.6E-03	1.8E-02	2.9E-02	5.3E-02	4.0E-01
7	5.0E-06	1.1E-03	4.2E-03	9.0E-03	1.6E-02	2.7E-02	5.2E-02	4.6E-01
8	4.5E-06	1.2E-03	4.5E-03	9.6E-03	1.7E-02	2.8E-02	5.3E-02	4.8E-01
9	5.2E-06	1.2E-03	4.2E-03	9.0E-03	1.6E-02	2.8E-02	5.2E-02	4.9E-01
10	3.5E-06	8.6E-04	3.3E-03	6.8E-03	1.2E-02	1.9E-02	2.9E-02	6.1E-02
11	3.8E-06	8.6E-04	3.2E-03	6.8E-03	1.2E-02	1.9E-02	2.9E-02	6.0E-02
12	4.0E-06	8.5E-04	3.2E-03	6.8E-03	1.2E-02	1.8E-02	2.8E-02	5.3E-02
13	5.4E-06	1.1E-03	4.3E-03	9.3E-03	1.7E-02	2.8E-02	5.1E-02	3.9E-01
14	5.2E-06	1.1E-03	4.4E-03	9.5E-03	1.7E-02	2.8E-02	5.1E-02	3.5E-01
15	5.7E-06	1.2E-03	4.3E-03	9.0E-03	1.6E-02	2.7E-02	5.1E-02	4.0E-01
16	4.7E-06	1.2E-03	4.4E-03	9.4E-03	1.7E-02	2.8E-02	5.2E-02	4.2E-01
17	4.5E-06	1.1E-03	4.2E-03	8.9E-03	1.6E-02	2.7E-02	5.2E-02	4.6E-01
18	4.4E-06	1.2E-03	4.4E-03	9.7E-03	1.7E-02	2.9E-02	5.4E-02	4.5E-01
19	4.2E-06	8.5E-04	3.2E-03	6.9E-03	1.2E-02	1.8E-02	2.8E-02	5.5E-02
20	4.0E-06	7.8E-04	3.0E-03	6.6E-03	1.2E-02	1.8E-02	2.8E-02	5.3E-02
21	5.1E-06	1.2E-03	4.5E-03	9.6E-03	1.7E-02	2.9E-02	5.3E-02	4.9E-01
22	5.0E-06	1.2E-03	4.5E-03	9.7E-03	1.7E-02	2.9E-02	5.2E-02	4.1E-01
23	3.8E-06	9.1E-04	3.4E-03	7.0E-03	1.2E-02	1.9E-02	3.1E-02	8.1E-02
24	5.9E-06	1.2E-03	4.4E-03	9.2E-03	1.6E-02	2.7E-02	4.8E-02	2.9E-01
25	4.7E-06	1.2E-03	4.5E-03	9.7E-03	1.7E-02	2.8E-02	5.2E-02	4.4E-01
26	4.7E-06	1.1E-03	4.4E-03	9.6E-03	1.7E-02	2.9E-02	5.3E-02	4.0E-01
27	3.5E-06	8.4E-04	3.3E-03	7.0E-03	1.2E-02	1.9E-02	2.9E-02	6.1E-02
28	3.4E-06	9.1E-04	3.4E-03	7.2E-03	1.2E-02	2.0E-02	3.1E-02	6.8E-02
29	6.6E-06	1.2E-03	4.6E-03	9.8E-03	1.7E-02	2.8E-02	4.7E-02	2.7E-01
30	6.4E-06	1.3E-03	4.8E-03	1.0E-02	1.8E-02	2.9E-02	5.1E-02	3.8E-01
31	3.5E-06	9.0E-04	3.4E-03	7.1E-03	1.2E-02	1.9E-02	3.1E-02	8.0E-02
32	3.2E-06	8.8E-04	3.4E-03	6.9E-03	1.2E-02	1.9E-02	3.0E-02	6.9E-02

Table 4.6: *Quantization Table for $L_{Block} = 8, L_{Texture} = 16$ and $L_{Bright} = 8$ Part 1.*

L	000	001	010	011	100	101	110	111
33	3.7E-06	1.1E-03	4.3E-03	9.4E-03	1.7E-02	2.9E-02	5.5E-02	4.7E-01
34	6.0E-06	1.2E-03	4.5E-03	9.4E-03	1.7E-02	2.8E-02	5.2E-02	4.2E-01
35	5.6E-06	1.2E-03	4.4E-03	9.3E-03	1.7E-02	2.7E-02	5.0E-02	3.6E-01
36	5.5E-06	1.2E-03	4.5E-03	9.5E-03	1.7E-02	2.8E-02	5.0E-02	3.3E-01
37	2.1E-06	1.1E-03	4.3E-03	9.1E-03	1.6E-02	2.5E-02	4.1E-02	1.1E-01
38	1.8E-06	9.6E-04	3.8E-03	8.1E-03	1.4E-02	2.2E-02	3.5E-02	8.6E-02
39	2.3E-06	9.0E-04	3.5E-03	7.5E-03	1.3E-02	2.1E-02	3.3E-02	7.4E-02
40	2.8E-06	8.5E-04	3.2E-03	6.7E-03	1.2E-02	1.8E-02	2.9E-02	6.8E-02
41	3.4E-06	1.1E-03	4.1E-03	9.0E-03	1.6E-02	2.8E-02	5.3E-02	4.8E-01
42	5.1E-06	1.2E-03	4.5E-03	9.6E-03	1.7E-02	2.9E-02	5.4E-02	5.2E-01
43	5.0E-06	1.3E-03	4.7E-03	9.8E-03	1.7E-02	2.8E-02	5.0E-02	3.4E-01
44	4.8E-06	1.2E-03	4.6E-03	9.8E-03	1.7E-02	2.8E-02	5.0E-02	3.7E-01
45	2.8E-06	1.2E-03	4.9E-03	1.1E-02	1.9E-02	3.1E-02	5.6E-02	3.3E-01
46	2.7E-06	1.2E-03	5.0E-03	1.1E-02	1.9E-02	3.2E-02	5.9E-02	3.9E-01
47	2.6E-06	8.4E-04	3.2E-03	6.8E-03	1.2E-02	1.9E-02	3.0E-02	6.2E-02
48	2.6E-06	8.4E-04	3.3E-03	6.8E-03	1.2E-02	1.8E-02	2.9E-02	6.2E-02
49	2.9E-06	1.2E-03	4.7E-03	1.0E-02	1.8E-02	2.9E-02	5.2E-02	2.3E-01
50	2.0E-06	9.3E-04	3.8E-03	8.0E-03	1.4E-02	2.2E-02	3.7E-02	9.8E-02
51	3.5E-06	9.4E-04	3.5E-03	7.2E-03	1.2E-02	2.0E-02	3.1E-02	7.6E-02
52	3.3E-06	9.5E-04	3.5E-03	7.3E-03	1.3E-02	2.0E-02	3.2E-02	7.2E-02
53	2.7E-06	1.2E-03	4.5E-03	9.6E-03	1.7E-02	2.9E-02	5.4E-02	3.2E-01
54	2.9E-06	1.2E-03	4.7E-03	1.0E-02	1.8E-02	3.0E-02	5.4E-02	3.3E-01
55	3.7E-06	1.2E-03	4.4E-03	9.3E-03	1.7E-02	2.9E-02	5.7E-02	4.4E-01
56	3.1E-06	1.1E-03	4.2E-03	9.0E-03	1.6E-02	2.8E-02	5.5E-02	3.8E-01
57	4.7E-06	1.2E-03	4.6E-03	9.8E-03	1.7E-02	2.9E-02	5.1E-02	2.9E-01
58	2.1E-06	9.8E-04	3.9E-03	8.2E-03	1.4E-02	2.2E-02	3.6E-02	8.6E-02
59	1.9E-06	8.7E-04	3.5E-03	7.4E-03	1.3E-02	2.1E-02	3.3E-02	7.4E-02
60	2.9E-06	9.9E-04	3.8E-03	7.8E-03	1.3E-02	2.1E-02	3.2E-02	6.7E-02
61	3.3E-06	1.2E-03	4.6E-03	9.8E-03	1.8E-02	3.0E-02	5.7E-02	4.1E-01
62	3.4E-06	1.2E-03	4.4E-03	9.5E-03	1.7E-02	2.9E-02	5.6E-02	4.2E-01
63	3.1E-06	1.1E-03	4.2E-03	9.1E-03	1.6E-02	2.8E-02	5.4E-02	3.7E-01
64	2.8E-06	1.1E-03	4.4E-03	9.5E-03	1.7E-02	3.0E-02	5.7E-02	4.0E-01

Table 4.7: *Quantization Table for $L_{Block} = 8, L_{Texture} = 16$ and $L_{Bright} = 8$ Part 2.*

image n. Then the $AP(q)$ is calculated. The MAP is calculated for each benchmarking image database, being the average of the $AP(q)$s of all database queries.

To compare the ratio, retrieval efficiency with descriptor size, experiments were carried out using 7 approaches, as described in Table 4.8.

Approach	L_{Blocks}	$L_{Texture}$	L_{Bright}	Scanning Method	Size in bytes
E1	1	8	8	None	24
E2	1	8	16	None	48
E3	1	16	8	None	48
E4	4	16	8	Hilbert	768
E5	4	16	8	Z-Grid	768
E6	8	16	8	Hilbert	3072
E7	8	16	8	Z-Grid	3072

Table 4.8: *The 7 approaches used in the experiments*

4.5.1   Experiments on IRMA 2007 Medical Image Database

The IRMA 2007 database consists of 12000 fully classified medical radiographs taken randomly from medical routine at the RWTH Aachen University Hospital. 10000 of these were released together with their classification as training data; another 1000 were also published with their classification as validation data to allow for tuning classifiers in a standardized manner. In addition, the database includes 1000 images which comprise the query images.

Each of the 10000 images is described with the IRMA code. The IRMA code is a method for describing medical images and includes information relating to the following:

• Technical code (T) describes the imaging modality

• Directional code (D) models body orientations

• Anatomical code (A) refers to the body region examined

• Biological code (B) describes the biological system examined.

The 1000 query images are also described by the IRMA CODE. Each query image has all the images from the set of the 10000 with the same IRMA CODE as ground truth. In total, 116 different IRMA codes occur in the database.

The IRMA 2007 database was used in the ImageCLEF 2007 image retrieval evaluation for the automatic annotation task.

First, experiments were carried out to identify which method of measuring the distance works better with the presented descriptor. Using the 3rd approach ($L_{Blocks} = 1$, $L_{Texture} = 16$, and $L_{Bright} = 8$) three similarity metric techniques were tested in 100 queries.

The distance $D(a,b)$ of two image descriptors X_a and X_b was calculated using 3 different approaches.

First, the distance was calculated using the Euclidean metric, so that the results could be compared with the implementation of the Tamura features in the LIRe Demo retrieval system [117] (which uses the Euclidean distance to compare the Tamura directionality histogram of the images).

Then, the Jensen-Shannon divergence [152] was attempted. This similarity matching method was used in order to compare the Tamura Features on [103] and [60] and computed using the following formulas:

$$\tilde{X}(i) = \frac{X_a(i) + X_b(i)}{2} \tag{4.10}$$

$$D(a,b) = \sum_i X_a(i) \log \frac{X_a(i)}{\tilde{X}(i)} + \sum_i X_b(i) \log \frac{X_b(i)}{\tilde{X}(i)} \tag{4.11}$$

Finally, the similarity between the images was calculated using the non binary Tanimoto Coefficient [93].

Table 4.9 shows th MAP results for the presented descriptor using the 3 similarity metric techniques. As the results show, the non-binary Tanimoto coefficient presented the best results.

Approach	Similarity Metric	Number Of Queries	MAP
E3	Euclidean	100	35.45
E3	Jensen-Shannon	100	34.79
E3	Tanimoto Coefficient	100	**37.14**

Table 4.9: *MAP results using several similarity metric techniques*

Therefore, by using the Tanimoto coefficient, all the approaches were tested on all the queries.

When spatial information is integrated into the presented descriptor, the similarity matching is differentiated, in order to take into account the information about the sequence with which the histograms of the Sub-Images forms the final histogram. Depending on the fractal scanning technique selected during descriptor extraction, the histograms of the Sub-Images are placed in a different order. The presented descriptor is defined as $H(i)$, and contains the information extracted from k Sub-Images ($k = L_{Blocks}^2$). This histogram can be analyzed as follows:

$$H(i) = H(h_1(j), h_2(j), h_3(j) \ldots h_k(j)) \tag{4.12}$$

$$i \in [0, k \times L_{Textute} \times L_{Brightness}], j \in [0, L_{Textute} \times L_{Brightness}]$$

109

Where $h_k(j)$ are the histograms resulting from each Sub-Image S_j. It is noted that every such histogram is the presented descriptor for $L_{Texture} = n$ and $L_{Brightness} = m$, without any spatial distribution information.

The neighborhood of each sub-image S_j is defined as the neighborhood with $r = 1$

$$S_{(j_0)}^M = (j) : |j - j_0| <= r \qquad (4.13)$$

In total, L_{Blocks} neighborhoods are defined for each $H(i)$. The distance between 2 images is defined as the sum of the distances between $S(j)$ neighborhoods according to Tanimoto Coefficient.

$$D(a,b) = \sum_{j=0}^{k=L_{Blocks}^2} D_{Tanimoto}(S_a(j), S_b(j)) \qquad (4.14)$$

Experimental results have shown that in the case of distance measurement of the BTD-H Descriptor with Spatial Distribution Information, the results are slightly better if the Tanimoto Coefficient is replaced with the Ordinal distance [163]. The reason for this is that the histogram of the presented descriptor displays a number of zero values. However, the calculation cost necessary for conversion of the histogram to a signature, and more specifically to extended signatures [163], is quite high, and slows the retrieval process down considerably.

The presented descriptor retrieval results are compared with the corresponding results of the following descriptors: Tamura Directionality Histogram, Gray value Histogram and MPEG-7: Edge Histogram (EHD) [120] [194]. Implementations of these low level features are available in [117].

Given that the presented descriptor is a combination of Tamura directionality histogram and the Gray Value Histogram, it would be useful to compare the obtained retrieval results with the results that would come from other combination processes of these characteristics.

One way of combining the retrieval results that come from different low level features is the Borda Count. Initially, the Borda count was presented as a single-winner election method in which voters rank candidates in order of preference. In the field of retrieval, it was originally suggested by [81]. The way by which the Borda count was applied in order to combine the results of Tamura directionality histogram and the Gray Value Histogram is described as follows:

Let the query Q consisting of q images. The search is performed on a database of images that includes N images. The results that come from the Tamura directionality histogram are classified according to the distance D, that each image presents from the image Q. Each image l, depending on the position shown in the results, is scored as follows:

110

$$Rank'(l) = \frac{N - RA}{N} \tag{4.15}$$

where N is the total number of the images in the database and RA is the Rank of the image l after the classification.

The same procedure is also applied on the results coming from the Gray Value Histogram. The results are classified and each image is scored with $Rank(l)''$.

Finally, for each l image the $Rank(l) = Rank(l)' + Rank(l)''$ is calculated and a final classification of the results according to the Rank of each image is being made. The evaluation process of the results through the MAP, after this classification, is the same as the evaluation process, that has been described.

Descriptor	MAP	Descriptor	MAP
BTDH Descriptor E7	**36.81**	BTDH Descriptor E3	20.4
BTDH Descriptor E6	36.78	Tamura Directionality Histo.	15.1
BTDH Descriptor E5	35.1	Borda Count	14.7
BTDH Descriptor E4	35.0	Gray Value Histogram	12.4
MPEG-7: Edge Histogram	28.1	BTDH Descriptor E1	10.3
BTDH Descriptor E2	20.9		

Table 4.10: *MAP results on IRMA 2007 Medical Image Database*

Observation of the results can easily lead to the following conclusions: The results of the compact versions of the presented descriptor are directly related to the size of the descriptor. Approaches E2 and E3 produced decidedly better results than approach E1. In addition, when comparing the results of E2 and E3 to each other, we observe that their results are similar, thus strengthening the conclusion that the system's performance is related to the number of bins of the descriptor.

It is taken for granted that the integration of information about the spatial distribution further enhances the system's performance. However, it is observed that in this case the descriptor size does not correlate with the retrieval accuracy. The size difference in approaches E4 and E5 with E6 and E7 is not reflected in the results. It could be concluded that result improvement is achieved through integration of spatial information, and it approaches maximum performance either when using a small number L_{Blocks}, or a large one.

4.5.2 Experiments on IRMA 2005 Medical Image Database

The IRMA 2005 database consists of 10000 annotated radiographs. The images are separated into 9000 training images and 1000 test images. The images are subdivided into 57 classes. For CBMIR, the relevances are defined by the classes, given a query image from a certain class, all database images from the same class are considered relevant. [41]

The IRMA 2005 database was used in the ImageCLEF 2005 image retrieval evaluation for the automatic annotation task.

Descriptor	MAP	Descriptor	MAP
BTDH Descriptor E7	**44.28**	Gray Value Histogram	26.1
BTDH Descriptor E6	44.26	Gabor histogram	25.2
BTDH Descriptor E5	42.8	inv. feature histogram (mon.)	24.4
BTDH Descriptor E4	42.7	inv. feature histogram (relational)	24.1
32x32 image	40.9	LF patches signature	23.0
Xx32 image	35.0	Borda Count	23.0
LF SIFT histogram	32.7	Tamura Directionality Histo.	21.5
LF patches histogram	31.4	LF SIFT global search	20.9
BTDH Descriptor E3	28.3	LF patches global	17.6
BTDH Descriptor E2	28.3	global texture feature	16.4
BTDH Descriptor E1	28.0	LF SIFT signature	10.9
Gabor vector	27.7	MPEG-7: Edge Histogram	10.9

Table 4.11: *MAP results on IRMA 2005 Medical Image Database*

Table 4.11 shows the MAP results in this database. The values of the remaining descriptors are taken from [41].

Observation of the experiment results strengthens the conclusions that resulted from experiments on the IRMA2007 database. The sole exception is perhaps the high performance that approach E1 produced, which is however considered unsuitable due to the inconsistency of its results. Finally, it is worth noting that use of different fractal scanning methods leads to equally good results, with the Z-Grid method displaying slightly better results. Another conclusion that arises, is related to the information described in the presented descriptor. Considering the results of both experiments and comparing them with the results that come from the Borda Count between the Tamura directionality histogram and the Gray Value Histogram, we perceive that the presented descriptor (without the E1 approach) shows much better results than the Borda Count. Hence, the combination of Tamura Directionality Histogram and the Gray Value Histogram through the presented descriptor is better than the combination made by the Borda Count. In addition, the difference between the sizes of the XML files using the 2 approaches, is notable. The size of the file, which carries the information that uses the Borda Count to describe the number of 9000 images for IRMA2005, is 8.47 MB, while for the E3 approach the file size is not exceeding 1.3 MB.

Having studied both experiments, we have reached the conclusion that the approach displaying the best correlation between size and result is approach E5.

The AP results for all the queries are available on line[3].

---
[3]http://www.ee.duth.gr/acsl/results

4.6 Conclusions and Future Works

This chapter presented a new method combining Brightness and Texture information in one scalable descriptor. Furthermore, the presented descriptor includes the spatial distribution of the information it describes. The most important feature of the presented descriptor is that its size adapts according to the storage capabilities of the application that is using it. This characteristic render the descriptor appropriate for use in large medical (or greyscale) image databases.

The experimental results showed that the presented descriptor can be used for the retrieval of medical images more successfully than other state of art low level features.

BTDH is an extension of the state of art Tamura Texture to which, in the Directionality histogram, brightness and spatial distribution information is added. The presented method can be used as part of a broader retrieval system that uses more characteristics, replacing the Tamura Texture Directionality Histogram extraction unit.

The presented descriptor's capability of achieving reliable retrieval results, even in its compact versions, allows the possibility of an additional element that can be integrated into the header of DICOM files. DICOM is an all-encompassing data transfer, storage and display protocol, built and designed to cover all functional aspects in digital imaging [141]. The combination of visual characteristics described by BTDH descriptor with the textual characteristics already included in the DICOM header could create a hybrid retrieval system with very good results. Corresponding systems that have been developed [34] [15], [45] use non compact descriptors which are extracted from the images in advance and saved in appropriate databases.

Integration of the presented descriptor into DICOM files would contribute to the development of a CAD (computer-aided diagnosis) system. Nowadays, doctors can search for similar cases based on the textual information included in DICOM files. With the presented method, they would also be able to use the visual information. For example, for a patient exhibiting an unexpected image on a chest MRI scan, the doctor would use the terms "Chest" and "MRI" as textual information and would supply the CAD with the patient's radiology images. The system will return similar cases entered in the database as well as the diagnosis/treatment followed in said cases. It should be noted that by no means does the system offer a diagnosis, but rather a reference to similar cases.

Additionally, by using BTDH, it is also possible to design a quick retrieval system for medical images. A significant factor influencing the speed of a retrieval system is the distance computational time. The presented descriptor can be used to design a multi-level database which would include different sizes of the descriptor. During the first retrieval phase, a compact version of the descriptor would be used, which may not achieve the best retrieval results, yet it would locate and reject those images least relevant to the query image and exclude them from the next phase of the process. In the next stage, a less compact version of the descriptor would be used, concluding in the final stage where the largest descriptor version would be used, but applied to a very small number of images.

Finally, an element which could improve the performance of the presented descriptor is the application of a detection technique for the minimum boundary rectangle of the images, and the extraction of features only from the pixels enclosed within it.

5

Accelerating the Retrieval Procedure

$\mathbf{A}$s the use of computers, Internet and cameras is getting more popular by the minute, efficient content-based image retrieval is more essential than ever.The requirements of the modern retrieval systems are not limited to the achievement of good retrieval results, but extend to their ability for quick results. The majority of the Internet users accept a reduction in the accuracy of the results in order to save time from searching.

Image retrieval, as well as text retrieval, may be described by the similarity search paradigm [79]. Efficient approaches that allow application on generic similarity search problems still need to be investigated [4]. A promising direction to address this issue is the *approximate* similarity search paradigm [201, 29, 2, 53]. Approximate similarity search provides an improvement in search performance at the price of some imprecision in the results. An interesting approach of approximate similarity search was proposed in [4]. The idea at the basis of this technique is that when two objects are very close to each other they 'see' the world around them in the same way.

In order to achieve image retrieval from large scale databases, the representation of images by Latent Dirichlet Allocation (LDA) [10] models for content-based image retrieval is studied in [68]. Image representations are learned in an unsupervised fashion, and each image is modeled as a mixture of its depicted topics or object parts.

This chapter[1] [2] describes a different approach for searching in large-scale databases. First of all, in order to ensure quality of the results, the Color and Edge Directivity Descriptor (CEDD) is utilized. The size of this descriptor, as mentioned in chapter 2, is 54 bytes/image. Subsequently, the Binary Haar Wavelet Transform [175] applied on the CEDD, is used for the extraction of a second descriptor. This second descriptor, which describes the CEDD content with less than 2 bytes, is employed during the retrieval procedure instead of the image. In this way, reduced retrieval times are achieved.

In order to shape B-CEDD, we follow and evaluate three different approaches. First,

---

[1]Part of the material presented in this chapter has been awarded with the"**Best Paper Award**" at the "The Fifth International Multi-Conference on Computing in the Global Information Technology (ICCGI 2010)"
[2]This Chapter is Based on:[156][24]

we consider CEDD as a single vector and apply the Binary Haar Wavelet Transform up to 15 coefficients. Second, we consider CEDD as a result of early fusion of two independent vectors, one capturing color and the other texture information. Also in this case, the resulting compact descriptor consists of 15 coefficients. In final third approach, we again consider CEDD as a result of early fusion of 6 independent vectors and apply Binary Haar Wavelet Transform to each of the vectors separately. The length of the resulting descriptor is now 18 coefficients. In Section 5.4, we will describe these three approaches in detail.

During the search process, an image query is entered and the system returns images with a similar content. Initially, the similarity/distance between the query and each image in the database is calculated with the presented descriptor, and only if the distance is smaller than a predefined threshold, the comparison of their CEDDs is performed.

5.1 Binary Haar Wavelet Transform

The Binary Haar Wavelet Transform coefficients of the histogram are calculated with the use of following Haar Wavelet Transform [175]:

$$\psi(x) = \begin{cases} 1 & 0 \leq x < 0.5 \\ -1 & 0.5 \leq x < 1 \\ 0 & else \end{cases} \tag{5.1}$$

Figure 5.1 shows the four basis functions of the Haar wavelet of length eight. The Haar wavelet coefficients are obtained by taking the inner product of the basis functions with the given histogram. This transformation is very fast as it does not involve multiplications.

The Haar coefficients capture the qualitative aspects of the histogram [99]. For example, the second coefficient (from the basis function 2 in Figure 5.1) is positive if the sum of the left half of the histogram bins is greater than the right half and negative otherwise. Similarly, the third coefficient is positive if the sum of the first quarter of the histogram bins is greater than the second quarter and negative otherwise. In the Binary Haar descriptor, each of these coefficients is quantized to '0' or '1', depending on whether its value is negative or positive, hence a binary representation is obtained.

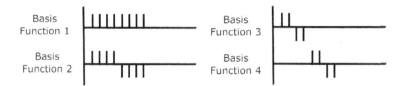

Figure 5.1: *Four basis functions of the Haar wavelet of length eight.*

At the first level, the k bins of the histogram are divided into two halves. If the sum of the histogram values in the left half is greater than the sum of the histogram values in the right half then the second bit of descriptor is '1', while is '0' otherwise. Note that the first coefficient corresponds to the sum of all probabilities in a histogram and it is always positive. Therefore is quantized to 1 and is not used in similarity matching.

At the second level, the $k/2$ bins of each half of the histogram are divided into two halves. If the sum of the histogram values in the first half is greater than the sum of the histogram values in the second half then the second bit of descriptor is '1' else it is '0'. Similar, if the sum of the third half is greater than the sum in the fourth half, then the third bit of descriptor is '1' else it is '0'. This is repeated recursively for the third and the fourth level.

5.2 Binary CEDD (B-CEDD)

In order to describe the contents of CEDD with another descriptor significantly smaller in storage needs, we followed 3 different approaches with the use the Binary Haar Wavelet Transform.

5.2.1 Approach 1: B-CEDD$_1$

The first approach considers CEDD as a 144-dimensional vector, in which we apply 4-level Binary Haar Wavelet Transform. In the first level, the 144 elements are split in two groups of 72 elements. If the sum of the coefficients of the first group is greater or equal to the corresponding sum of the second group, then the first output coefficient of the transform is 1; otherwise, it is 0.

In the second level, the 144 elements are split in groups of 36 elements, and compared in consequent pairs using the same method as in the first level. The output of the transform consists of two coefficients. The third level of the transform compares consequent pairs of 18 elements, producing another 4 output coefficients.

Finally, the fourth level compares consequent pairs of 9 elements, producing another 8 coefficients. Overall, the output vector of the transform consists of 15 coefficients. We chose to apply the transform four times in order to produce an output vector of 2 bytes. In the rest of this chapter, the result obtained from the application of the Binary Haar Transform on the CEDD descriptor will be referred as Binary CEDD with index 1 (B-CEDD$_1$).

5.2.2 Approach 2: B-CEDD$_2$

The second approach considers CEDD as the results of early fusion of two independent vectors; a vector capturing the color information of the image described by the CEDD, and a vector describing the texture information. To apply the Binary Haar Wavet Transform, we work as follows: First, we isolate the color and texture information from the descriptor in two independent vectors, the CEDD_Color vector consisting of 24 elements and the

CEDD_Texture vector consisting of 6 elements. The separation is straightforward since each information item is distinctively placed in the descriptor. The separation pseudocode is the following:

```
for (int i = 0; i LT 6; i++)
  {
    for (int j = 0; j LT 24; j++)
      {
          CEDD#Color [j] += CEDD[24 * i + j];
      }
  }

for (int i = 0; i LT 6; i++)
  {
    for (int j = 0; j LT 24; j++)
      {
          CEDD#Texture [i] += CEDD[24 * i + j];
      }
  }
```

The Binary Haar Transform is applied on the CEDD_Color vector up to the third level resulting in 7 coefficients (1 coefficient from the first transformation level, 2 coefficients from the second transformation level, and 3 from the third level).

Regarding the CEDD_Texture vector, given that the resulting 2 halves include 3 elements, the problem arising is that the transform may be applied only once. In order to overcome this constraint, whenever this is met during the transform application, we present the following solution: During the first transform level, the 6 elements are divided in 2 triads. To apply the second level, the middle element of each triad is cloned. The 2 identical elements replace the original element from which they came from. In this way, each triad is replaced by a quartet of elements, which now the transform may be applied on. In the third level of the Binary Haar Transform the cloned elements are removed and the transform is applied directly on the vector, comparing this time the elements per pair. On the whole, 8 elements are created (1 from the first transform level, 4 from the second level and 3 from the third). The complete extraction procedure of the Modified Binary Haar Wavelet Transform from CEDD_Texture is illustrated in Figure 5.2.

At the end of the procedure, the 2 resulting vectors are placed consecutively. The size of the produced descriptor is limited to 15 binary bins and its storage requirements are much smaller than 2 bytes per image (15 bits). In the rest of this chapter, this descriptor will be referred to as Binary CEDD with index 2 (B-CEDD$_2$).

5.2.3   Approach 3: B-CEDD$_3$

The third approach splits CEDD to 6 independent vectors in 24 dimensions. Each vector corresponds to one of the 6 texture areas used by the descriptor. The transform is applied twice to each of the vectors, splitting the vectors to groups of 12 and then to 6. From each vector, 3 coefficients are produced. We produce B-CEDD$_3$ by taking consequently the 18

118

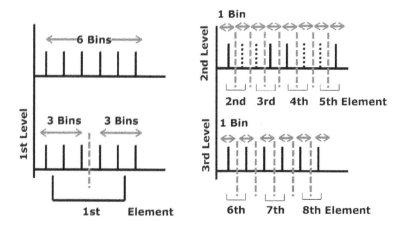

Figure 5.2: *Extraction procedure of the Modified Binary Haar Wavelet Transform from CEDD_Texture.*

output coefficients ($3 \times 6 = 18$). This approach results to the largest descriptor size and is closer to the essence of Compact Composite Descriptors where CEDD belongs to, but as we will see in Section 5.7 it does not lead to the best end-results.

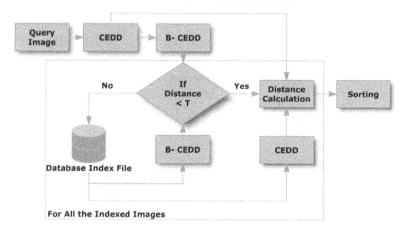

Figure 5.3: *Searching using the 2 descriptors.*

5.3 System Overview

One of the most important attributes of the Binary CEDD is that it is extracted directly from the CEDD with no intervention of the described image. This results in its immediate extraction from the already existent index files.

The search procedure based on the use of the 2 descriptors, CEDD and B-CEDD, is illustrated in Figure 5.3. The user enters a query image in the system. From this image, both the CEDD and the B-CEDD descriptors are extracted. The system uses an image database in which the indices are described by both descriptors. During data retrieval from databases, the length of the retrieved information is of great significance. For this reason, in a first phase the system retrieves only the B-CEDD descriptor, which, due to its small storage requirements as well as its small length, is retrieved practically in an instance.

For each database image, the distance between the B-CEDD descriptor with the corresponding B-CEDD descriptor of the query image is calculated by a simple X-OR gate. In the case of 2 identical descriptors, the X-OR output is equal to 0, while in the worst scenario the obtained distance is 15 (equal to the B-CEDD length). The logic gate X-OR requires much less computing resources than the Tanimoto coefficient. The Tanimoto coefficient is used to calculate the distance between CEDD descriptors.

If the distance of the 2 descriptors is found to be smaller than a threshold T, then the CEDD descriptor is retrieved from the database and its distance from the corresponding CEDD descriptor of the query image is calculated. The procedure is repeated for all the database images.

After the completion of the procedure, the classified results are shown to the user in ascending order of the distance obtained during the CEDD descriptors comparison.

The most important issue that should be taken into consideration during the aforementioned procedure is the determination of the threshold T. This threshold defines whether an image is potentially similar to the query image. If it is, then the retrieval of the image's CEDD is requested and the process for its comparison with the corresponding CEDD of the query image is activated. The T value investigation is described in detail in the following section.

5.4   Investigating the T Value

In order to determine an appropriate T value, we work as follows: We choose 35 images from the Wang database and regard them as historical queries. The historical queries idea comes from the text retrieval area and has been used to normalize retrieval scores of documents in cases of fusion and distributed information retrieval [5, 54].

For each one of the historical queries, searching is performed in the database from which they originate. In particular, the distances between the B-CEDD descriptors of each historical query and each image of the database are calculated and a ranking list, in which the database images are ordered according to their distance from the historical query, is obtained. The procedure is repeated for all the historical queries. At the end of the process, 35 ranking lists emerge. Since the Wang database includes 1000 images, 35000 values (35 ranking list $\times$ 1000 images) are finally obtained. By plotting these values the distance distribution is obtained. As depicted in Figure 5.4, which shows score distributions from the three B-CEDD approaches, the first two approaches produce similar distributions.

Subsequently, the set of these 35000 values for each approach, enters in a Gustafson Kessel fuzzy classifier. The Gustafson Kessel is an extension of the Fuzzy C-Means algorithm. The Gustafson Kessel parameters are selected as: Clusters = 4, Repetitions = 3000, $e = 0.001$ and $m = 2$.

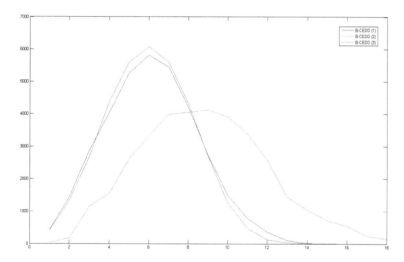

Figure 5.4: *Distribution of the B-CEDD distances for 35 historical queries.*

The four resulting classes were used to form a single input fuzzy system for each approach. The fuzzy system includes four membership functions which are labeled as: 'Low', 'Medium', 'High' and 'Highest' The centers of the classes, as they result from Gustafson Kessel classifier, correspond to the tops of the membership functions. Given that the score distribution of the B-CEDD$_1$ and B-CEDD$_2$ are similar to each other, the fuzzy systems that come from the Gustafson Kessel classifier output are identical.

The fuzzy system that was shaped operates as follows: The system gets as input the distance between the B-CEDD descriptors of the query image and any other image. The vertical axis shows the distance that may be obtained during the comparison of the 2 B-CEDD descriptors, while the horizontal axis shows the activation degree for the membership function of each class. Consider, for instance, that the distance between 2 B-CEDD descriptors was found to be equal to 4 (see Figure 5.5). This value activates both the first and the second membership function by 0.5.

For the simplest scenario of the model usage we should specify that if the 'Low' membership function is activated with a value greater than the activation value of any other membership function, then the image under study is likely to be visually similar to the query image. Thus, the CEDD descriptor should be also retrieved in order to perform the comparison.

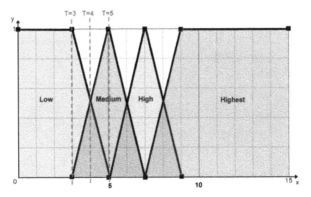

Figure 5.5: *Outcome of the historical queries distances distribution classification in 4 classes.*

Similarly, if the 'Low' activation degree is smaller than that of another membership function, the image is discarded. In the next section, the experimental results of a threshold tuning attempt are presented.

5.5 Experimental Results

To the best of our knowledge, there is no large scale image database with ground truths data available that could be used for the performance evaluation of the presented method. For this reason, experiments have been performed on two known small scale benchmarking databases.

For the performance evaluation the following measures were used:

1. Recall at n, where n is the number of the retrieved through the presented method images. This measure presents the number of relevant documents retrieved by a search divided by the total number of existing relevant documents.

2. ANMRR at n. The ANMRR ranges from 0 to 1. The smaller the value of this measure is, the better the retrieval quality.

This method is implemented in the retrieval system img(Rummager). For better time measurements, each experiment was repeated 10 times. All the experiments were performed on an Intel Core 2 Quad Q9550 @2.83GHz PC with 3GB of RAM.

As elaborated in the previous section, the necessity for accurate estimation of the T threshold value which defines whether the CEDD descriptor of an image should be retrieved, is imperative. In order to determine the appropriate threshold, we experiment with the following scenarios: Initially, for each of the approaches of B-CEDD, we consider that the two images may be potentially similar (and calculate the distance between the two CEDD descriptors) if the distance of their B-CEDD descriptors activates the membership function 'Low' with value equal to 1. This threshold is defined as $T1$.

According to the second scenario, two images may be potentially similar if the distance of their B-CEDD descriptors activates the membership function 'Low' with value greater than 0.5. This threshold is defined as $T2$. At the end, according to the third scenario, two images may be potentially similar if the distance of their B-CEDD descriptors activates the membership function 'Low' with value greater than 0. This threshold is defined as $T3$.

The values of T for all the approaches are given in Table 5.1, while in the case of B-CEDD$_1$ and B-CEDD$_2$ the threshold values are depicted in Figure 5.6 with a dashed line.

	$T1$	$T2$	$T3$
B-CEDD$_1$ Thresholds	3	4	5
B-CEDD$_2$ Thresholds	3	4	5
B-CEDD$_3$ Thresholds	5	7	8

Table 5.1: *Threshold Values*

Initially, our experiments were performed using Wang database. For each query, the time of the retrieval through the presented system is measured, as well as the time required when only the CEDD descriptor is used. Table 5.2 illustrates the mean results for the 20 queries of the Wang database for all the approaches and all the T values. The Recall index represents the ratio of the correct image retrievals for each query (images that belong to the ground truth of the query) to the size of the ground truth. Therefore, the Recall @ n describes the percentage of the correct images that were retrieved for all the queries. On the other hand, the ANMRR index evaluates the order in which the results were placed after the completion of the procedure. Thus, in order to assess the systems effectiveness properly both measures should be taken into account.

Considering these results, it can be readily observed that the presented method improves the searching procedure times significantly. For $T1$, all approaches are capable of retrieving almost 112,000 images per second. But in all three approaches both Recall @ n and ANMRR have a very small value. This means that a lot of images from the ground truth were absorbed during the retrieval procedure. By comparing the three approaches, B-CEDD$_1$ seems to perform better.

The threshold $T2$, which retrieves almost 83,333 images per second and its performance is found satisfactory for both the Recall @ n and the ANMRR, could be considered as the 'golden-mean' solution. Compared to the CEDD method, the presented method with $T2$ retrieves almost four times more images per second. Also in this case, B-CEDD$_1$ seems to advance, although it requires slightly more time than the B-CEDD$_2$

CEDD Time	45.2ms		
	$T1$	$T2$	$T3$
B-CEDD$_1$ Time	10.0ms	13.1ms	19.0ms
B-CEDD$_2$ Time	9.1ms	12.2ms	19.0ms
B-CEDD$_3$ Time	9.1ms	13.7ms	19.1ms
B-CEDD$_1$ Retrieved Im.	242.95	404.35	562.20
B-CEDD$_2$ Retrieved Im.	218.40	381.45	563.15
B-CEDD$_3$ Retrieved Im.	212.20	445.75	599.65
B-CEDD$_1$ Recall @ n	**0.6476**	**0.8188**	**0.9234**
B-CEDD$_2$ Recall @ n	0.5441	0.7074	0.8675
B-CEDD$_3$ Recall @ n	0.4971	0.7715	0.8704
CEDD ANMRR	0.2528		
B-CEDD$_1$ ANMRR	**0.4011**	**0.3100**	**0.2636**
B-CEDD$_2$ ANMRR	0.4836	0.3747	0.2902
B-CEDD$_3$ ANMRR	0.5322	0.3397	0.2824

Table 5.2: *Experiments on the WANG database*

(8.33% more time / 1 ms), it improves the Recall @ n by 16.6% compared to the performance of B-CEDD$_2$. Better performance is observed also in ANMRR where B-CEDD$_1$, having the value of 0.31, is better than B-CEDD$_3$ by 8.74%.

With $T3$, good results were achieved from all the approaches for both the Recall @ n and the ANMRR but the searching time was over doubled in comparison to the corresponding time for $T1$. Also in this case B-CEDD$_1$ performs better than the other two approaches, with its value of Recall @ $n = 0.9234$ approaching the CEDD performance, consider that the value of ANMRR is smaller by 4% from the corresponding value that the CEDD descriptor presents.

In the sequel, experiments were performed using the UCID Database. The results for all the three B-CEDD extraction approaches, for all the T values are illustrated in Table 5.3.

In this database we observe that even the smallest values of T retrieve more images compared to the images that were retrieved for the corresponding values of T on Wang database. We also observe that even for very small T, as for $T1$, there are good results for Recall @ n from all the three approaches that we used. Also in this case, B-CEDD$_1$ performs way better than the other two approaches, showing improvement from the B-CEDD$_3$ by 6.83%, while the improvement from B-CEDD$_2$ equals to 11.64%. B-CEDD $_1$ ANMRR value is by 5.24% smaller than the corresponding value of the CEDD descriptor, but the system retrieves twice as many images in the same time.

For $T2$, B-CEDD$_1$ performance is approaching the performance of CEDD. With Recall @ n value at 0.9457, ANMRR presents deviation from the corresponding CEDD value by just 0.35%. Significant improvements also presented by the other two approach-

CEDD Time	60.3ms		
	T1	*T2*	*T3*
B-CEDD$_1$ Time	22.7ms	25.2ms	34.0ms
B-CEDD$_2$ Time	19.5ms	25.9ms	33.3ms
B-CEDD$_3$ Time	16.0ms	18ms	27.4ms
B-CEDD$_1$ Retrieved Im.	550.13	785.68	1007.61
B-CEDD$_2$ Retrieved Im.	472.08	825.04	987.37
B-CEDD$_3$ Retrieved Im.	379.14	618.90	866.44
B-CEDD$_1$ Recall @ *n*	**0.8920**	**0.9457**	**0.9734**
B-CEDD$_2$ Recall @ *n*	0.7990	0.8926	0.9478
B-CEDD$_3$ Recall @ *n*	0.8349	0.9424	0.9653
CEDD ANMRR	0.2823		
B-CEDD$_1$ ANMRR	**0.2971**	**0.2833**	**0.2823**
B-CEDD$_2$ ANMRR	0.3258	0.2905	0.2831
B-CEDD$_3$ ANMRR	0.3140	0.2874	0.2848

Table 5.3: *Experiments on the UCID database*

es.

Finally, for $T3$, the performance of B-CEDD$_1$ is identical to the CEDD performance. At the same time, the other two methods also improve their performance, with B-CEDD$_2$ to behave slightly better than B-CEDD$_3$.

Observing the results in the two databases, is obvious that the B-CEDD$_1$ approach performs better than the other two approaches. Considering the threshold value, is obvious that by $T2$, a satisfactory trade-off between the acceleration rate of the retrieval procedure and the performance rate of the system is ensured. But how important is the reduction in the results? In order to quantize the reduction that is observed, we use a significance test. Significance tests tell us whether an observed effect, such as a difference between two means or a correlation between two variables, could reasonably occur 'just by chance' in selecting a random sample [127]. We used a bootstrap test, one-tailed, at significance levels 0.05(*), 0.01 (**), and 0.001 (***), against the CEDD results baseline in UCID database . The significance test was applied on Mean Average Precision (MAP).

CEDD MAP	0.6748		
	T1	*T2*	*T3*
B-CEDD$_1$ MAP	**0.6598****	**0.6720-**	**0.6748-**
B-CEDD$_2$ MAP	0.6324***	0.6639**	0.6730-
B-CEDD$_3$ MAP	0.6747***	0.6685**	0.6720-

Table 5.4: *Significance Test Results*

Observing the results of Table 5.4, we conclude that all three approaches for $T3$ have non-significant reductions in their results. On the other hand, for $T2$ B-CEDD$_1$ is the only approach which has a non-significant reduction. The significance test results support the conclusion that the best method is B-CEDD$_1$ for $T2$.

5.6 Conclusions

We presented an extension of the Color and Edge Directivity Descriptor which improves the speed efficiency of the CEDD. Through the application of the Modified Binary Haar Wavelet Transform on the CEDD, the presented method achieves the extraction of a second, smaller (15 bits length), descriptor. Essentially, each CEDD descriptor is described by another compact binary descriptor. During the image searching process, the compact versions of the descriptors are employed, and only when their distance is smaller than a given threshold the searching continues with the CEDD. The distance between the B-CEDD descriptors is calculated by using a simple X-OR gate. The logic gate X-OR has much less computational cost than the Tanimoto coefficient. One of the most important attributes of the Binary CEDD (B-CEDD) is that it is extracted directly from the CEDD, without the need of the described image. This enables its immediate extraction from pre-existing index files. The effectiveness of the presented method was demonstrated through experiments. Finally, it is worth noting that the presented method can be applied to all Compact Composite Descriptors.

6
Selection of the Most Appropriate Descriptor

Observing the results in various queries, it is easy to ascertain that in some of the queries, better retrieval results are achieved by using CEDD, and in others by using FCTH. Could these 2 descriptors be combined to improve the retrieval results? This chapter[1] e-laborates in this issue presenting alternative schemes for combining the 2 descriptors.

6.1 Joint Composite Descriptor

Based on the fact that the color information given by the 2 descriptors comes from the same fuzzy system, we can assume that joining the descriptors will rely on the combination of similar texture areas carried by each descriptor. Therefore, uniting CEDD and FCTH will lead to a new descriptor that will be made up of a combination of CEDD and FCTH texture areas.

The combined descriptor is called Joint Composite Descriptor (JCD). It is made up of 7 texture areas, with each area made up of 24 sub-regions that correspond to color areas. The texture areas are as follows: JCD(0) Linear Area, JCD(1) Horizontal Activation, JCD(2) 45 Degrees Activation, JCD(3) Vertical Activation, JCD(4) 135 Degrees Activation, JCD(5) Horizontal and Vertical Activation and JCD(6) Non Directional Activation.

In order to make the combination process of CEDD and FCTH clear, we model the problem as follows: Let CEDD and FCTH be available for one image (j). The indicator $m \in [0, 23]$ symbolizes the bin of the color of each descriptor while $n \in [0, 5]$ and $n' \in [0, 7]$ determine the texture area for the CEDD and FCTH respectively. Each descriptor can be described in the following way: $\text{CEDD}(j)_n^m, \text{FCTH}(j)_{n'}^m$.

For example, the symbol $\text{CEDD}(j)_2^5$ corresponds to the $\text{bin}(2 \times 24 + 5 = 53)$ of the CEDD descriptor of image (j). The formulas producing the elements of the Joint Composite Descriptor are given in the following equations:

$$\text{JCD}(j)_0^i = \frac{\text{FCTH}(j)_0^i + \text{FCTH}(j)_4^i + \text{CEDD}(j)_0^i}{2} \tag{6.1}$$

---
[1] This Chapter is Based on: [23], [22], [157]

$$JCD(j)_1^i = \frac{FCTH(j)_1^i + FCTH(j)_5^i + CEDD(j)_2^i}{2} \tag{6.2}$$

$$JCD(j)_2^i = CEDD(j)_4^i \tag{6.3}$$

$$JCD(j)_3^i = \frac{FCTH(j)_2^i + FCTH(j)_6^i + CEDD(j)_3^i}{2} \tag{6.4}$$

$$JCD(j)_4^i = CEDD(j)_5^i \tag{6.5}$$

$$JCD(j)_5^i = FCTH(j)_3^i + FCTH(j)_7^i \tag{6.6}$$

$$JCD(j)_6^i = CEDD(j)_1^i \tag{6.7}$$

with $i \in [0,23]$. The above formulas were produced in order to combine the similar texture areas of each descriptor.

In order to measure the similarity of the images on the basis of JCD the Tanimoto coefficient is used, just as in the CEDD and FCTH.

6.2 Auto Descriptor Selection (ADS)

With the two descriptors (CEDD and FCTH) available, it is possible to design a system that will decide on the best descriptor for each image entered into the system. In other words for each indexed image the most appropriate descriptor can be found based on the descriptor values without knowledge of the whole image database. The term *appropriate descriptor* designates the descriptor that carries the largest amount of information to describe the image from which it is extracted. Similar techniques were applied to select the most appropriate MPEG-7 descriptor [50] [173], by extracting information from all the images of a dataset. The aim of these techniques was to select the best descriptor in each dataset and not for each query.

As the amount of information is assessed on a per image basis we can select a descriptor for each image. In retrieval scenarios however a combination of different feature spaces within a single query is often not possible. Therefore we approached the problem with two different strategies:

- The searching descriptor is chosen based on the query image. In this case the most appropriate descriptor for the query image is used for all similarity assessments throughout a single query.

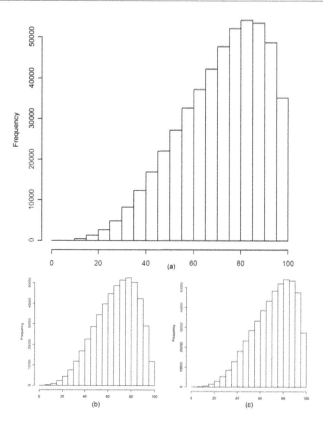

Figure 6.1: *Distribution of (a) CEDD, (b) FCTH and (c) JCD similarities / Wang 1000 image database.*

- The most appropriate descriptor is chosen at similarity assessment time, so within a single query the chosen descriptor can be different for different image pairs.

To allow meaningful combination of different features within one query however, similarities in the feature spaces have to be distributed in a similar fashion.

Experiments on the Wang [189] data set have shown that with normalized similarities (mean of 0 and standard derivation of 1) distributions are similar enough to be combined (see Figure 6.1 and Table 6.1 for the results of the Kolomogorov Smirnov Test). Note that in our experiments the second strategy performs better.

Given that the color information in all two descriptors (CEDD and FCTH) is the same, the factor that will determine the suitability and capability of each descriptor is mainly found in the texture information.

The system that determines the most appropriate descriptor is a Mamdani [204] fuzzy system of three inputs and one fuzzy output. The centroid method was used to defuzzify

	CEDD	FCTH	JCD
CEDD	-	0.0246	0.0056
FCTH		-	0.0195
JCD			-

Table 6.1: *Results of the Kolomogorov Smirnov test of pair wise similarities normalized to a mean of 0 and a standard derivation of 1 of the different descriptors within the Wang data set, p-value < 0.01 for all tests.*

the output of the Mamdani model.

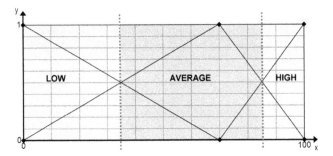

Figure 6.2: *The fuzzy output of the presented system.*

The values of 3 criteria, adopted to decide the suitability of the descriptors, are used as inputs to the system. These criteria are as follows:

- **Criterion 1:** Maximum amount of information. Due to the fuzzy form of the systems used to extract the CCDs, the image blocks (the 1600 sections of the images used to extract the descriptor) can be classified in more than one area, either color or texture. Based on this factor, together with the fact that each histogram (descriptor graph) is quantized with a different quantization table, histograms are created with different quantities of information. For example, let the CCD values of the normalized bin $n = 4$ and $m = 0$ of one image (j) be equal to the value 0.0391.

$$CEDD(j)_0^4 = FCTH(j)_0^4 = 0.0391$$

After the quantization process, these values do not remain equal:

$$CEDD(j)_0^4 = 3, FCTH(j)_0^4 = 7$$

The first Criterion shows which CCD contains the largest quantity of information. Its extraction process is as follows: For one image (j) the total information $S(j)$ contained within the two descriptors is first calculated:

$$S(j) = \sum_{m=0}^{24} \left(\sum_{n=0}^{7} FCTH(j)_n^m + \sum_{n=0}^{5} CEDD(j)_n^m \right) \tag{6.8}$$

Then, the normalized percentage of information carried by each descriptor is calculated:

$$C_1^{CEDD} = \frac{\sum_{m=0}^{24} \sum_{n=0}^{5} CEDD(j)_n^m}{S(j)} \tag{6.9}$$

$$C_1^{FCTH} = \frac{\sum_{m=0}^{24} \sum_{n=0}^{7} FCTH(j)_n^m}{S(j)} \tag{6.10}$$

The values C_1 of the two descriptors constitute input values in the first input of the fuzzy system.

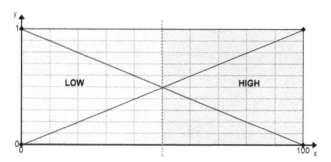

Figure 6.3: *The fuzzy input for the first Criterion.*

- **Criterion 2:** Percentage of information in non-uniform texture areas. Each of the two CCDs contains at least one area in which image blocks that don't present uniform texture areas are classified. The second Criterion considers that the most appropriate descriptor is the one that contains the smallest percentage of non uniform image blocks.

$$C_2^{CEDD} = \frac{\sum_{m=1}^{24} CEDD(j)_n^m}{S(j)} \tag{6.11}$$

$$C_2^{FCTH} = \frac{\sum_{m=0}^{24} FCTH(j)_1^m + \sum_{m=0}^{24} FCTH(j)_7^m}{S(j)} \tag{6.12}$$

- **Criterion 3:** The percentage of information in texture areas.

The third Criterion considers the most appropriate descriptor to be the one that has the smallest percentage of image blocks present in linear areas. Given that the CCD are intended to be used for natural images, which usually include a large number

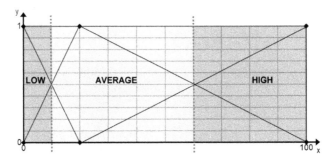

Figure 6.4: *The fuzzy input for the second Criterion.*

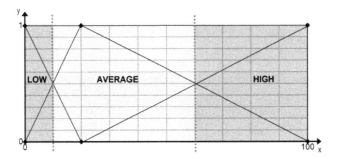

Figure 6.5: *The fuzzy input for the third Criterion.*

of different complex texture types, the classification of a large percentage of image blocks in linear areas signifies an inability to approach the image content.

For an image j, the total information $G(j)$ found in each descriptor is initially calculated.

$$G(j)^{CEDD} = \sum_{m=0}^{24} \sum_{n=0}^{5} CEDD(j)_n^m \qquad (6.13)$$

$$G(j)^{FCTH} = \sum_{m=0}^{24} \sum_{n=0}^{7} FCTH(j)_n^m \qquad (6.14)$$

Then, the normalized percentage of information carried by each descriptor in linear areas is calculated.

$$C_3^{CEDD} = \frac{\sum_{m=0}^{24} \sum_{n=1}^{5} CEDD(j)_n^m}{G(j)^{CEDD}} \qquad (6.15)$$

$$C_3^{FCTH} = \frac{\sum_{m=0}^{24} \sum_{n=1}^{3} FCTH(j)_n^m + \sum_{m=0}^{24} \sum_{n=5}^{7} FCTH(j)_n^m}{G(j)^{FCTH}} \qquad (6.16)$$

The values C_3 of the two descriptors constitute input values in the third entry of the fuzzy system.

By using 18 rules (See Appendix D) the fuzzy system evaluates each descriptor. The descriptor with the highest value is considered to be the most appropriate for the query image.

6.3 Experiments

Experiments were carried out on 3 benchmarking image databases. Initially, experiments were carried out in Wang's database of 1000 images [189]. In particular, queries and ground truths presented by the MIRROR [195] image retrieval system are used. MIRROR separates the WANG database into 20 queries. Experiments were also carried out in the UCID image database [161]. This database currently consists of 1338 uncompressed TIFF images. All the UCID images were subjected to manual relevance assessments against 262 selected images, creating 262 ground truth image sets for performance evaluation. Finally, experiments were also carried out using the Nister [136] image database.

The objective Averaged Normalized Modified Retrieval Rank (ANMRR) is employed to evaluate the performance of the image retrieval system that uses the presented method in the retrieval procedure.

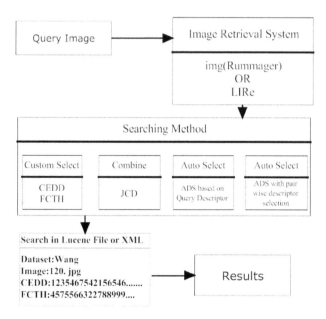

Figure 6.6: *Experimental process.*

133

The way in which the experiments were carried out is illustrated in Figure 6.6. The query image is entered into the image retrieval system img(Rummager). The user selects one of four retrieval methods (Custom Select Descriptor, JCD, Auto Descriptor Selection based on Query Descriptor and ADS with pair wise descriptor selection) and the system carries out the search in the database's index file.

In case of ADS based on query image descriptor, CEDD and FCTH descriptors from the query image are calculated. The two vectors are imported in the ADS (Auto Descriptor Selection) unit. This unit selects the descriptor which describes better the image. This descriptor is then used for all similarity assessments throughout a single query. In case of ADS with pair wise descriptor selection, the retrieval procedure is illustrated in Figure 6.7 and is described as follows:

CEDD and FCTH descriptors are calculated from the query image and the proper descriptor is selected. The two CCDs, from each indexed image are also imported in the ADS unit. In the sequel, a unit compares the descriptors that were selected for each image (query and indexed image). If the query image proper descriptor is the same with the indexed image proper descriptor then, this descriptor is used in order to compare the two images. If the query image proper descriptor is not the same with the indexed image proper descriptor then Joint Composite Descriptor is used for comparing the images. In order to use multiple different descriptors within one query, the ADS unit needs also to normalize the similarities based on their distribution. Based on experiments we used the normalization values given in Table 6.2 (under the assumption that the Tanimoto Coefficient is normalized). The process is repeated for each pair of images (query image and indexed image).

	CEDD	FCTH	JCD
Ranking	$\frac{d_{CEDD}-0.71646}{0.18035}$	$\frac{d_{FCTH}-0.66659}{0.17942}$	$\frac{d_{JCD}-0.70775}{0.18014}$

Table 6.2: *Normalization of the distribution to a common mean of 0 and a common standard derivation of 1, whereas d_x is the normalized Tanimoto coefficient of the x-th descriptor.*

	WANG	UCID	NISTER
CEDD	0.25283	0.28234	0.11297
FCTH	0.27369	0.28737	0.09463
JCD	0.25606	0.26832	0.085486
ADS Based on Query descriptor	0.24948	0.27952	0.09291
ADS Based on Pair wise descriptor	0.24876	0.27722	0.09291

Table 6.3: *Early Fusion Results*

As shown in Table 6.3, the JCD succeeds in approaching an average between the

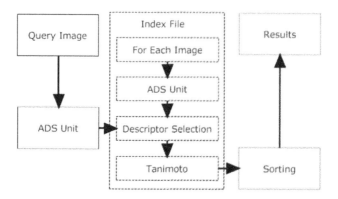

Figure 6.7: *ADS with pair wise descriptor selection retrieval procedure.*

ANMRR of CEDD and FCTH in the Wang database, whereas in the remaining databases it presents better results than the other two CCD. The auto descriptor selector (ADS) methods demonstrated better results than CEDD and FCTH in all of the databases it was tested on.

6.4 Conclusions

This chapter presented an extension of Compact Composite Descriptors CEDD and FCTH. It presents a technique combining CEDD and FCTH into a new descriptor, the Joint Composite Descriptor (JCD), and a system for the automatic selection of the most appropriate descriptor, to achieve the best results in the retrieval process. JCD and ADS methods are not suggested to improve the retrieval procedure. The goal is to approach the best ANMRR that would result from CEDD and FCTH. Nevertheless, the new JCD shows an increase in retrieval performance for all experiments compared to FCTH and for 2 out of 3 experiments for CEDD. The methods for automatic selection of the most appropriate descriptor (ASD) for retrieval increases the retrieval performance in all 3 experiments. Note that ASD decides solely on image basis without knowledge on the data set as a whole, so the overhead compared to the use of a single descriptor is reasonably small. Furthermore the auto selection for indexed images can take place at index time (for the ADS Based on Query descriptor). Even though in certain results, JCD appears to have better retrieval score, the use of ADS methods is more robust, since they accomplished the improvement of the ANMRR in all the databases it was tested on.

7

Late Fusion and Distributed Image Retrieval

The quality of the Compact Composite Descriptors has so far been evaluated through retrieval from homogeneous benchmarking databases, containing images of only the type that each CCD is intended for. For example, the JCD is tested on Wang, UCID and NISTER databases which contain natural color images, the BTDH on the IRMA database consisting of grayscale medical radiology images, and the SpCD on two benchmarking databases with artificially generated images.In this chapter[1], we evaluate the retrieval effectiveness of late fusion techniques which enable the combined use of the JCD, BTDH, and SpCD, on heterogeneous databases as well as in distributed image retrieval systems.

7.1   CCDs Late Fusion

We created a heterogeneous database with 20230 images by joining the following: 9000 grayscale images from the IRMA 2005 database; 10200 natural color images from the NISTER database and 1030 artificially generated images from the Flags database [21]. We used 40 queries: The first 20 natural color image queries from the NISTER database and the first 20 grayscale queries of the IRMA 2005 database.

Fusion methods consist of a score normalization and a score combination component. We mainly focus on the normalization, using each time the combination method more natural to the normalization at hand, although we investigated other possibilities in initial experiments not reported here. Six fusion methods were tested:

- **CombSUM**: This is a classic method for integrating results from different ranking lists. The sum of the deviation presented in each ranking list is defined as the deviation of each image. Finally, the images are ranked on the basis of this sum. In general, this method is described as the addition of all scores per image, without normalization.

- **Borda Count + CombSUM**: The Borda Count originates from social theory in voting. The image with the highest rank on each ranked list gets n votes, where n

---
[1]This Chapter is Based on: [23][22]

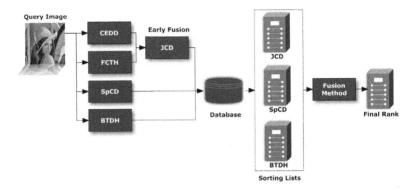

Figure 7.1: *Late Fusion Implementation Process.*

is the collection size. Each subsequent rank gets one vote fewer than the previous. Votes across ranked-lists are naturally combined with CombSUM.

Let the query be A. The search is performed on a database according to the JCD. The results are sorted according to the distance D, which each image presents from the query A. Each image l, depending on the position shown in the results, is scored as follows:

$$Rank'(l) = N - R(l) \qquad (7.1)$$

where N is the total number of the images in the database and $R(l)$ is the Rank of the image l after classification.

The same procedure is followed for the BTDH and the SpCD descriptors. The results are classified and each image is scored with $Rank(l)''$ and $Rank(l)''$ respectively. Finally, for each l image the $Rank(l) = Rank(l)' + Rank(l)'' + Rank(l)'''$ is calculated and a final classification of the results according to the $Rank$ of each image is made.

- **IRP**: The Inverse Rank Position merges ranked lists in the decreasing order of the inverse of the sum of inverses of individual ranks.

The operating principle of the method is as follows: A search is performed using each of the 3 descriptors. The IRP Rank of each image is determined as:

$$IRP(l) = \frac{1}{\sum\limits_{D=0}^{2} \frac{1}{Rank_D(l)}} \qquad (7.2)$$

Where $Rank_D(l)$ is the position where the image was found when the search was performed with descriptor d, $d \in \{0,2\}$. At the end of the process the images are ranked on the basis of their IRP distance.

138

- **Z-SCORE**: A standard method for score normalization that takes the SD (score distribution) into account is the Z-SCORE. Scores are normalized, per topic and engine, to the number of standard deviations by which they are higher (or lower) than the mean score:

  Assume that for query A there were 3 ranking lists, one for each descriptor. For each image l, its Z-Score is calculated for each of the ranking lists according to the function:

  $$s'(l) = \frac{s(l) - \mu}{\delta} \qquad (7.3)$$

  Where $s(l)$ is the distance that image l presents when query image A is applied, μ the average value of the distances, and δ the typical deviation.

  When the process is completed, the $s'(l)$ values of each image for each ranking list are summed and the final ranking is done on the basis of these values.

  The mean and standard deviation depend on the length of the ranking. Z-SCORE seems to assume a normal distribution of scores, where the mean would be a meaningful "neutral" score. As it is well-known, actual SDs are highly skewed and clearly violate the assumption underlying the Z-SCORE. Although not very popular in information retrieval, Z-SCORE was used with reasonable success in [88]. In the field of image retrieval, it was used by [55].

- **Z-SCORE with Median**: In order to compensate for any skews in the score distributions of the descriptors we replaced the mean value with the median.

- **Aggregate Historical CDF (HIS)**: HIS is a non-linear normalization which maps each score to the probability of a historical query scoring a collection image below that score. This enables normalization of scores to probabilities - albeit not of relevance - comparable across different engines. Per engine, the presented normalization is:

  $$s'(l) = F^{-1}(P(S \leq s(l))) \qquad (7.4)$$

  Where $P(S \leq s(l))$ is the cumulative density function (CDF) of the probability distribution of all scores aggregated by submitting a number of queries to the engine, and F is the CDF of the score distribution of an ideal scoring function that matches the ranking by actual relevance. The F^{-1} transformation is called *standardization step*, it is common across all engines participating in a fusion or distributed setup, and is considered critical to the method for compensating for potential individual system biases.

  Further study of this method in [5] demonstrated that this is a very promising method, albeit unnecessarily complicated.

The same study presented the Aggregate Historical CDF Simplified according to which:

$$HIS : s'(l) - P(S_{HIS} \leq s(l)) \qquad (7.5)$$

where HIS refers to the fact that historical queries are used for aggregating the SD that the random variable SHIS follows. HIS normalizes input scores $s(l)$ to the probability of a historical query scoring at or below $s(l)$. The aggregate historical SD is a distance histogram produced by applying sufficient number of queries. This set of queries forms the so called 'average' query. In this respect, HIS normalizes the SD of the 'average' query to uniform in $[0, 1]$. This is equivalent to the Cormack model [64], assuming such an 'average' query is reasonable and exists. It should be noted that this approach is used for the first time in image retrieval.

As historical queries we used 50 images drawn randomly from the database. Since HIS returns probabilities, the natural combination would be multiplication; addition gave inferior results in initial experiments.

We evaluated with two measures: the Average Normalized Modified Retrieval Rank (ANMRR), and the Mean Average Precision (MAP). Since the goal of fusion is to achieve better results than those achieved by any of the CCDs in isolation, we used the performance of SpCD as a baseline, as shown in Table 7.1.

All fusion methods beat the baseline. Best effectiveness overall is achieved by Z-score which beats the baselines of the individual CCDs by wide margins. Both versions (with the mean or median) perform similarly. While HIS performs better than IRP and close to BC, it lags behind Z-score and the bare CombSUM. We tried using more than 50 historical queries (up to 1000) in order to deduce smoother normalization functions, but the effectiveness of HIS did not improve. This is in line with [5], where 50 queries were deemed sufficient to achieve a performance plateau.

The performance of the bare CombSUM is remarkable. Although it is considered a naive method [6], it is found to be effective and robust. On further investigation it transpired that the reason for this is the similarity of the SDs, in both shape and range, across the CCDs (Fig. 7.2).

7.2 Distributed Image Retrieval

With the growing popularity of digital databases, the focus of research in the area of CBIR has shifted toward content query from distributed databases. A peer-clustering model for the query is presented in [134], with the assumption that the image collection at each peer node falls under one category. In [102], a novel approach is introduced studying practical scenarios where multiple image categories exist in each individual database in

Descriptor / Fused	40 Queries	
	ANMRR	MAP
JCD	0.3554	0.5899
BTDH	0.4015	0.5555
SpCD	**0.3081**	**0.6311**
CombSUM	0.2491	0.7121
BC + CombSUM	0.2678	0.6848
Z-score with Mean + CombSUM	**0.2400**	**0.7194**
Z-score with Median + CombSUM	0.2420	0.7193
IRP	0.2729	0.6674
HIS + multiplication	0.2664	0.6846

Table 7.1: *Late Fusion Results*

a distributed storage network. In [80], the behavior of a CBIR engine in an interactive distributed environment is examined. In the latter approach, the query image is sent to all registered databases in the network.

The response of each database is then collected and transferred to a local server where a supervised relevance identification approach is applied to identify the final outcome of the search. The issue of fusing results returned by different image repositories is also examined in [9].

In this section, we assume databases with disjointed content, and simply merge results by first normalizing the scores assigned to retrieved images by the individual libraries. The libraries in the current setup are described by a variety of single compact composite descriptors. The query is forwarded to all libraries, without any resource selection. Each library extracts from the query its own descriptor and executes the search. In [5] is postulated that effective normalization methods should be non-linear taking into account the shape of score distributions (SDs) especially for non-text descriptors where a wider variety of SDs is assumed. In this respect, we adapt and employ two non-linear methods. We compare against linear functions, as well as the simple ranked-based merging with round-robin.

In the previous section, in fusing result-lists obtained for individual CCDs from a heterogeneous database, we found that simple score normalization and combination methods, such as combining by adding bare or linearly normalized scores with Z-score, work best. This was due to the similarity of the SDs, in both shape and range, across the CCDs, resulting in compatible scores. This implies that merging without normalization may be a good baseline.

In order to overcome the baseline, we initially attempted the classic round-robin method. Round-robin merges results by simply sorting ranks produced by individual descriptors, ignoring scores.

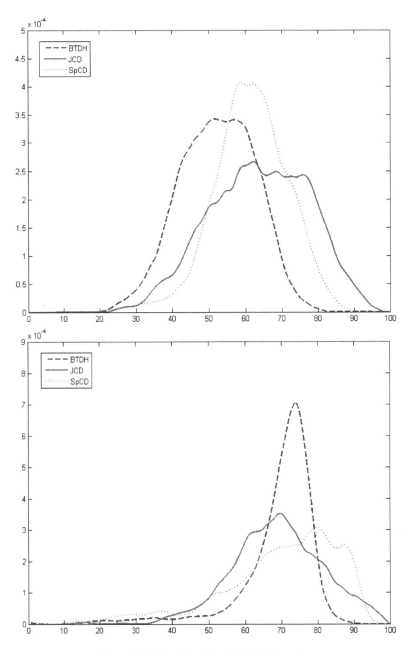

Figure 7.2: *SDs of the three CCDs for 2 queries.*

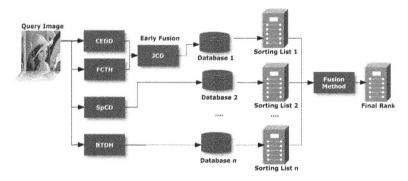

Figure 7.3: *Distributed Image Retrieval Implementation Process.*

We also tried the MinMax method. MinMax normalization maps the resulting score range linearly to the $[0,1]$ interval. Its two obvious drawbacks are: outlier scores have a large impact, and it creates a round-robin effect at the merged ranking due to the top normalized score in all engines being 1.

We then attempted to merge the results with the Z-SCORE and Z-SCORE with Median methods.

For non-linear normalization we attempted the HIS method. Having no historical queries available, we used 50 images drawn randomly from the union of databases (HIS-rfu). We also tried the alternative method of using 50 random images drawn for each database from its content (HIS-rfe).

We created a distributed image retrieval testbed consisting of 6 databases with disjointed content of the same type: 9000 grayscale images from the IRMA 2005 database indexed with the BTDH are randomly partitioned to 2 libraries; 10200 natural color images from the Nister indexed with the JCD partitioned to 2 libraries; 1030 artificially generated images from the Flags database [199] indexed with the SpCD partitioned to 2 libraries. We used 40 queries: the first 20 natural color image queries from the NISTER database and the first 20 grayscale queries of the IRMA 2005 database.

We evaluated using four measures: the Average Normalized Modified Retrieval Rank (ANMRR), the Mean Average Precision (MAP), and the Precision at 1 and 5.

Table 7.2 summarizes the merging results. The effectiveness of round-robin depends on the order of the engines. To deal with this arbitrariness, we repeated the experiment 6 times with random engine orderings, and presented the average effectiveness; round-robin is clearly the worst method.

We removed the engine ordering arbitrariness similarly for the top result per engine also for MinMax, which performs slightly better than round-robin. Z-score is the best performer of both linear methods and much better than round-robin.

There is a clear advantage of the non-linear HIS methods over the linear ones, although they lag slightly behind in the bare score merging. Using compatible descriptors from the

Normal. Method	40 Queries			
	ANMRR	MAP	P@1	P@5
No-Normaliz.	**0.3812**	**0.5520**	**0.6750**	0.5150
Round Robin	0.6464	0.2126	0.1750	0.2350
MinMax	0.6450	0.2794	0.1750	0.2800
Z-Score Mean	0.4200	0.4408	0.3500	0.2800
Z-Score Median	0.4230	0.4382	0.3500	0.2800
HISrfu	0.4475	0.5068	0.6250	**0.5400**
HISrpe	0.4161	0.5170	**0.6750**	0.4900

Table 7.2: *Distributed Image Retrieval Results*

family of CCDs and merging with bare non-normalized scores works best.

7.3 Conclusions

While [5] postulates that effective normalization methods should be non-linear taking into account the shape of SDs especially for non-text descriptors where a wilder variety of SDs is assumed we found these claims to be not necessarily true. Using compatible descriptors from the family of CCDs, combined with adding bare or linearly normalized scores with Z-score works best.

Finally, the use of CCDs in distributed image retrieval was attempted. In observing the results, we found that non-linear normalizations are better than linear. By using compatible descriptors from the family of CCDs, merging by bare non-normalized scores works best.

8

Relevance Feedback

$\mathbf{H}$igh retrieval scores in content-based image retrieval systems can be attained by adopting relevance feedback mechanisms. These mechanisms require the user to grade the quality of the query results by marking the retrieved images as being either relevant or not. Then, the search engine uses this grading information in subsequent queries to better satisfy users' needs. It is noted that while relevance feedback mechanisms were first introduced in the information retrieval field[159], they currently receive considerable attention in the CBIR field. The vast majority of relevance feedback techniques presented in the literature are based on modifying the values of the search parameters so that they better represent the concept consistent with the user's option. Search parameters are computed as a function of the relevance values assigned by the user to all the images retrieved so far. For instance, relevance feedback is frequently formulated in terms of the modification of the query vector and/or in terms of adaptive similarity metrics. Pattern classification methods such as SVMs have been used [203] in Relevance Feedback (RF) techniques.

Moreover, the user searching for a subset of images using the above descriptors, sometimes has not a clear and accurate vision of these images. He/she has a general notion of the image in quest but not the exact visual depiction of it. Also, sometimes there is not an appropriate query image to use for retrieval. The presented Automatic Relevance Feedback (ARF) [1] algorithm attempts to overcome these problems by providing a mechanism to fine tune the retrieval results or to use a group of query images instead of one. The aforementioned is accomplished by manipulating the original query descriptor relying on the subsequent queries' images, while attempting to construct the ideal query descriptor.

---

[1]This Chapter is Based on: "ACCURATE IMAGE RETRIEVAL BASED ON COMPACT COMPOSITE DESCRIPTORS AND RELEVANCE FEEDBACK INFORMATION", S. A. Chatzichristofis, K. Zagoris, Y. S. Boutalis and N. Papamarkos, International Journal of Pattern Recognition and Artificial Intelligence (IJPRAI), Volume 24, Number 2 / February, 2010, pp. 207-244, Copyright @ 2010 World Scientific.

8.1 Relevance Feedback Algorithm

The goal of this Automatic Relevance Feedback (ARF) algorithm[155] is to optimally readjust or even change the initial retrieval results based on user preferences. During this procedure, the user selects from the first round of retrieved images one or more, as being relevant to his/her initial retrieval expectations. Information extracted from these selected images, is used to alter the initial query image descriptor.

Primarily, the initial image query one-dimensional descriptor is transformed to a three-dimensional (x,y,z) vector $W_{x,y,z}$ based on the inner features of the descriptor. The $x, x \in [1,n]$ dimension represents the texture with n being equal to the number of textures that the image descriptor contains. The $y, y \in [1,k]$ dimension corresponds to the dominant colors, where k is equal to the number of dominant colors contained in each texture. The $z, z \in [1,m]$ dimension depicts the variation of dominant colors where m is equal to the maximum variation that each color has. Table 8.1 depicts the values of n, k and m for each descriptor and Figure 8.1 illustrates the vector. The advantage of the above transformation is the easier access to the inner information of the descriptor through the x, y and z dimensions. For example, the extraction of the bin descriptor of the same variation (z axis) of a dominant color (y axis) for each different texture (x axis) is accomplished by holding the two dimensions (y,z) constant, while x dimension takes all its allowable values in the interval $[1,n]$. The transformation of the descriptor to the three-dimensional vector is based on:

$$i = (k \times m) \times x + m \times y + z \tag{8.1}$$

$$x = \left\lfloor \frac{i}{k \times m} \right\rfloor \tag{8.2}$$

$$y = \left\lfloor \frac{i - \lfloor \frac{i}{k \times m} \rfloor \times (k \times m)}{m} \right\rfloor \tag{8.3}$$

or

$$y = \left\lfloor \frac{i - x \times (k \times m)}{m} \right\rfloor \tag{8.4}$$

$$z = i - \left\lfloor \frac{i}{k \times m} \right\rfloor \times (k \times m) - \left\lfloor \frac{i - \lfloor \frac{i}{k \times m} \rfloor \times (k \times m)}{m} \right\rfloor \times m \tag{8.5}$$

or

$$z = i - x \times (k \times m) - y \times m \tag{8.6}$$

where i is the position of the bin inside the descriptor and x,y,z is the position of the same bin inside the three-dimensional vector $W_{x,y,z}$. Initially, the value of each vector element is equal to the value of the corresponding descriptor bin. When the user selects a relevant

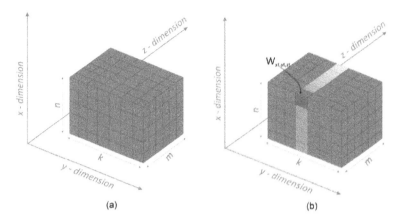

(a)   (b)

Figure 8.1: *(a) The three-dimensional vector $W_{x,y,z}$ (b) The alteration of the values of the vector element $W_{xt,yt,zt}$ and its associated elements.*

image from the retrieval results, each bin of that selected image's descriptor X_i updates the corresponding value of the $W_{x,y,z}$ vector in a Kohonen Self Organized Featured Map (KSOFM) [96, 95] manner, so that it moves closer to the new value emerging from X_i:

$$W_{xt,yt,zt}(t+1) = W_{xt,yt,zt}(t) + L(t) \times (X_{xt,yt,zt} - W_{xt,yt,zt}(t)) \qquad (8.7)$$

where

- $X_{xt,yt,zt}$ is the transformed three-dimensional vector of the selected image query descriptor X_i based on Eq. (8.1).

- xt, yt, zt are the x, y, z parameters for the selected image.

Each time a user selects another relevant image, an epoch t starts. This epoch ends after all the elements of vector $X_{xt,yt,zt}$ of the selected relevant image are used to update the corresponding values of $W_{xt,yt,zt}$ according to Eq. (8.7).
$L(t)$ function utilizes the same philosophy as the KSOFM learning rate function and defines the rate of the vector element readjustment. It is not constant; instead decreases each time a new query image descriptor is presented:

$$L(t) = E_{initial} \times \left(\frac{E_{Final}}{E_{Initial}} \right)^{\frac{t}{tmax}} \qquad (8.8)$$

In the present work: $E_{Initial} = 0.4$, $E_{Final} = 0.001$, $\forall t \in [0,30]$ and $tmax = 30$. According to Eq. (8.7), $L(t)$ is a decreasing function, getting values in the interval $E_{Initial}$ to E_{Final}. Additionally, each one of the other vector elements Wxq, yq, zq (except the Wxt, yt, zt) also readjust their values based on the following equation:

$$W_{xq,yq,zq}(t+1) = W_{xq,yq,zq}(t) + L(t) \times h(xq,yq,zq) \times (X_{xt,yt,zt} - W_{xt,yt,zt}(t)) \qquad (8.9)$$

xq,yq,zq are the x,y,z parameters for the query image.

The $h(xq,yq,zq)$ function utilizes the same philosophy as the KSOFM neighborhood function and defines the readjustment rate of the associated descriptor bins:

$$h(xq,yq,zq) = \frac{k \times m}{100} \ \textit{where } yq = yt, \ zq = zt \qquad (8.10)$$

$$h(xq,yq,zq) = \frac{k}{100 \times |zt - zq|} \ \textit{when } xq = xt, \ yq = yt \qquad (8.11)$$

$$h(xq,yq,zq) = 0 \ \textit{otherwise} \qquad (8.12)$$

Equation 11.9 attempts to correct the descriptor errors (for example the quantization) as it readjusts the same color of the corresponding element $W_{xt,yt,zt}$ found within other texture areas (through x axis), and its other color variations found within the same texture area (through z axis) approaching the X_i value.

The readjustment rate of the colors belonging to the other textures is constant and depends on the number $(k \times m)$ of descriptor bins that a texture contains. The readjustment rate of the similar variants of the dominant color is not constant but rather decreases inversely proportional to the distance between the variant colors. Also, the rate depends on the amount of the dominant color (k) that a texture contains.

The final descriptor to query the image database is formed by the values of the three-dimensional vector $W_{x,y,z}$ using Eq. (8.1). The above procedure is repeated every time the user selects a relevant image. Figure 8.2 depicts the entire process of the presented technique.

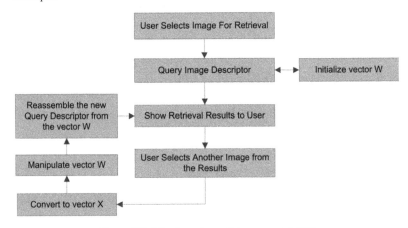

Figure 8.2: *The flow-chart of the presented ARF.*

148

	CEDD	FCTH	C.CEDD	C.FCTH
n	6	8	6	8
k	8	8	10	10
m	3	3	1	1

Table 8.1: *The n,k,m values for each presented descriptor*

8.2 Experimental Results

Table 8.2 illustrates the improvements achieved by the presented Automatic Relevance Feedback algorithm for queries on the WANG Database after one, two and three repetitions while Table 8.3 illustrates the achieved improvements on the MPEG-7 CCD database. As shown from the results, the presented method improves the retrieval scores significantly.

8.3 Conclusions

The goal of the presented ARF algorithm is to optimally readjust or even change the initial retrieval results based on user preferences. During this procedure, the user selects from the first round of retrieved images one or more, as being relevant to his/her initial retrieval expectations. Information extracted from these selected images, is used to alter the initial query image descriptor. Though extremely simple to implement, the presented method significantly improves image retrieval scores.

Descriptor	Query					ANMRR
	204	327	522	600	703	
Default Results						
CEDD	0.314	0.127	0.347	0.059	0.115	0.25283
FCTH	0.235	0.114	0.323	0.026	0.092	0.27369
C.CEDD	0.316	0.140	0.452	0.069	0.088	0.30637
C.FCTH	0.320	0.224	0.493	0.013	0.116	0.31537
First Repetition						
RF Image	285	317	551	609	791	
CEDD	0.303	0.085	0.386	0.046	0.093	0.23332
FCTH	0.204	0.089	0.324	0.019	0.079	0.25443
C.CEDD	0.265	0.109	0.441	0.034	0.084	0.29229
C.FCTH	0.274	0.186	0.324	0.010	0.093	0.30220
Second Repetition						
RF Image	240	346	535	633	796	
CEDD	0.294	0.071	0.293	0.065	0.090	0.21341
FCTH	0.183	0.083	0.308	0.022	0.075	0.23442
C.CEDD	0.251	0.116	0.370	0.104	0.081	0.26887
C.FCTH	0.245	0.171	0.308	0.012	0.090	0.29776
Third Repetition						
RF Image	284	320	503	644	761	
CEDD	0.273	0.045	0.285	0.034	0.081	0.19776
FCTH	0.214	0.049	0.316	0.016	0.067	0.20834
C.CEDD	0.230	0.073	0.365	0.035	0.077	0.25336
C.FCTH	0.241	0.108	0.316	0.012	0.081	0.27557

Table 8.2: *Results on WANG Image Database.*

Descriptor	Query			ANMRR
	i0121_add5	img00133_add3	img00438_s3	
		Default Results		
CEDD	0	0	0.033	0.08511
FCTH	0	0.037	0.003	0.10343
C.CEDD	0	0.014	0.167	0.12655
C.FCTH	0	0.065	0	0.15977
		First Repetition		
RF Image	i0123_add5	img00134_add3	img00444_s3	
CEDD	0	0	0.022	0.05334
FCTH	0	0.060	0	0.09883
C.CEDD	0	0.009	0.031	0.11341
C.FCTH	0	0.097	0.000	0.14333
		Second Repetition		
RF Image	i26e_add1	img00131_add3	img00439_s3	
CEDD	0	0	0.033	0.03445
FCTH	0	0	0	0.08788
C.CEDD	0	0.005	0.008	0.10443
C.FCTH	0	0.009	0.000	0.12221
		Third Repetition		
RF Image	0131_add5	img00135_add3	img00440_s3	
CEDD	0	0	0	0.03122
FCTH	0	0.014	0	0.07322
C.CEDD	0	0	0.006	0.10443
C.FCTH	0	0.009	0	0.11322

Table 8.3: *Results on MPEG-7 CCD Image Database.*

9

Software Tools

Img(Rummager)[20] software was employed for the demonstration of the results of the research undertaken for the book[1]. In addition to the developed descriptors, the software utilize a large number of descriptors from the literature (amongst which are the MPEG-7 descriptors), so that the application constitutes a platform for retrieving images via which the behavior of a number of descriptors can be studied. The application can evaluate the retrieval results, both via the use of the new image retrieval evaluation method as well as via MAP and ANMRR. The application was programmed using C# and is freely available via the "Automatic Control, Systems and Robotics Laboratory" webpage, Department of Electrical and Computer Engineering, Democritus University of Thrace.

img(Anaktisi)[199] software was developed in collaboration with "Electrical Circuit Analysis Laboratory", Department of Electrical and Computer Engineering, Democritus University of Thrace (Prof. N. Papamarkos and Dr. K. Zagoris), and is an Internet based application which possesses the capability of executing image retrieval using CCDs in a large number of images. The application is programmed in C# .NET.

Moreover, CCDs were included into the free and open source library, LIRe. This library is programmed in JAVA and includes implementations for the most important descriptors used for image retrieval. The program was developed in collaboration with the ALPEN-ADRIA University of Information Technology in Klagenfurtm Austria, Distributed Multimedia Systems Research Group (Ass. Prof. M. Lux).

In this chapter the structure and the abilities of the first two software tools are presented along with user guide instructions. More details can be found on-line in the respective web sites.

---

[1]This Chapter is Based on: [20][199]

9.1 img(Rummager)

9.1.1 Technical Details

img(Rummager) application is programmed in C# and requires a Windows XP+ Operating System with a 3.0 .NET Framework. This is a portable application that does not require installation. The index files it creates can be stored in any part of the user's hard disk, or even on a local network. They are normal XML files where documents consisting of fields each one having a name and a value. img(Rummager) is available online along with documentation and video tutorials on http://www.img-rummager.com.

The application environment can be divided into 3 sections:

1. Image Laboratory Section

2. Image Retrieval Section

3. Extras Section

9.1.2 Image Laboratory Section

In this section of the application, the low level features used by the application for retrieval procedure are visually depicted.

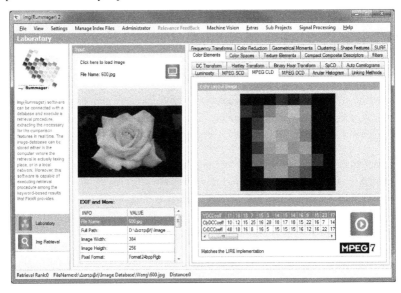

Figure 9.1: *Image Laboratory Section*

This section includes graphic representation of the low level features of the query image, and provides information extracted from them. A complete list of the low level features that are demonstrated in this section is given in Table 9.1.

154

Feature	Tab	Feature	Tab
Luminosity Histograms	Color	Lab Color Histograms	Color Spaces
MPEG-7 SCD	Color	RGB Color Histograms	Color Spaces
MPEG-7 CLD	Color	HSV Color Histograms	Color Spaces
MPEG-7 DCD	Color	HSL Color Histograms	Color Spaces
Annular Histogram	Color	MPEG-7 HMMD	Color Spaces
Color Linking Methods	Color	Co-Occurrance Matrices	Texture
- Fuzzy HSV 10 Bin		Laws Texture	Texture
- Fuzzy HSV 8 Bin		Tamura Feature	Texture
- Fuzzy HSV 24 Bin		Wang Wavelet	Texture
- Fuzzy Lab 10 Bin		Modified Wang Wavelet	Texture
- Spatial Fuzzy Linking		MPEG-7 EHD	Texture
- Color Histograms		Gabor Histogram	Texture
Auto Correlograms	Color	FCTH	CCDs
SpCD	Color	Spatial FCTH	CCDs
Binary Haar Transform	Color	CEDD	CCDs
-on Lab		BTDH	CCDs
-on RGB		Compact CEDD	CCDs
-on HSV		Compact FCTH	CCDs
Hartlay Transform	Color	Scalable BTDH	CCDs
-on Lab		JCD	CCDs
-on RGB		Wavelet	Freq. Trans.
-on HSV		Fourier	Freq. Trans.
DCT Haar Transform	Color	Hu Moments	Moments
-on Lab		Zernike Moments	Moments
-on RGB		SURF Features	LF
-on HSV		Projections	Shape
TSRD	Shape	More than 60 Filtes	Filters
Connected Components	Shape	CLF XOR	Filters
CSPD	Shape	Face Detection	Filters
Color Reduction	Filters	Auto Color Correction	Filters
-Using K-Means		Auto Brightness Correction	Filters
-Gustafson Kessel		Edge Extraction Methods	Filters
-Fuzzy C-Means		Visual Words Histogram	LF
Color Visual Words	LF		

Table 9.1: *Low Level Features in img(Rummager)*

9.1.3   Image Retrieval Section

The application offers 3 different search options:

1. Search from XML index files

2. Search in local / network folder.

3. Search from the application server

Search from XML index files

The application supports the creation of XML files containing information from a group
of images selected by the user. An XML index file can include information from 13
different descriptors [2].

Descriptor	XML Size (KB)
CEDD	210
FCTH	258
SpCD	152
Compact CEDD	131
Compact FCTH	151
JCD - ADS	412
MPEG -7 SCD	231
MPEG -7 CLD	**103**
MPEG -7 EHD	147
BTDH	195
Tamura Directionality Histogram	373
RGB Histograms	761
Correlograms	27336
Visual Words (SURF)	Dynamic
Visual Words (SIFT)	Dynamic
Color Visual Words (SURF)	Dynamic
Color Visual Words (SIFT)	Dynamic
All Descriptors	30176

Table 9.2: *Descriptors contained in the img(Rummager) and the index file size for the
Wang's [189] database.*

The user selects which descriptors to include for each file. The searching procedure
is as follows: The user enters a query image and an index file. In the case that the index file contains information about more than one descriptor, the user must also select a

---

[2]The source code for the MPEG-7 Descriptors is a modification of the implementation that
can be found in the LIRe [117] retrieval library.

descriptor. The application executes the search using the similarity matching technique recommended for each descriptor. When the procedure is completed, the application arranges the images contained in the index file according to their proximity to the query image, and presents the user with the results.

The user then has the option to select those images matching the ground truth of the query image, and the application calculates the normalized modified retrieval rank(NMRR), MNRO and/or the average precision (AP) for that query. This feature of img(Rummager) allows for easy retrieval evaluation to find the most appropriate descriptor for an arbitrary domain, where a ground truth has been defined.

An auto relevance feedback technique to tune the retrieval results is also provided to the user. The user selects one or more images, as being relevant to the initial retrieval expectations from the first round of retrieved images. After that, the technique re-adjusts the initial retrieval results.

The query image does not need to belong to the index file. The user may use an image and the application extracts the descriptors for that image during the search process.

By pressing "**f5**" the user may provide a list of queries among their ground truth files and img(Rummager) application executes the retrieval procedure for all the files calculating the ANMRR, ANMRO and/or AP. This function is known as "Batch Mode".

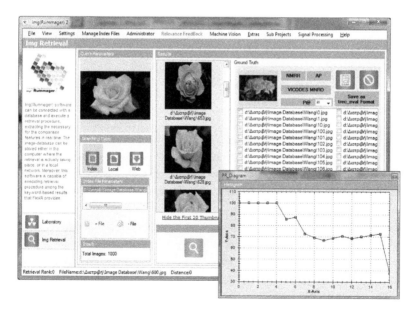

Figure 9.2: *Screenshot from the XML file search and the Precision / Recall graph.*

157

9.1.4 Search from Local / Network Folder

In this case, the user designates the query image and allocates one or more folders where the search is to be executed. Next, one of the descriptors from Table 9.2 may be selected, or a custom retrieval method can be designated, through the selection determining which low level features are to be used. These features include elements from the color histograms RGB, YIQ, HSL, the Direct Cosine Transform from an array of histograms, the Binary Harr Wavelet Transform from an array of histograms, Fuzzy Linking techniques, Moments, and others.

Every feature selected by the user comprises an independent unit. A permissible deviation limit at every unit of the system is designated. If the image is within limits, it will be led either to the outlet or to the next level. In every other case the image will be rejected.

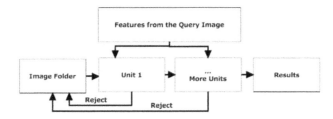

Figure 9.3: *Flowchart of the customization process of image searching from image folder.*

Upon completion of the process, all the images that successfully passed all units are presented to the user.

9.1.5 Search from the application server

Searching for images via the application server is differentiated from the two previous search methods, as apart from visual similarity, it also includes **keywords**. The server side part of the img(Rummager) undertakes the execution of image retrieval based on **Flickr**[3] keywords (tags) and creates XML index files containing the descriptors of these images.

When the user of the img(Rummager) client version selects the application server search, the img(Rummager) automatically connects to its server version and downloads an XML file with the available keywords. So far the application supports 100 keywords. The options appear in a drop down menu.

The user selects the desired keyword, preferred descriptor for the search, and imports a query image. The application downloads a second XML file containing the descriptors for 500 images tagged with the keyword specified by the user.

---

[3]http://www.flickr.com

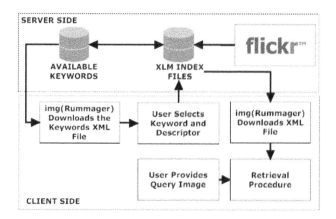

Figure 9.4: *Searching from the application server.*

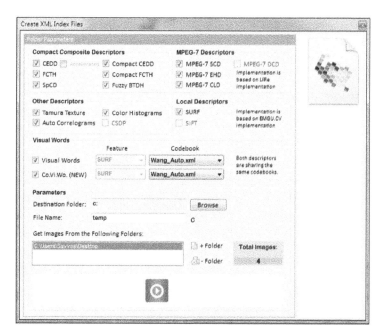

Figure 9.5: *img(Rummager) Index File Generator.*

159

9.1.6   Extras Section

The img(Rummager) application integrates several additional applications:

- **img(Finder):** The img(Finder) connects to Facebook[4], using the user's personal account. Subsequently, it downloads an XML file from the Facebook server, which includes the addresses of the images that have been uploaded by the user's "friends". The application extracts the Joint Composite Descriptor for each image and creates a new XML index file. During the retrieval process, the user inserts an image in order to check whether this image has been used at Facebook.

- **img(Paint.Anaktisi)** The img(Paint.Anaktisi) uses the MPEG-7 Color Layout Descriptor to retrieve images using color rough sketches. Color Layout Descriptor descriptor effectively represents the spatial distribution of color of visual signals in a very compact form. The img (Paint.Anaktisi) uses the same XML files with img(Rummager) application.

- **Fuzzy Classifier** This demo performs a fuzzy classification on multi-dimensional data using either Fuzzy C-Means or Gustafson Kessel classifier.

- **Real Time Face Detection and Tracking** Using several face detection techniques, this demo provides a real time face tracking.

- **Puzzle Solver** This application demonstrates a novel approach for solving two dimensional puzzles and its application at several robotic arms. Despite many classical methods concerning resolving puzzles, the implemented method is characterized by low computational cost and ease of development. In order to achieve the shape recognition, classical techniques from the field of image processing are combined with efficient techniques. A camera captures an image from the whole disassembled puzzle, whose pieces are scattered at the workspace of the robotic arm. At the beginning, Otsu's method converts this image to a binary form. Then, the connected components are identified and their inclination is being corrected. In order to achieve the recognition of every single shape, Morphological Associative Memories (MAMs) that have been initially trained are used. After the object recognition the system communicates with the robotic arm so as to solve the puzzle.

Morphological Neural Networks (MNNs) represent artificial neural networks whose neurons perform an elementary operation of mathematical morphology [184]. Unlike Hopfield network [67], MNNs provide the result in one pass through the network, without any significant amount of training. The underlying algebraic system used in these models is the set of real numbers R together with the operations of addition and multiplication and the laws governing these operations. Morphological associative memories (MAMs) are based on the algebraic lattice structure

---

[4]http://www.facebook.com

$(R, +, \wedge, \vee)$. They have been initially proposed in [148] for associating binary pattern vectors and are far more robust to noise than the conventional linear associative memories.

- **img(Encryption)** This application demonstrates a new method for visual multimedia content encryption using Cellular Automata (CA). The encryption scheme is based on the application of an attribute of the CLF XOR filter, according to which the original content of a cellular neighborhood can be reconstructed following a predetermined number of repeated applications of the filter.

  The encryption is achieved using a key image of the same dimensions as the image being encrypted. This technique is accompanied by the one-time pad (OTP) encryption method, rendering the proposed method reasonably powerful, given the very large number of resultant potential security keys. This method makes encryption possible in cases where there is more than one image with the use of just one key image. A further significant characteristic of the method is that it demonstrates how techniques from the field of image retrieval can be used in the field of image encryption.

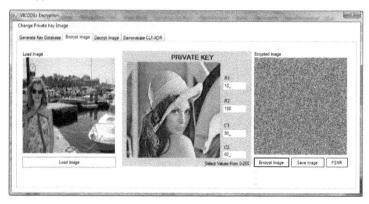

Figure 9.6: *img(Encryption) Screenshot.*

img(Encryption) encryption method is further strengthened by the fact that the resulting encrypted image for a given key image is different each time. The encryption result depends on the structure of an artificial image produced by the superposition of four 1-D CA timespace diagrams as well as from a CA random number generator. A semi-blind source separation algorithm is used to decrypt the encrypted image. The result of the decryption is a lossless representation of the encrypted image. Simulation results demonstrate the effectiveness of the encryption method. More details about this method are given in [25].

- **Real Time Color Correction** This demo performs real time color correction on the frames captured by a web camera using an algorithm for digital images unsupervised enhancement with simultaneous global and local effects. This algorithm is known as ACE (Automatic Color Equalization). It is based on a computational model of the human visual system that merges the two basic *Gray World* and *White Patch* global equalization mechanisms[149].

9.2 img(Anaktisi)

img(Anaktisi)[5] is a C#/.NET content based image retrieval application suitable for the web. It provides efficient retrieval services for various image databases using as a query a sample image, an image sketched by the user and keywords. The image retrieval engine is powered by the compact composite descriptors.

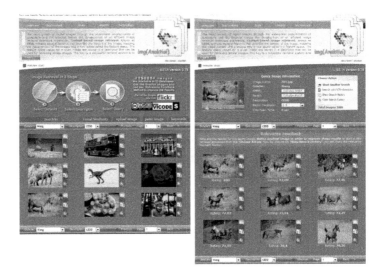

Figure 9.7: *img(Anaktisi) Screenshot.*

The Auto Relevance Feedback (ARF) technique presented in Chapter 8 readjusts the initial retrieval results based on user preferences improving the retrieval score significantly. img(Anaktisi) can be found at http://www.anaktisi.net.

9.2.1 Implementation

Firstly, the user can select among different ways to describe the query image. These ways are:

---

[5]This work results from collaboration with "Electrical Circuit Analysis Laboratory", Department of Electrical and Computer Engineering, Democritus University of Thrace (Prof. N. Papamarkos and Dr. K. Zagoris)

1. **Sample image from the database or from the user:** The user can select an image from the section that displays the database images or he/she can upload his/her image from the flash-based upload utility that the web site provides.

2. **Draw Rough Stretch:** The user can paint a rough stretch of the query image.

3. **Keywords:** The user can describe the query image as series of keywords.

Next, the application based on the user query information search the database and presents to the user the most similar images. This is accomplished by a group of descriptors. These are: the Color and edge directivity descriptor (CEDD), the Fuzzy color and texture histogram (FCTH), their compact variants which are described in the first part of this dissertation and the Join Composite Descriptor (JCD).

img(Anaktisi) provides eleven image databases to search. These are: Wang (1000 images), MIR flickr [73] (25.000 images), flickr (103746 images), MPEG-7 CCD (5473 images), UCID (1338 images), Nister (10200 images), Television (3520 images), Rummager (9680 images), Paintings (1771 images), Chinese Art (3646 images), Textures Collection (2862 images) and Cars (1051 images).

It is worth worth noticing that img(Anaktisi) implements a cache between the application and the database in order to speed up the retrieval procedure. The database cache is constructed based on the frequency that a database is used.

Moreover, the user searching for a subset of images using the above descriptors, sometimes has a general notion of the image in quest but not the exact visual depiction of it. The Automatic Relevance Feedback (ARF) algorithm attempts to overcome these problems by providing a mechanism to tune the retrieval results or to use a group of query images instead of one. During this procedure, the user selects from the first round of retrieved images one or more, as being relevant to his/her initial retrieval expectations.

9.2.2 Technical Details

The img(Anaktisi) web application is developed in C#/.NET Framework 3.5 and it requires a fairly modern browser to use it (Mozilla Firefox 2+, Microsoft Internet Explorer 7+). It uses AJAX, Adobe Flash and Microsoft Silverlight technologies.

Concerning the server, the img(Anaktisi) uses the Microsoft SQL Server 2005 Database to store and retrieve the images.

$$10$$

Conclusions and Discussion

This book is composed of 9 chapters. Each chapter has its own conclusions, which are presented at the end of the respective chapter. Here, we only give a short overview on the individual sections and provide with hints or ideas for future work. Moreover, this section provides a short reference to the impact that this work already has in the research efforts of other researchers.

10.1 Compact Composite Descriptors

The core of this book includes a set of descriptors for each kind of images. It's the first approach of developing descriptors oriented to the content of the images. The descriptors has been designed in a way to be able to be used in large scale databases. Their storage needs do not exceed the 72 bytes per image. For their calculation, efficient techniques has been used.

The idea of integrating more than one characteristic in their structure, proved to enhance their performance in retrieval systems. Experimental results show that the descriptors developed show better results from the vast majority of other descriptor of the literature.

The medical image retrieval technique might be used in several medical applications, helping the development of intelligent systems for diagnostic support. Integration of BTDH descriptor into DICOM files would contribute to the development of a CAD (computer-aided diagnosis) system. Nowadays, doctors can search for similar cases based on the textual information included in DICOM files. With the presented method, they would also be able to use the visual information. For example, for a patient exhibiting an unexpected image on a chest MRI scan, the doctor would use the terms *Chest* and *MRI* as textual information and would supply the CAD with the patient's radiology images. The system will return similar cases entered in the database as well as the diagnosis/treatment followed in said cases. It should be noted that by no means does the system offer a diagnosis, but rather a reference to similar cases.

The ability of the descriptors to be incorporated in the MPEG-7 scheme allows their use in existing image databases, without any modifications to them.

Another issue that arises is how to combine all the descriptions that have been developed in order to achieve better retrieval results. The methods that were tested for late fusion of the descriptors shows that retrieval results can be improved significantly, especially if the experiments are performed in heterogeneous image databases.

In the sequel, we are proposing several plans for future work:

- Implementation on Graphics Processing unit. One possible solution is a *Compute Unified Device Architecture* (CUDA), which is a *C* compiler and a set of development tools for programmers to code algorithms for execution on a graphics processing unit (GPU) provided by NVIDIA[1]. This allows parallel computation of a given task. In this way the main unit is capable of computing other threads while the description is done automatically by the GPU. Similar implementations have been proposed for the MPEG-7 descriptors [89].

- Development of a fuzzy rule based fusion system. As observed from experiments conducted in this book, the failure of one of the descriptors in some images punish the system. The aim is to develop a system that will identify the possible failure and not take into account the contribution of the descriptor in the final result.

- Development of a new way for searching and retrieving information through XML files. The approach could be followed to support and extend FTMnodes [39].

- Development of a content based tag recommendation system for images.

10.2 Software

Software implementations enable the use of the presented techniques by other researchers in the field.

img(Rummager) provides a platform that can be used as a tool for testing new techniques for visual multimedia content retrieval from third parties.

Given that all the software applications are open source, several collaborative groups, both in research and industrial level can contribute to their expansion.

In addition, the open source libraries that has been developed, invites researchers from different research fields to use them on their applications, techniques from the field of image retrieval.

10.3 Impact of the Developed Methods

In this section we present some example applications of the literature, using techniques presented in this book.

---

[1]CUDA for GPU Computing. http://tinyurl.com/yeu937t

10.3.1 Similarity Content Search in Centric Networks

Content searching and downloading are the two dominant actions of the Internet users today, despite the fact that the Internet was not originally architected to serve such actions. Content Centric Networking is the new trend in the research community to build network architectures that route content by name and not by the host's network address so as to efficiently deal with content persistence, availability and authenticity issues. In [140], authors proposed an extension to the Content Centric Network protocol in order to support content search as a native process of the network.

By using object descriptors such as Color and Edge Directivity Descriptor (CEDD) to represent the actual content objects and integrate these descriptors in the network protocol they manage to search and retrieve content from the network not only by name but also by the content itself. In this approach, searching for information is a process distributed to the reachable network. Moreover, content aggregation is handled by the end user and not by content aggregation portals, thematic content search engines or information curators. By doing so, search is not any more an application but part of the network and can pave the way for many novel applications which have never been thought until today.

10.3.2 Tag Recommendation for Image Annotation

Recent advances in the fields of digital photography, networking and computing, have made it easier than ever for users to store and share photographs. However without sufficient metadata, e.g., in the form of tags, photos are difficult to find and organize. In [119], authors describe a system that recommends tags for image annotation. Authors of this paper postulate that the use of Color and Edge Directivity Descriptor (CEDD), proposed in this book, can improve the quality of the tag recommendation process when compared to a baseline statistical method based on tag co-occurrence. This paper also present results from experiments conducted using photos and metadata sourced from the Flickr photo website that suggest that the use of visual features improves the mean average precision (MAP) of the system and increases the system's ability to suggest different tags, therefore justifying the associated increase in complexity.

10.3.3 Exploiting External Knowledge to Improve Video Retrieval

Vallet et al. [185] proposed a set of techniques to automatically obtain additional query visual examples from different external knowledge sources, such as DBPedia, Flickr and Google Images, which have different coverage and structure characteristics. The proposed strategies attempt to exploit the semantics underlying the above knowledge sources to reduce the ambiguity of the query, and to focus the scope of the image searches in the repositories.

This work analyses the role of the external Knowledge Sources (KS) for providing relevant visual examples, without extra effort from the user, unlike manually providing examples, or without techniques that require collections indexed with additional features, such as pseudo-relevance feedback. They study three different external KSs: 1) a highly structured, collaborative built KS, with a low semantic coverage in multimedia sources, such as DBPedia; 2) a folksonomy-based KS, freely defined by users, with a greater coverage, such as Flickr; and 3) a low structured KS such as Google Images, but with a high coverage (the Web).

Authors of this paper are using Color and Edge Directivity Descriptor (CEDD) and Fuzzy Color and Texture Histogram (FCTH) to describe the visual content of the images.

10.3.4   A Classification-Driven Similarity Matching Framework for Retrieval of Biomedical Images

This paper [145] presents a classification-driven biomedical image retrieval system to bride the semantic gap by transforming image features to their global categories at different granularity, such as image modality, body part, and orientation. To generate the feature vectors at different levels of abstraction, both the visual concept feature based on the "bag of concepts" model that comprise of local color and texture patches and various low-level global color, edge, and texture related features are extracted. Since, it is difficult to find a unique feature to compare images effectively for all types of queries, we utilize a similarity fusion approach based on the linear combination of individual features. However, instead of using the commonly used fixed or hard weighting approach, authors rely on the image classification to determine the importance of a feature at real time. For this, a supervised multi-class classifier based on the support vector machine (SVM) is trained on a set of sample images and classifier combination techniques based on the rules derived from the Bayes's theorem are explored.

After the combined prediction of the classifiers for a query image category, the individual pre-computed weights of different features are adjusted in the similarity matching function for effective query-specific retrieval. Experiment is performed in a diverse medical image collection of 67000 images of different modalities. It demonstrates the effectiveness of the category-specific similarity fusion approach with a mean average precision (MAP) score of 0.0265 when compared to using only a single feature or equal weighting of each feature in similarity matching.

In addition to the visual concept feature, authors of this paper are using Color and Edge Directivity Descriptor (CEDD) and Fuzzy Color and Texture Histogram (FCTH) to describe the visual content of the images.

10.3.5   Mining Personal Image Collection for Social Group Suggestion

Popular photo-sharing sites have attracted millions of people and helped construct massive social networks in cyberspace. Different from traditional social relationship, users actively interact within groups where common interests are shared on certain types of events or topics captured by photos and videos. Contributing images to a group would greatly promote the interactions between users and expand their social networks. In [198], authors intend to produce accurate predictions of suitable photo-sharing groups from a user's images by mining images both on the Web and in the user's personal collection. To this end, a new approach designed to cluster popular groups into categories by analyzing the similarity of groups via SimRank. Both visual content and its annotations are integrated to understand the events or topics depicted in the images. The Color and Edge Directivity Descriptor (CEDD) describes the visual content of the images. Experiments on real user images demonstrate the feasibility of the proposed approach.

10.3.6   Visual Diversification of Image Search Results

Due to its reliance on the textual information associated with an image, image search engines on the Web lack the discriminative power to deliver visually diverse search results.

The textual descriptions are key to retrieve relevant results for a given user query, but at the same time provide little information about the rich image content.

In [186] authors investigate three methods for visual diversification of image search results. The methods deploy lightweight clustering techniques in combination with a dynamic weighting function of the visual features, to best capture the discriminative aspects of the resulting set of images that is retrieved. A representative image is selected from each cluster, which together form a diverse result set.

The Color and Edge Directivity Descriptor (CEDD) is one of the low level features that describes the visual content of the images.

Based on a performance evaluation authors found that the outcome of the methods closely resembles human perception of diversity, which was established in an extensive clustering experiment carried out by human assessors.

10.3.7   A novel tool for summarization of arthroscopic videos

Arthroscopic surgery is a minimally invasive procedure that uses a small camera to generate video streams, which are recorded and subsequently archived. In [118] authors proposed a video summarization tool and demonstrate how it can be successfully used in the domain of arthroscopic videos.

Arthroscopic videos have certain distinguishing characteristics and requirements, which bear implications for video analysis and summarization. For example, the video coding method and visual quality of video streams are constrained by restrictions on the sensor, the sterile environment of the operating room and the requirement that surgical instruments need to be error-free during the course of a surgery. The way by which the video is acquired, encoded, and storedusing an expensive proprietary equipmentcannot be changed. Additionally, the recorded videos are typically short (6070 s in average), as the surgeon only records the most important parts of the surgery. Despite the fact that only a small set of videos per arthroscopy is recorded for archival purposes, the total number of stored videos quickly builds up, as a result of the large number of surgeries performed by a surgeon. Consequently, the video archives of arthroscopists grow to a size for which multimedia information management is crucial.

In order to describe the visual content of the Arthroscopic videos, the Color and Edge Directivity Descriptor (CEDD) was used (among with other descriptors from the literature).

The proposed tool generates a keyframe-based summary, which clusters visually similar frames based on user-selected visual features and appropriate dissimilarity metrics. This paper describes how this tool can be used for arthroscopic videos, taking advantage of several domain-specific aspects, without losing its ability to work on generalpurpose videos. Experimental results confirm the feasibility of the proposed approach and encourage extending it to other application domains.

10.3.8 An Image Retrieval Approach Based on Composite Features and Graph Matching

Content-Based Image Retrieval (CBIR) considers the characteristics of the image itself, for example its shapes, colors and textures. The Current approaches to CBIR differ in terms of which image features are extracted. Recent work deals with combination of distances or scores from different and independent representations.

The work in [65] attempts to induce high level semantics from low level descriptors, such as Fuzzy Color and Texture Histogram (FCTH). In this paper, authors proposed a new approach that integrates techniques of salient, color and texture features. This approach extracts interest salient regions that work as local descriptors. A greedy graph matching algorithm with a proposed modified scoring function is applied to determine the final image rank. The proposed approach is appropriate for accurately retrieving images even in distortion cases such as geometric deformations and noise. This approach was tested on proprietary image databases. Also an offline case study is developed where our approach is tested on images retrieved from Google keyword based image search engine. The results show that a combination of our approach as a local image descriptor with another global descriptor outperforms other approaches.

Essential Tools

A.1   Gustafson Kessel Fuzzy Classifier

One major problem of the standard algorithms is that it produces spherical classes. For example, if the sets of points illustrated at Fig. 1(a) pass through the fuzzy C-mean algorithm for partitioning into four classes, the result will not be the optimal (Fig 1(b)). If we replace the Euclidean distance in the fuzzy C-mean algorithm with another metric, the calculation of which will include a positive symmetrical table, it will allow ellipsoid clusters to be recognized, as well as spherical ones. Such an algorithm has been designed by Gustafson and Kessel (GK) [61].

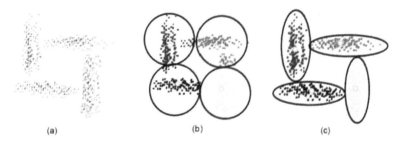

(a)   (b)   (c)

Figure A.1: *(a) The points in the 2D space which must separate to four classes. (b) Four classes obtained by using the fuzzy C-mean algorithm. (c) The four classes obtained through the Gustafson - Kessel algorithm.*

Let the total of prototypes $X = \{x_1, x_2, \ldots, x_n\}$ with $X_i \in R^p$, which we want to classify into L clusters. If $\{v_1, v_2, \ldots, v_L\}$ are the vectors of the cluster centers then Mahalanobis distance of every prototype x_k of the cluster (v_i, A_i) is equal to:

$$d_{ik}^2 = (x_k - v_i)^T \times A_i \times (x_k - v_i) \tag{A.1}$$

Where $A_i = C_i^{-1}$, with C_i the covariance matrix of the cluster i given by:

$$C_i = \sum_{k=1}^{n} u_{ik}^m (x_k - v_i) \times (x_k - v_i)^T \tag{A.2}$$

Where u_{ik}^m is described in equation B.14. In every repetition of the GK algorithm the vectors of the center v_i of the clusters are determined as:

$$v_i = \frac{1}{\sum\limits_{k=1}^{n} u_{ik}^m} \sum_{k=1}^{n} u_{ik}^m x_k \quad i = 1,2,\ldots,n \quad k = 1,2,\ldots,n \tag{A.3}$$

The GK algorithm is consist of the following steps:

Step 1: The number of L clusters and the largest number of repetitions are determined.

Step 2: The U^0 table of participatory functions is started, either at random or based on a particular approach. The centers of V^0 clusters and the covariance matrices C^0 are calculated. Then, the tables A^0 of the clusters are calculated. Next, the U^0 tables are recalculated. A value is set for m. Indicator $a = 0$.

Step 3: Given table U^a the centers of V^a clusters are calculated according to equation B.11.

Step 4: Given the V^a, the covariance matrices C^a of every cluster are calculated:

$$C_i = \sum_{k=1}^{n} u_{ik}^m (x_k - v_i)(x_k - v_i)^T \quad i = 1,2,\ldots,L \quad k = 1,2,\ldots,n \tag{A.4}$$

Step 5: Given the covariance matrices C^a, the A^a of every cluster are calculated

$$A_i = \sqrt[p]{\det(C_i)}(C_i)^{-1} \quad i = 1,2,\ldots,L \tag{A.5}$$

Step 6: Given the A^a table, the distance of every prototype x_k from the center of cluster is calculated according to the equation $d_{ik}^2 = (x_k - v_i)^T A_i (x_k - v_i)$. Next, the new participatory functions U^a of every prototype in every cluster are calculated.

$$u_{ik} = \frac{\left[\frac{1}{d_{ik}^2}\right]^{\frac{1}{m-1}}}{\sum\limits_{j=1}^{L} \left[\frac{1}{d_{ik}^2}\right]^{\frac{1}{m-1}}} \quad i = 1,2,\ldots,L \quad k = 1,2,\ldots,n \tag{A.6}$$

Step 7: The process is completed if $\left|u_{ik}^{(a)} - u_{ik}^{(a-1)}\right| \le e$ or if $a = Repetitions$. Otherwise make $a = a + 1$ and the process is repeated from step 3.

Steps 1 and 2 are executed only once, during the algorithm initiation, while steps 3, 4, 5 and 6 are repeatedly executed until at least one of the conditions described in step 7 is satisfied. The parameters calculated in steps 3, 4 and 5 are used in the repetition during which they are calculated while parameter U^a, calculated in step 6, is used both to check that the condition for algorithm termination is satisfied, and as data for the next repetition.

CEDD & FCTH Fuzzy Inference Parameters

IF *HUE* IS	AND *S* IS	AND *V* IS	THEN OUTPUT IS
Any Color	0	0	Black
Any Color	1	0	Black
Any Color	0	2	White
Any Color	0	1	Gray
Red to Orange	1	1	Red
Red to Orange	1	2	Red
Orange	1	1	Orange
Orange	1	2	Orange
Yellow	1	1	Yellow
Yellow	1	2	Yellow
Green	1	1	Green
Green	1	2	Green
Cyan	1	1	Cyan
Cyan	1	2	Cyan
Blue	1	1	Blue
Blue	1	2	Blue
Magenta	1	1	Magenta
Magenta	1	2	Magenta
Magenta to Red	1	1	Red
Magenta to Red	1	2	Red

Table B.1: *The Fuzzy inference rules which bind the Fuzzy 10-bin Histogram.*

IF INPUT S IS	AND INPUT V IS	THEN OUTPUT IS
1	1	Color
0	0	Dark Color
0	1	Light Color
1	0	Dark Color

Table B.2: *The Fuzzy inference rules which bind the Fuzzy 24-bin Histogram.*

IF F_{HH} IS	AND F_{HL} IS	AND FLH IS	THEN OUTPUT IS
0	0	0	Low Energy Linear
0	0	1	Low Energy Horizontal
0	1	0	Low Energy Vertical
0	1	1	Low Energy Horizontal & Vertical
1	0	0	High Energy Linear
1	0	1	High Energy Horizontal
1	1	0	High Energy Vertical
1	1	1	High Energy Horizontal & Vertical

Table B.3: *The Fuzzy inference rules which bind the Fuzzy 8-bin Texture Histogram.*

Fuzzy 10-bin Color System

Membership Function	Activation Value			
	0	1	1	0
	Domain of the MFs			
HUE				
Red to Orange	0	0	5	10
Orange	5	10	35	50
Yellow	35	50	70	85
Green	70	85	150	165
Cyan	150	165	195	205
Blue	195	205	265	280
Magenta	265	280	315	330
Magenta to Red	315	330	360	360
SATURATION				
0	0	0	10	75
1	10	75	255	255
VALUE				
0	0	0	10	75
1	10	75	180	200
2	180	200	255	255

Fuzzy 24-bin Color System

Membership Function	Activation Value			
	0	1	1	0
	Domain of the MFs			
SATURATION				
0	0	0	68	188
1	68	188	255	255
VALUE				
0	0	0	68	188
1	68	188	255	255

Table B.4: *Fuzzy Color System.*

Membership Function	Activation Value			
	0	1	1	0
	Domain of the MFs			
F_{LH} and F_{HL}				
0	0	0	20	90
1	20	90	255	255
F_{HH}				
0	0	0	20	80
1	20	80	255	255

Table B.5: *Fuzzy 6-bin Texture System.*

Fuzzy Inference Parameters for SpCD

Membership Function	Activation Value			
	0	1	1	0
	Domain of the MFs			
HUE				
Red I (0)	0	0	5	55
Yellow (1)	5	55	60	115
Green (2)	60	115	120	175
Cyan (3)	120	175	180	235
Blue (4)	180	235	240	295
Magenta (5)	240	295	300	355
Red II (6)	300	355	360	360
SATURATION				
Gray	0	0	25	55
Color	25	55	255	255
VALUE				
White	0	0	100	156
Black	100	156	255	255

Table C.1: *Fuzzy 8-bin Color System*

If HUE is	And SATURATION is	And VALUE is	Then OUT is
Red I (0)	Gray	White	White
Red I (0)	Gray	Black	Black
Red I (0)	Color	White	Red
Red I (0)	Color	Black	Red
Yellow (1)	Gray	White	White
Yellow (1)	Gray	Black	Black
Yellow (1)	Color	White	Yellow
Yellow (1)	Color	Black	Yellow
Green (2)	Gray	White	White
Green (2)	Gray	Black	Black
Green (2)	Color	White	Green
Green (2)	Color	Black	Green
Cyan (3)	Gray	White	White
Cyan (3)	Gray	Black	Black
Cyan (3)	Color	White	Cyan
Cyan (3)	Color	Black	Cyan
Blue (4)	Gray	White	White
Blue (4)	Gray	Black	Black
Blue (4)	Color	White	Blue
Blue (4)	Color	Black	Blue
Magenta (5)	Gray	White	White
Magenta (5)	Gray	Black	Black
Magenta (5)	Color	White	Magenta
Magenta (5)	Color	Black	Magenta
Red II (6)	Gray	White	White
Red II (6)	Gray	Black	Black
Red II (6)	Color	White	Red
Red II (6)	Color	Black	Red

Table C.2: *Fuzzy Interface Rules.*

Fuzzy Inference Parameters for ADS

	Activation Value		
	0	1	0
Membership Function	Domain of the MFs		
C_1			
	-100	0	100
	0	100	200
C_2			
	-18	0	18
	0	18	100
	18	100	118
C_3			
	-20	0	20
	0	20	100
	20	100	120
out			
	-70	0	70
	0	70	100
	70	100	170

Table D.1: *Membership Function Limits.*

If C_1 is	And C_2 is	And C_3 is	Then *out* is
High	Low	Average	Average
High	Average	High	Low
High	High	High	Low
High	Low	Average	Average
High	Low	Low	High
High	Average	Average	Low
High	Average	Low	High
High	High	Average	Low
High	High	High	Low
Low	Low	Average	Average
Low	Average	High	Low
Low	High	High	Low
Low	Low	Average	Average
Low	Low	Low	High
Low	Average	Average	Low
Low	Average	Low	High
Low	High	Average	Low
Low	High	High	Low

Table D.2: *Fuzzy Interface Rules.*

Bibliography

[1] Mohamed Aly, Peter Welinder, Mario E. Munich, and Pietro Perona. Automatic discovery of image families: Global vs. local features. In *ICIP*, pages 777–780, 2009.

[2] G. Amato, F. Rabitti, P. Savino, and P. Zezula. Region proximity in metric spaces and its use for approximate similarity search. *ACM Transactions on Information Systems (TOIS)*, 21(2):192–227, 2003.

[3] G. Amato and P. Savino. Approximate similarity search in metric spaces using inverted files. In *Proceedings of the 3rd international conference on Scalable information systems*, page 28. ICST (Institute for Computer Sciences, Social-Informatics and Telecommunications Engineering), 2008.

[4] G. Amato and P. Savino. Approximate similarity search in metric spaces using inverted files. In *Proceedings of the 3rd international conference on Scalable information systems*, page 28. ICST (Institute for Computer Sciences, Social-Informatics and Telecommunications Engineering), 2008.

[5] A. Arampatzis and J. Kamps. A signal-to-noise approach to score normalization. In *Proceeding of the 18th ACM conference on Information and knowledge management*, pages 797–806. ACM, 2009.

[6] Avi Arampatzis, Stephen Robertson, and Jaap Kamps. Score distributions in information retrieval. In *ICTIR*, pages 139–151, 2009.

[7] M. Batko, V. Dohnal, D. Novak, and J. Sedmidubsky. Mufin: A multi-feature indexing network. In *2009 Second International Workshop on Similarity Search and Applications*, pages 158–159. IEEE, 2009.

[8] H. Bay, T. Tuytelaars, and L. Van Gool. Surf: Speeded up robust features. In *Computer Vision–ECCV 2006*, pages 404–417. Springer, 2006.

183

[9] S. Berretti, A. Del Bimbo, and P. Pala. Merging results for distributed content based image retrieval. *Multimedia Tools and Applications*, 24(3):215–232, 2004.

[10] D.M. Blei, A.Y. Ng, and M.I. Jordan. Latent dirichlet allocation. *The Journal of Machine Learning Research*, 3:993–1022, 2003.

[11] S.A. Bloom. Similarity indices in community studies: potential pitfalls. *Mar. Ecol. Prog. Ser*, 5(2):125–128, 1981.

[12] M. Bober. Mpeg-7 visual shape descriptors. *IEEE Transactions on Circuits and Systems for Video Technology*, 11(6):716–719, 2001.

[13] P. Bolettieri, A. Esuli, F. Falchi, C. Lucchese, R. Perego, T. Piccioli, and F. Rabitti. Cophir: a test collection for content-based image retrieval. *CoRR, abs/0905.4627 v2*, 2009.

[14] P. Brodatz. *Textures: a photographic album for artists and designers.* Dover Pubns, 1966.

[15] J. Caicedo, F. Gonzalez, E. Triana, and E. Romero. Design of a medical image database with content-based retrieval capabilities. *Advances in Image and Video Technology*, 4872:919–931, 2007.

[16] C. Carson, S. Belongie, H. Greenspan, and J. Malik. Blobworld: Image segmentation using expectation-maximization and its application to image querying. *IEEE Transactions on Pattern Analysis and Machine Intelligence*, 24(8):1026–1038, 2002.

[17] S. Chatzichristofis and Y. Boutalis. A hybrid scheme for fast and accurate image retrieval based on color descriptors. In *Proceedings of The Eleventh IASTED International Conference on Artificial Intelligence and Soft Computing*, pages 280–285. ACTA Press, 2007.

[18] S. Chatzichristofis and Y. Boutalis. Cedd: Color and edge directivity descriptor: A compact descriptor for image indexing and retrieval. *Computer Vision Systems*, 5008:312–322, 2008.

[19] S. A. Chatzichristofis and Y. S. Boutalis. Fcth: Fuzzy color and texture histogram a low level feature for accurate image retrieval. In *, IEEE Computer Society*, pages 191–196, Klagenfurt, 2008. IEEE Computer Society.

[20] S. A. Chatzichristofis, Y. S. Boutalis, and M. Lux. Img(rummager): An interactive content based image retrieval system. In *, IEEE Computer Society*, pages 151–152, Prague, 2009. IEEE Computer Society.

[21] S. A. Chatzichristofis, Y. S. Boutalis, and M. Lux. Spcd - spatial color distribution descriptor - a fuzzy rule based compact composite descriptor appropriate for hand drawn color sketches retrieval. In *2nd International Conference on Agents and Artificial Intelligence (ICAART)*, pages 58–63, 2010.

[22] S.A. Chatzichristofis and A. Arampatzis. Late fusion of compact composite descriptors for retrieval from heterogeneous image databases. In *Proceeding of the 33rd international ACM SIGIR conference on Research and development in information retrieval*, pages 825–826. ACM, 2010.

[23] S.A. CHATZICHRISTOFIS, A. ARAMPATZIS, and Y.S. BOUTALIS. Investigating the behavior of compact composite descriptors in early fusion, late fusion and distributed image retrieval. *Radioengineering*, 19(4):725, 2010.

[24] S.A. Chatzichristofis, Y.S. Boutalis, and A. Arampatzis. Accelerating image retrieval using binary haar wavelet transform on the color and edge directivity descriptor. In *Computing in the Global Information Technology (ICCGI), 2010 Fifth International Multi-Conference on*, pages 41–47. IEEE.

[25] S.A. Chatzichristofis, D.A. Mitzias, G.C. Sirakoulis, and Y.S. Boutalis. A novel cellular automata based technique for visual multimedia content encryption. *Optics Communications*, 2010.

[26] E. Chavez, K. Figueroa, and G. Navarro. Effective proximity retrieval by ordering permutations. *IEEE Transactions on Pattern Analysis and Machine Intelligence (TPAMI)*, 30(9):1647–1658, 2008.

[27] P.C. Chen and T. Pavlidis. Segmentation by texture using a co-occurrence matrix and a split-and-merge algorithm. *Computer Graphics and Image Processing*, 10(2):172–182, 1979.

[28] WW Chu, C.C. Hsu, AF Cardenas, and RK Taira. Knowledge-based image retrieval with spatial and temporalconstructs. *IEEE Transactions on Knowledge and Data Engineering*, 10(6):872–888, 1998.

[29] P. Ciaccia and M. Patella. Pac nearest neighbor queries: Approximate and controlled search in high-dimensional and metric spaces. In *ICDE*, page 244. Published by the IEEE Computer Society, 2000.

[30] L. Cieplinski. Mpeg-7 color descriptors and their applications. In *Computer Analysis of Images and Patterns*, pages 11–20. Springer, 2001.

[31] L. Cinque, G. Ciocca, S. Levialdi, A. Pellicano, and R. Schettini. Color-based image retrieval using spatial-chromatic histograms. *Image and Vision Computing*, 19(13):979–986, 2001.

[32] D. Comaniciu, P. Meer, D. Foran, and A. Medl. Bimodal system for interactive indexing and retrieval of pathologyimages. In *Fourth IEEE Workshop on Applications of Computer Vision, 1998. WACV'98. Proceedings.*, pages 76–81, 1998.

[33] Oana G. Cula and Kristin J. Dana. Compact representation of bidirectional texture functions. In *CVPR (1)*, pages 1041–1047, 2001.

[34] A. da Luz, DD Abdala, AV Wangenheim, and E. Comunello. Analyzing dicom and non-dicom features in content-based medical image retrieval: A multi-layer approach. In *19th IEEE International Symposium on Computer-Based Medical Systems, 2006. CBMS 2006*, pages 93–98, 2006.

[35] R. Datta, D. Joshi, J. Li, and J.Z. Wang. Image retrieval: Ideas, influences, and trends of the new age. *ACM Computing Surveys*, 40(2):160, 2008.

[36] I. Daubechies. *Ten lectures on wavelets*. Society for Industrial Mathematics, 1992.

[37] R. De Maesschalck, D. Jouan-Rimbaud, and DL Massart. The mahalanobis distance. *Chemometrics and Intelligent Laboratory Systems*, 50(1):1–18, 2000.

[38] AP De Vries and T. Westerveld. A comparison of continuous vs. discrete image models for probabilistic image and video retrieval. In *Image Processing, 2004. ICIP'04. 2004 International Conference on*, volume 4, 2004.

[39] F. Del Razo Lopez, A. Laurent, P. Poncelet, and M. Teisseire. Ftmnodes: Fuzzy tree mining based on partial inclusion. *Fuzzy Sets and Systems*, 160(15):2224–2240, 2009.

[40] T. Deselaers, D. Keysers, and H. Ney. Fire–flexible image retrieval engine: Imageclef 2004 evaluation. *Multilingual Information Access for Text, Speech and Images*, 3497:688–698, 2005.

[41] T. Deselaers, D. Keysers, and H. Ney. Features for image retrieval: An experimental comparison. *Information Retrieval*, 11(2):77–107, 2008.

[42] T. Deselaers, D. Keysers, and H. Ney. Features for image retrieval: An experimental comparison. *Information Retrieval*, 11(2):77–107, 2008.

[43] T. Deselaers, H. Muller, P. Clough, H. Ney, and T.M. Lehmann. The clef 2005 automatic medical image annotation task. *International Journal of Computer Vision*, 74(1):51–58, 2007.

[44] T. Deselaers, L. Pimenidis, and H. Ney. Bag-of-visual-words models for adult image classification and filtering. In *Pattern Recognition, 2008. ICPR 2008. 19th International Conference on*, pages 1–4. IEEE, 2008.

[45] T. Deselaers, T. Weyand, D. Keysers, W. Macherey, and H. Ney. Fire in imageclef 2005: Combining content-based image retrieval with textual information retrieval. *Accessing Multilingual Information Repositories*, 4022:652–661, 2006.

[46] Thomas Deselaers. *Image Retrieval, Object Recognition, and Discriminative Models*. PhD thesis, Von der Fakultat fur Mathematik, Informatik und Naturwissenschaften der RWTH Aachen University zur Erlangung, 2008.

[47] A.P. Dhawan. *Medical image analysis*. Wiley-Interscience, 2003.

[48] G. Dorko and C. Schmid. Object class recognition using discriminative local features. *IEEE Transactions on Pattern Analysis and Machine Intelligence*, -:-, 2005.

[49] R. Dubes and A. Jain. Random field models in image analysis. *Journal of Applied Statistics*, 16(2):131–164, 1989.

[50] H. Eidenberger. How good are the visual mpeg-7 features? In *SPIE & IEEE Visual Communications and Image Processing Conference, Lugano, Switzerland*. Citeseer, 2003.

[51] A. Esuli. Mipai: using the pp-index to build an efficient and scalable similarity search system. In *Proceedings of the 2009 Second International Workshop on Similarity Search and Applications*, pages 146–148. IEEE Computer Society, 2009.

[52] H. Ferhatosmanoglu, E. Tuncel, D. Agrawal, and A. El Abbadi. Vector approximation based indexing for non-uniform high dimensional data sets. In *Proceedings of the ninth international conference on Information and knowledge management*, pages 202–209. ACM, 2000.

[53] H. Ferhatosmanoglu, E. Tuncel, D. Agrawal, and A. El Abbadi. Approximate nearest neighbor searching in multimedia databases. In *Proceedings of the International Conference on Data Engineering*, pages 503–514. Citeseer, 2001.

[54] M. Fernandez, D. Vallet, and P. Castells. Using historical data to enhance rank aggregation. In *Proceedings of the 29th annual international ACM SIGIR conference on Research and development in information retrieval*, page 644. ACM, 2006.

[55] X. Fu, Y. Li, R. Harrison, and S. Belkasim. Content-based image retrieval using gabor-zernike features. In *Proceedings of the 18th International Conference on Pattern Recognition*, volume 2, 2006.

[56] A. Gil, O.M. Mozos, M. Ballesta, and O. Reinoso. A comparative evaluation of interest point detectors and local descriptors for visual slam. *Machine Vision and Applications*, 21(6):905–920, 2010.

[57] T. Glatard, J. Montagnat, and I.E. Magnin. Texture based medical image indexing and retrieval: application to cardiac imaging. In *Proceedings of the 6th ACM SIG-MM international workshop on Multimedia information retrieval*, pages 135–142. ACM, 2004.

[58] M. Grubinger and C. Leung. A benchmark for performance calibration in visual information search. In *Proceedings of The 2003 International Conference on Visual Information Systems (VIS 2003)*, pages 414–419, 2003.

[59] M.O. Gueld, D. Keysers, T. Deselaers, M. Leisten, H. Schubert, H. Ney, and T.M. Lehmann. Comparison of global features for categorization of medical images. In *Proceedings SPIE*, volume 5371, pages 211–222. Citeseer, 2004.

[60] M. Guld, C. Thies, B. Fischer, and T. Lehmann. Content-based retrieval of medical images by combining global features. *Accessing Multilingual Information Repositories*, 4022:702–711, 2006.

[61] D.E. Gustafson and W.C. Kessel. Fuzzy clustering with a fuzzy covariance matrix. In *IEEE Conference on Decision and Control including the 17th Symposium on Adaptive Processes*, volume 17, 1978.

[62] C. Harris and M. Stephens. A combined corner and edge detector. In *Alvey vision conference*, volume 15, page 50. Manchester, UK, 1988.

[63] T. Hastie and R. Tibshirani. Discriminant adaptive nearest neighbor classification. *IEEE Transactions on Pattern Analysis and Machine Intelligence*, 18(6):607–616, 1996.

[64] D. Hawking and S. Robertson. On collection size and retrieval effectiveness. *Information retrieval*, 6(1):99–105, 2003.

[65] M.A.E. Helala, M.M. Selim, and H.H. Zayed. An image retrieval approach based on composite features and graph matching. In *2009 Second International Conference on Computer and Electrical Engineering*, pages 466–473. IEEE, 2009.

[66] F.S. Hillier, G.J. Lieberman, and G.J. Liberman. *Introduction to operations research*. McGraw-Hill, New York, 2001.

[67] J.J. Hopfield. Neural networks and physical systems with emergent collective computational abilities. *Proceedings of the National Academy of Sciences of the United States of America*, 79(8):2554, 1982.

[68] E. Hoster, R. Lienhart, and M. Slaney. Image retrieval on large-scale image databases. In *Proceedings of the 6th ACM international conference on Image and video retrieval*, page 24. ACM, 2007.

[69] J. Hou, J. Kang, and N. Qi. On vocabulary size in bag-of-visual-words representation. *Advances in Multimedia Information Processing-PCM 2010*, pages 414–424, 2010.

[70] M.K. Hu. Visual pattern recognition by moment invariants. *Information Theory, IRE Transactions on*, 8(2):179–187, 1962.

[71] J. Huang, S.R. Kumar, M. Mitra, and W.J. Zhu. Image indexing using color correlograms. *US Patent 6,246,790*, 12:1–16, June 12 2001. US Patent 6,246,790.

[72] PW Huang, SK Dai, and PL Lin. Texture image retrieval and image segmentation using composite sub-band gradient vectors. *Journal of Visual Communication and Image Representation*, 17(5):947–957, 2006.

[73] M.J. Huiskes and M.S. Lew. The mir flickr retrieval evaluation. In *Proceeding of the 1st ACM international conference on Multimedia information retrieval*, pages 39–43. ACM, 2008.

[74] W.S. Hwang, J.J. Weng, M. Fang, and J. Qian. A fast image retrieval algorithm with automatically extracted discriminant features. In *IEEE Workshop on Content-Based Access of Image and Video Libraries*, 1999.

[75] ISO/IEC/15938-3. Information technology - multimedia content description interface / part 3: Visual, 2002.

[76] ISO/IEC/JTC1/SC29/WG11. Description of core experiments for mpeg-7 color/-texture descriptors, 1999.

[77] J., Huang, Q., Dom, B., Gorkani, M., Hafner, J., Lee, D., Petkovic, D., Steele, D., Flickner. Query by image and video content: the qbic system. *Computer*, 28(9):2332, 1995.

[78] C.E. Jacobs, A. Finkelstein, and D.H. Salesin. Fast multiresolution image querying. In *Proceedings of the 22nd annual conference on Computer graphics and interactive techniques*, pages 277–286. ACM New York, NY, USA, 1995.

[79] HV Jagadish, A.O. Mendelzon, and T. Milo. Similarity-based queries. In *Proceedings of the fourteenth ACM SIGACT-SIGMOD-SIGART symposium on Principles of database systems*, page 45. ACM, 1995.

[80] K. Jarrah and L. Guan. Content-based image retrieval via distributed databases. In *International conference on Content-based image and video retrieval*, pages 389–394. ACM, 2008.

[81] S. Jeong, K. Kim, B. Chun, J. Lee, and Y.J. Bae. An effective method for combining multiple features of image retrieval. In *Proc. IEEE Region 10 Conf*, 1999.

189

[82] A. Jian Yaoa, Z.M. Zhanga, S. Antanib, R. Longb, and G. Thomab. Automatic medical image annotation and retrieval. *Neurocomputing*, 71:2012–2022, 2008.

[83] Y.G. Jiang, C.W. Ngo, and J. Yang. Towards optimal bag-of-features for object categorization and semantic video retrieval. In *Proceedings of the 6th ACM international conference on Image and video retrieval*, pages 494–501. ACM, 2007.

[84] ISO/IEC JTC1/SC29/WG11N6828. Mpeg-7 overview, 2004.

[85] F. Jurie and C. Schmid. Scale-invariant shape features for recognition of object categories. In *CVPR*. IEEE Computer Society, 2004.

[86] T. Kadir and M. Brady. Scale, saliency and image description. *International Journal of Computer Vision*, 45(2):83–105, 2001.

[87] T. Kadir, A. Zisserman, and M. Brady. An affine invariant salient region detector. *Computer Vision-ECCV 2004*, pages 228–241, 2004.

[88] J. Kamps, M. De Rijke, and B. Sigurbjornsson. Combination methods for crosslingual web retrieval. *Lecture Notes in Computer Science*, 4022:856, 2006.

[89] R. Kapela, P. Sniatala, and A. Rybarczyk. Real-time visual content description system based on mpeg-7 descriptors. *Multimedia Tools and Applications*, pages 1–32, 2010.

[90] E. Kasutani and A. Yamada. The mpeg-7 color layout descriptor: a compact image featuredescription for high-speed image/video segment retrieval. In *Image Processing, 2001. Proceedings. 2001 International Conference on*, volume 1, 2001.

[91] R. Keys. Cubic convolution interpolation for digital image processing. *IEEE Transactions on Acoustics, Speech and Signal Processing*, 29(6):1153–1160, 1981.

[92] Kim, W.Y. and Kim, Y.S. and Kim, YS. A new region-based shape descriptor, 1999.

[93] G.J. Klir and B. Yuan. *Fuzzy sets and fuzzy logic: theory and applications*. Prentice Hall Upper Saddle River, NJ, 1995.

[94] Marian Kogler and Mathias Lux. Bag of visual words revisited: an exploratory study on robust image retrieval exploiting fuzzy codebooks. In *Proceedings of the Tenth International Workshop on Multimedia Data Mining*, MDMKDD '10, pages 3:1–3:6, New York, NY, USA, 2010. ACM.

[95] T. Kohonen. The self-organizing map. *Proceedings of the IEEE*, 78(9):1464–1480, 1990.

[96] T. Kohonen and P. Somervuo. Self-organizing maps of symbol strings. *Neurocomputing*, 21(1-3):19–30, 1998.

[97] K. Konstantinidis, A. Gasteratos, and I. Andreadis. Image retrieval based on fuzzy color histogram processing. *Optics Communications*, 248(4-6):375–386, 2005.

[98] P. Korn, N. Sidiropoulos, C. Faloutsos, E. Siegel, and Z. Protopapas. Fast and effective retrieval of medical tumor shapes. *IEEE Transactions on Knowledge and Data Engineering*, 10(6):889–904, 1998.

[99] S. Krishnamachari and M. Abdel-Mottaleb. Compact color descriptor for fast image and video segment retrieval. In *IS&T/SPIE Conference on Storage and Retrieval of Media Databases 2000*. Citeseer, 2000.

[100] K.I. Laws. *Texture Energy Measures*. Storming Media, 1979.

[101] K.I. Laws. *Textured image segmentation*. University of Southern California, Los Angeles Image Processing Institute, 1980.

[102] I. Lee and L. Guan. Semi-automated relevance feedback for distributed content based image retrieval. In *ICME*, volume 3, 2004.

[103] T.M. Lehmann, M.O. Guld, D. Keysers, T. Deselaers, H. Schubert, B. Wein, and K. Spitzer. Similarity of medical images computed from global feature vectors for content-based retrieval. In *Knowledge-Based Intelligent Information and Engineering Systems*, pages 989–995. Springer, 2004.

[104] M.S. Lew, N. Sebe, C. Djeraba, and R. Jain. Content-based multimedia information retrieval: State of the art and challenges. *ACM Transactions on Multimedia Computing, Communications, and Applications (TOMCCAP)*, 2(1):19, 2006.

[105] J. Li and J.Z. Wang. Automatic linguistic indexing of pictures by a statistical modeling approach. *IEEE Transactions on Pattern Analysis and Machine Intelligence*, 25(9):1075–1088, 2003.

[106] J. Li and J.Z. Wang. Real-time computerized annotation of pictures. In *Proceedings of the 14th annual ACM international conference on Multimedia*, page 920. ACM, 2006.

[107] T. Li, T. Mei, and I.S. Kweon. Learning optimal compact codebook for efficient object categorization. In *Applications of Computer Vision, 2008. WACV 2008. IEEE Workshop on*, pages 1–6. IEEE.

[108] X. Li, L. Chen, L. Zhang, F. Lin, and W.Y. Ma. Image annotation by large-scale content-based image retrieval. In *Proceedings of the 14th annual ACM international conference on Multimedia*, page 610. ACM, 2006.

[109] Xirong Li, Le Chen, Lei Zhang, Fuzong Lin, and Wei-Ying Ma. Image annotation by large-scale content-based image retrieval. In *ACM Multimedia*, pages 607–610, 2006.

[110] S. Lim and G. Lu. Spatial statistics for content based image retrieval. In *Information Technology: Coding and Computing [Computers and Communications], 2003. Proceedings. ITCC 2003. International Conference on*, pages 155–159, 2003.

[111] B. Lin, X. Wang, R. Zhong, and Z. Zhuang. Continuous optimization based-on boosting gaussian mixture model. In *Pattern Recognition, 2006. ICPR 2006. 18th International Conference on*, volume 1, 2006.

[112] T. Lindeberg. Feature detection with automatic scale selection. *International Journal of Computer Vision*, 30(2):79–116, 1998.

[113] F. Long, H. Zhang, and D.D. Feng. *Fundamentals of content-based image retrieval*. Springer, 2003.

[114] D.G. Lowe. Object recognition from local scale-invariant features. In *iccv*, page 1150. Published by the IEEE Computer Society, 1999.

[115] D.G. Lowe. Distinctive image features from scale-invariant keypoints. *International journal of computer vision*, 60(2):91–110, 2004.

[116] G. Loy and A. Zelinsky. Fast radial symmetry for detecting points of interest. *IEEE Transactions on Pattern Analysis and Machine Intelligence*, pages 959–973, 2003.

[117] M. Lux and S. A. Chatzichristofis. Lire: Lucene image retrieval - an extensible java cbir library. In *ACM International Conference on Multimedia 2008, (ACM MM), Open Source Application Competition*, pages 1085–1087, Vancouver, BC, 2008.

[118] M. Lux, O. Marques, K. Schoffmann, L. Boszormenyi, and G. Lajtai. A novel tool for summarization of arthroscopic videos. *Multimedia Tools and Applications*, 46(2):521–544, 2010.

[119] M. Lux, A. Pitman, and O. Marques. Can global visual features improve tag recommendation for image annotation? *Future Internet*, 2(3):341–362, 2010.

[120] BS Manjunath, J.R. Ohm, VV Vasudevan, and A. Yamada. Color and texture descriptors. *IEEE Transactions on circuits and systems for video technology*, 11(6):703–715, 2001.

[121] BS Manjunath, P. Salembier, and T. Sikora. *Introduction to MPEG-7: multimedia content description interface*. John Wiley & Sons Inc, 2002.

[122] O. Marques and B. Furht. *Content-based visual information retrieval*. Springer (formerly Kluwer Academic Publishers), 2002.

[123] J. Matas, O. Chum, M. Urban, and T. Pajdla. Robust wide-baseline stereo from maximally stable extremal regions. *Image and Vision Computing*, 22(10):761–767, 2004.

[124] BG Mertzios and K. Tsirikolias. Applications of coordinate logic filters in image analysis and pattern recognition. *Circuits, Systems, and Signal Processing*, 17:517–538, 2005.

[125] K. Mikolajczyk and C. Schmid. A performance evaluation of local descriptors. *IEEE Transactions on Pattern Analysis and Machine Intelligence*, 27(10):1615–1630, 2005.

[126] S.K. Mitra and G.L. Sicuranza. *Nonlinear image processing*. Academic Pr, 2001.

[127] D.S. Moore and L. Sorenson. *Introduction to the Practice of Statistics SPSS Manual*. WH Freeman, 2005.

[128] H Moravec. Obstacle avoidance and navigation in the real world by a seeing robot rover. Technical report, Carnegie-Mellon University, Robotics Institute, 1980.

[129] MPEG-7. *Subjective Evaluation of the MPEG-7 Retrieval Accuracy Measure (ANMRR)*. ISO/WG11, Doc. M6029, 2000.

[130] H. Muller, N. Michoux, D. Bandon, and A. Geissbuhler. A review of content-based image retrieval systems in medical applications–clinical benefits and future directions. *International journal of medical informatics*, 73(1):1–23, 2004.

[131] H. Muller, W. Muller, D.M.G. Squire, S. Marchand-Maillet, and T. Pun. Performance evaluation in content-based image retrieval: Overview and proposals. *Pattern Recognition Letters*, 22(5):593–601, 2001.

[132] A. Natsev, W. Jiang, M. Merler, J.R. Smith, J. Tešic, L. Xie, and R. Yan. Ibm research trecvid-2008 video retrieval system. In *Proc. of TRECVID 2008*. Citeseer, 2008.

[133] Navneet Dalal, Bill Triggs. Histograms of oriented gradients for human detection. In *IEEE Computer Society Conference on Computer Vision and Pattern Recognition*, 2005.

[134] C.H. Ng, K.C. Sia, and CH Chang. Advanced peer clustering and firework query model in the peer-to-peer network. In *World Wide Web Conference (WWW)*, 2003.

[135] N. Nikolaou and N. Papamarkos. Color image retrieval using a fractal signature extraction technique. *Engineering Applications of Artificial Intelligence*, 15(1):81–96, 2002.

[136] D. Nister and H. Stewenius. Scalable recognition with a vocabulary tree. In *Proc. CVPR*, volume 5. Citeseer, 2006.

[137] D.K. Park, Y.S. Jeon, C.S. Won, S.J. Park, and S.J. Yoo. A composite histogram for image retrieval. In *2000 IEEE International Conference on Multimedia and Expo, 2000. ICME 2000*, volume 1, 2000.

[138] G. Pass, R. Zabih, and J. Miller. Comparing images using color coherence vectors. In *Proceedings of the fourth ACM international conference on Multimedia*, page 73. ACM, 1997.

[139] A. Pentland, RW Picard, and S. Sclaroff. Photobook: Content-based manipulation of image databases. *International Journal of Computer Vision*, 18(3):233–254, 1996.

[140] Petros Daras, Theodoros Semertzidis, Lambros Makris and Michael G. Strintzis. Similarity content search in content centric networks. In *ACM Multimedia 2010*, 2010.

[141] O.S. Pianykh. *Digital imaging and communications in medicine (DICOM): a practical introduction and survival guide*. Springer Verlag, 2008.

[142] Adrian Popescu, Pierre-Alain Moëllic, Ioannis Kanellos, and Rémi Landais. Lightweight web image reranking. In *ACM Multimedia*, pages 657–660, 2009.

[143] S. Poullot, O. Buisson, and M. Crucianu. Z-grid-based probabilistic retrieval for scaling up content-based copy detection. In *Proceedings of the 6th ACM international conference on Image and video retrieval*, page 355. ACM, 2007.

[144] P. Prusinkiewicz and J. Hanan. *Lindenmayer systems, fractals, and plants*. Springer Verlag, 1989.

[145] M.M. Rahman, S.K. Antani, and G.R. Thoma. A classification-driven similarity matching framework for retrieval of biomedical images. In *Proceedings of the international conference on Multimedia information retrieval*, pages 147–154. ACM, 2010.

[146] A. Rao, RK Srihari, and Z. Zhang. Spatial color histograms for content-based image retrieval. In *11th IEEE International Conference on Tools with Artificial Intelligence, 1999. Proceedings*, pages 183–186, 1999.

[147] Aibing Rao, Rohini K. Srihari, and Zhongfei Zhang. Spatial color histograms for content-based image retrieval. In *ICTAI*, pages 183–186, 1999.

[148] G.X. Ritter, P. Sussner, and J.L. Diaz-de Leon. Morphological associative memories. *IEEE Transactions on Neural Networks*, 9(2):281, 1998.

[149] A. Rizzi, C. Gatta, and D. Marini. A new algorithm for unsupervised global and local color correction. *Pattern Recognition Letters*, 24(11):1663–1677, 2003.

[150] Y.M. Ro and K. Yoo. Texture featuring and indexing using matching pursuit in radonspace. In *Image Processing, 1999. ICIP 99. Proceedings. 1999 International Conference on*, volume 2, 1999.

[151] Carles Ventura Royo. Image-based query by example using mpeg-7 visual descriptors. Master's thesis, Universitat Polit'ecnica de Catalunya Enginyeria T'ecnica Superior de Telecomunicacions Image and Video Processing Group, 2010.

[152] Y. Rubner, J. Puzicha, C. Tomasi, and J.M. Buhmann. Empirical evaluation of dissimilarity measures for color and texture. *Computer Vision and Image Understanding*, 84(1):25–43, 2001.

[153] Y. Rubner, C. Tomasi, and L.J. Guibas. The earth mover's distance as a metric for image retrieval. *International Journal of Computer Vision*, 40(2):99–121, 2000.

[154] B.C. Russell, A. Torralba, K.P. Murphy, and W.T. Freeman. Labelme: a database and web-based tool for image annotation. *International Journal of Computer Vision*, 77(1):157–173, 2008.

[155] S. A. Chatzichristofis, K Zagoris, Y. S. Boutalis and N. Papamarkos. Accurate image retrieval based on compact composite descriptors and relevance feedback information. *International Journal of Pattern Recognition and Artificial Intelligence (IJPRAI)*, 2:207–244, 2010.

[156] S. A. Chatzichristofis, Y. S. Boutalis and Avi Arampatzis. Fast retrieval from image databases via binary haar wavelet transform on the color and edge directivity descriptor. *International Journal On Advances in Networks and Services*, -:–, 2001.

[157] S. A. Chatzichristofis, Y. S. Boutalis, and M. Lux. Selection of the proper compact composite descriptor for improving content based image retrieval. In *SPPRA*, pages 134–140, 2009.

[158] H. Sagan and J. Holbrook. *Space-filling curves*. Springer-Verlag New York, 1994.

[159] G. Salton and M.J. McGill. *Introduction to modern information retrieval*. McGraw-Hill New York, 1983.

[160] M.S. Sarfraz and O. Hellwich. Head pose estimation in face recognition across pose scenarios. In *Int. conference on computer vision theory and applications VISAPP*, volume 1, pages 235–242, 2008.

[161] G. Schaefer and M. Stich. Ucid-an uncompressed colour image database. *Storage and Retrieval Methods and Applications for Multimedia 2004*, 5307:472–480, 2004.

195

[162] C. Schmid, R. Mohr, and C. Bauckhage. Evaluation of interest point detectors. *International Journal of computer vision*, 37(2):151–172, 2000.

[163] F. Serratosa and A. Sanfeliu. Signatures versus histograms: Definitions, distances and algorithms. *Pattern recognition*, 39(5):921–934, 2006.

[164] A. Shahbahrami, D. Borodin, and B. Juurlink. Comparison between color and texture features for image retrieval. In *Proceedings of the 19th Annual Workshop on Circuits, Systems and Signal Processing, ProRisc*, 2008.

[165] Linda G. Shapiro and George C. Stockman. *Computer Vision*. Prentice Hall, 2001.

[166] J. Shotton, J. Winn, C. Rother, and A. Criminisi. Textonboost: Joint appearance, shape and context modeling for multi-class object recognition and segmentation. In *Computer Vision–ECCV 2006*, pages 1–15. Springer, 2006.

[167] JR Smith. Image retrieval evaluation. In *IEEE Workshop on Content-Based Access of Image and Video Libraries, 1998. Proceedings*, pages 112–113, 1998.

[168] J.R. Smith and S.F. Chang. Visually searching the web for content. *IEEE Multimedia Magazine*, 4(3):12–20, 1997.

[169] J.R. Smith and S.F. Chang. Visualseek: a fully automated content-based image query system. In *Proceedings of the fourth ACM international conference on Multimedia*, pages 87–98. ACM, 1997.

[170] S.M. Smith and J.M. Brady. Susana new approach to low level image processing. *International journal of computer vision*, 23(1):45–78, 1997.

[171] D.M.G. Squire, W. Muller, H. Muller, and T. Pun. Content-based query of image databases: inspirations from text retrieval. *Pattern Recognition Letters*, 21(13-14):1193–1198, 2000.

[172] GN Srinivasan and G. Shobha. Statistical texture analysis. In *Proceeding of World Academy of Science, Engineering and Technology*, volume 36, pages 1264–1269, 2008.

[173] P. Stanchev, G. Amato, F. Falchi, C. Gennaro, F. Rabitti, and P. Savino. Selection of mpeg-7 image features for improving image similarity search on specific data sets. In *7-th IASTED International Conference on Computer Graphics and Imaging, CGIM*, pages 395–400. Citeseer, 2004.

[174] M. Stricker and M. Orengo. Similarity of color images. In *Proc. SPIE Storage and Retrieval for Image and Video Databases*, volume 2420, pages 381–392. Citeseer, 1995.

[175] Z. Struzik and A. Siebes. The haar wavelet transform in the time series similarity paradigm. *Principles of Data Mining and Knowledge Discovery*, 1:12–22, 1999.

[176] J. Sun, X. Zhang, J. Cui, and L. Zhou. Image retrieval based on color distribution entropy. *Pattern Recognition Letters*, 27(10):1122–1126, 2006.

[177] Junding Sun, Ximin Zhang, Jiangtao Cui, and Lihua Zhou. Image retrieval based on color distribution entropy. *Pattern Recognition Letters*, 27(10):1122–1126, 2006.

[178] M.T. Suzuki, Y. Yaginuma, and H. Kodama. A 2d texture image retrieval technique based on texture energy filters. Technical report, National Institute of Multimedia Education, 2010.

[179] H.D. Tagare, C.C. Jaffe, and J. Duncan. Medical image databases: A content-based retrieval approach. *Journal of the American Medical Informatics Association*, 4(3):184, 1997.

[180] H. Tamura, S. Mori, and T. Yamawaki. Textural features corresponding to visual perception. *IEEE Transactions on Systems, Man and Cybernetics*, 8(6):460–473, 1978.

[181] K. Tanimoto and Y. Yoshimoto. Theoretical and experimental study of reflection coefficient for wave dissipating caisson with a permeable front wall. *Report of the Port and Harbour Research Institute*, 21(3):44–77, 1982.

[182] K. Tsirikolias and BG Mertzios. Edge extraction and enhancement using coordinate logic filters. In *Proceedings of the International Conference on Image Processing: Theory and Applications*, pages 251–254, 1993.

[183] M. Unser. Texture classification and segmentation using wavelet frames. *IEEE Transactions on image processing*, 4(11):1549–1560, 1995.

[184] M.E. Valle and P. Sussner. A general framework for fuzzy morphological associative memories. *Fuzzy sets and systems*, 159(7):747–768, 2008.

[185] D. Vallet, I. Cantador, and J.M. Jose. Exploiting external knowledge to improve video retrieval. In *Proceedings of the international conference on Multimedia information retrieval*, 2010.

[186] R.H. van Leuken, L. Garcia, X. Olivares, and R. van Zwol. Visual diversification of image search results. In *Proceedings of the 18th international conference on World wide web*, pages 341–350. ACM, 2009.

[187] V. Vonikakis, I. Andreadis, and A. Gasteratos. Fast centre-surround contrast modification. *Image Processing, IET*, 2(1):19–34, 2008.

[188] H. Wang and M. Brady. Real-time corner detection algorithm for motion estimation. *Image and Vision Computing*, 13(9):695–703, 1995.

[189] J.Z. Wang, J. Li, and G. Wiederhold. Simplicity: Semantics-sensitive integrated matching for picture libraries. *IEEE Transactions on pattern analysis and machine intelligence*, 23:947–963, 2001.

[190] X.Y. Wang, J.F. Wu, and H.Y. Yang. Robust image retrieval based on color histogram of local feature regions. *Multimedia Tools and Applications*, 49(2):1323–345, 2010.

[191] Wikipedia, the free encyclopedia. Interest point detection, December 2009.

[192] P.M. Willy and K.H. Kufer. Content-based medical image retrieval (cbmir): an intelligent retrieval system for handling multiple organs of interest. In *Proceedings of the 17th IEEE Symposium on Computer-Based Medical Systems (CBMS04)*, volume 1063, pages 20–00, 2004.

[193] J. Winn, A. Criminisi, and T. Minka. Object categorization by learned universal visual dictionary. In *Tenth IEEE International Conference on Computer Vision, 2005. ICCV 2005*, volume 2, 2005.

[194] C.S. Won, D.K. Park, and S.J. Park. Efficient use of mpeg-7 edge histogram descriptor. *Etri Journal*, 24(1):23–30, 2002.

[195] K.M. Wong, K.W. Cheung, and L.M. Po. Mirror: an interactive content based image retrieval system. In *IEEE International Symposium on Circuits and Systems, 2005. ISCAS 2005*, pages 1541–1544, 2005.

[196] A. Yavlinsky. Behold: a content based image search engine for the world wide web, 2006.

[197] AG Yiannoulis, YS Boutalis, and BG Mertzios. Fast segmentation of colour images using the fuzzy k-means algorithm and different sampling approaches. In *Proceedings of the Ninth International Workshop on Systems, Signals and Image Processing, Manchester, UK*, pages 532–535, 2002.

[198] Jie Yu, Xin Jin, Jiawei Han, and Jiebo Luo. Mining personal image collection for social group suggestion. In *IEEE Data Mining Workshops, International Conference on*, 2009.

[199] K. Zagoris, S.A. Chatzichristofis, N. Papamarkos, and Y.S. Boutalis. Img (anaktisi): a web content based image retrieval system. In *2nd international workshop on similarity search and applications (SISAP)*, 2009.

[200] Konstantinos Zagoris, Kavallieratou Ergina, and Nikos Papamarkos. Image retrieval systems based on compact shape descriptor and relevance feedback information. *Journal of Visual Communication and Image Representation*, 22(5):378 – 390, 2011.

[201] P. Zezula, P. Savino, G. Amato, and F. Rabitti. Approximate similarity retrieval with m-trees. *The VLDB Journal*, 7(4):275–293, 1998.

[202] Shiliang Zhang, Qi Tian, Gang Hua, Qingming Huang, and Shipeng Li. Descriptive visual words and visual phrases for image applications. In *ACM Multimedia*, pages 75–84, 2009.

[203] X.S. Zhou and T.S. Huang. Relevance feedback in image retrieval: A comprehensive review. *Multimedia systems*, 8(6):536–544, 2003.

[204] H.J. Zimmermann. *Fuzzy sets, decision making, and expert systems*. Kluwer Academic Pub, 1987.

List of Figures

Dr. Savvas A. Chatzichristofis *received the diploma of Electrical and Computer Engineer in 2005 from the Democritus University of Thrace (DUTH), Greece. In 2010 he received his Ph.D. from the same department.*

Currently, he is a postdoctoral researcher at the Centre for Research and Technology Hellas (CE.R.T.H.), Informatics and Telematics Institute (I.T.I) involved in several European research projects. He is also a visiting professor at Cyprus University of Technology (C.U.T.), Department of Civil Engineering and Geomatics, Limassol, Cyprus

His research is focused on Computer Vision and Robotics, Image Retrieval, Image Processing and Analysis, Machine Intelligent and Pattern Recognition. He has published more than 30 papers in international scientific journals and proceedings of international conferences and he is co-author in book chapters of books published by international houses.

He has received numerous grants, including, the best paper award (Artificial Intelligence) in ICAART 2010, the best paper award in IC-CGI 2010 as well the best paper award in EUREKA 2010.

He has served as reviewer for scientific journals in the area of image processing, multimedia and fuzzy logic as well as member of Program Committees of several international conferences. He has given numerous talks during conferences, at universities, and in the industry.

Dr. Yiannis S. Boutalis *received the diploma of Electrical Engineer in 1983 from Democritus University of Thrace (DUTH), Greece and the phD degree in Electrical and Computer Engineering (topic Image Processing) in 1988 from the Computer Science Division of National Technical University of Athens, Greece.*

Since 1996, he serves as a faculty member, at the Department of Electrical and Computer Engineering, DUTH, Greece, where he is currently an Associate Professor and director of the Automatic Control Systems and Robotics Lab. Currently, he was also a Visiting Professor for research cooperation at Erlangen-Nuremberg University of Germany, chair of Automatic Control and has on-going research cooperation with other European Universities.

He served as an assistant visiting professor at University of Thessaly, Greece, and as a visiting professor in Air Defense Academy of General Staff of airforces of Greece. He also served as a researcher in the Institute of Language and Speech Processing (ILSP), Greece, and as a managing director of the R&D SME Ideatech S.A, Greece, specializing in pattern recognition and signal processing applications. His current research interests are focused in the development of Computational Intelligence techniques with applications in Control, Pattern Recognition, Signal and Image Processing Problems.

Dr. Boutalis teaches undergraduate and postgraduate lessons in the fields of Automatic Control, Robotis and Computational Intelligence Techniques. He has published more than 120 papers in international scientific Journals and proceedings of international conferences and he is co-author in book chapters of books published by international houses.

Dr. Boutalis has supervised a number of completed PhD and Master dissertations (11 until 2010) one of them being the dissertation of Dr. Chatsichristofis

www.ingramcontent.com/pod-product-compliance
Lightning Source LLC
LaVergne TN
LVHW042334060326
832902LV00006B/155